THE GHETTO

Kennikat Press
National University Publications
Interdisciplinary Urban Series

Advisory Editor
Raymond A. Mohl

THE GHETTO
Readings With Interpretations

Edited by
JOE T. DARDEN

National University Publications
KENNIKAT PRESS // 1981
Port Washington, N.Y. // London

Manufactured in the United States of America

Published by
Kennikat Press Corp.
Port Washington, N.Y. / London

Library of Congress Cataloging in Publication Data
Main entry under title:

The Ghetto: readings with interpretations.

(Interdisciplinary urban series) (National university publications)
Bibliography: p.
Includes index.
1. Afro-Americans—Social conditions—1975–
Addresses, essays, lectures. 2. Afro-Americans—Economic conditions—Addresses, essays, lectures. 3. Afro-Americans—Segregation—Addresses, essays, lectures. 4. United States—Social conditions—1960– —Addresses, essays, lectures. 5. United States—Economic conditions—1961– —Addresses, essays, lectures.
I. Darden, Joe T.
E185.86.G45   305.8'96073   80-27838
ISBN 0-8046-9277-7
ISBN 0-8046-9279-3 (pbk.)

*To my lovely and wonderful wife,
Doris, who continues to teach the
young the value of eliminating racism
and racial discrimination from
American society. She knows the true
meaning of this book.*

CONTENTS

Scholarly interest in the ghetto was relatively limited prior to the ghetto riots of the sixties. Such riots stimulated widespread interest, concern, fear, and increased attempts to understand the complexities of life in the ghetto. Now that we have entered a post-riot era, some of the fears have subsided, but a widespread lack of understanding of the ghetto remains and the problems of the ghetto continue to persist. Such a lack of understanding presents persistent obstacles to urban planners, politicians, city administrators, and social scientists who are concerned with finding solutions to the problems of cities. Because ghettos are inseparable parts of cities, the problems of cities cannot be solved without solving the problems of ghettos. The continuous flight to the suburbs serves only to exacerbate the problems. Social problems left unsolved have a tendency to diffuse spatially, uninhibited by artificial municipal boundaries. Thus what were specifically the problems of ghettos yesterday are the problems of cities today, and will become the problems of metropolitan areas engulfing the suburbs tomorrow.

The time has come to meet the challenge. This book is a response to that challenge. Although its contents have been selected from a variety of social science disciplines, the attempt has been made to view the ghetto from a geographic or spatial as well as a social perspective. Obviously several excellent papers on the ghetto have not been included, mainly because they were not appropriate to the themes presented. The reader who wants to investigate additional resources on the ghetto should consult the references given in the last chapter of this volume.

Few, if any comprehensive books on the present racial ghetto have been written. This lack of such works has already led scholars to edit such readers as *The Rise of the Ghetto* (Bracy et al., 1971); *The Enduring Ghetto* (Goldfield, 1973); *Politics and the Ghetto* (Warren, 1969); *Medicine in the Ghetto* Norman, 1969); and *Geography of the Ghetto* (Rose, 1972), all of which are highly specialized. Bracey (1971) and Goldfield (1973) have primarily provided a history of the ghetto. Warren (1969) surveys the political system and Norman (1969) informs us of the inadequate delivery of medical care in the ghetto. Even the work by Rose (1972), although less specialized than the others, falls short of providing a description and explanation of the nature and problems of the ghetto that are understandable to the average student. Indeed, frustration caused by the lack of a suitable volume for my own course on the ghetto led to the preparation of the present work.

Although the focus of this book is on the ghetto, particularly in the United States, no attempt to find agreement on a single definition of the ghetto has been made. In order, however, to avoid further widespread misconceptions of the concept, the editor felt that some discussion of the subject was appropriate. Thus the first section is devoted to the task of explaining the nature of the ghetto and its origin. Where did the concept originate? What does it mean? Why was the ghetto first created? The answers to these questions immediately lead the reader to conclude that the ghetto is an evolving or dynamic phenomenon, an urban reservoir for various religious, ethnic, and racial groups.

The second section focuses on the temporal dimension by comparing the experience of past residents of the ghetto—largely immigrants—with its present residents—largely blacks. By analyzing the similarities and differences between the two types of inhabitants the key issue—i.e., racism—and the consequent problems of the present racial ghetto are unveiled. This section demonstrates that the problems of the modern ghetto are not caused by class but by race.

Once this aspect has been understood, the succeeding section on how the ghetto spreads becomes apparent. However, as an additional illustration of the differences between racial and ethnic ghettos, the racial type of ghetto is viewed as analogous to an internal colony. Against this background, it is easy for a student or a layperson to grasp the complex problems of the racial—i.e., nonwhite—ghetto. These problems are then pinpointed in three areas; namely, the ghetto economy, the delivery of social services, and the lack of adequate political representation.

The next section searches for alternative solutions to the problems of today's ghetto, either through economic development or through redistribution of the population. To aid in such a search, a Bibliographic Guide has been provided for the final section. Since most of the material in this volume has been elsewhere published, journalistic style has throughout been adopted. Footnotes have been omitted or incorporated within the text, and tables and figures kept to a minimum. Therefore the reader should consult the original sources and/or the Bibliographic Guide if complete references are needed.

The study of the ghetto is not the domain of any one discipline. It can best be examined from an interdisciplinary perspective. The intention of this book is to give that focus. Although it was designed primarily for undergraduate students in urban geography, urban politics, urban economics, urban history, urban sociology, urban planning, and urban studies generally, graduate students in these disciplines may find several selections helpful as background material for seminars. The volume should also be helpful to students enrolled in courses of black studies in particular and courses of racial and ethnic studies in general.

Several individuals have helped to make this volume possible and to them I am most grateful. Donna Taxon, Alice Perrone, and Jackie Schwab typed the manuscript, and Karen Findlay provided the backup typing assistance when needed. The tedious task of preparing an index for this volume was done by Suzie Parel, one of my graduate research assistants. Mike Lipsey, production supervisor in the Center for Cartographic Research and Spatial Analysis, provided cartographic assistance.

Joe T. Darden

THE GHETTO

CONTRIBUTORS

Robert Blauner
Department of Sociology
Univeristy of California, Berkeley

Dennis Clark
Executive Director of Samuel S.
 Fels Fund
Philadelphia, Pennsylvania

William A. V. Clark
Department of Geography
University of California, Los Angeles

Joe T. Darden
Department of Geography & Urban
 Studies
Michigan State University

Donald Deskins, Jr.
Department of Geography
University of Michigan

Daniel Fusfeld
Department of Economics
University of Michigan

Barry Gruenberg
Department of Sociology
Wesleyan University

C. R. Hansell
Department of Geography
U. S. Military Academy

Clinton Jones
College of Urban Life
Georgia State University, Atlanta

John F. Kain
Department of City & Regional
 Planning
Harvard University

Peter Labrie
Oakland Office of Community
 Development
Oakland, California

**National Advisory Commission on
 Civil Disorders**
Washington, D. C.

Joseph Persky
Department of Economics
Fisk University

Gary Sands
Mayor's Committee on Community
 Renewal, Detroit

Howard Schuman
Department of Sociology
University of Michigan

Louis Wirth
Late Professor of Sociology
University of Chicago

PART ONE

THE CONCEPT AND ORIGIN OF THE GHETTO

INTRODUCTION

What is a ghetto? Where did the concept "ghetto" originate? As the papers in this volume show there is no consistent definition of the word "ghetto." However, implicit in each author's presentation is the belief that the ghetto contains a locational attribute, i.e., urban; a subgroup attribute, i.e., racial, religious or ethnic; a process attribute, i.e., discrimination in housing; and a pattern attribute, i.e., segregation.

An attempt to determine the extent of agreement among definitions of the term ghetto *is presented in the first article by Joe T. Darden. Darden examined more than a hundred studies and found that a number of writers did not give any explicit definition of the term even though the ghetto was the actual subject matter of their endeavor, and among those offering an explicit definition the degree of consensus was by no means complete. In general, however, two perspectives seem to exist— namely, the ghetto as an area of social pathologies, and the ghetto as a microcosm of the city as a whole. Such a basic lack of agreement has, however, implications for public policy and may indeed contribute to a perpetuation of the ghetto.*

The search for the origin of the ghetto concept is pursued in the second essay in this section by Louis Wirth; Wirth argues that the modern ghetto is of medieval urban European origin and that the term originally applied to European Jewish settlements which were segregated from the rest of the population. Wirth recognizes, however, that although the ghetto originated as a Jewish institution, there are ghettos in the United States that have never had Jewish occupants although the forces that underlie the formation and development of these areas bear a close resemblance to those that were at work in the early Jewish ghettos.

Wirth maintains that the typical ghetto is a densely populated, walled-in area usually found near the arteries of commerce. It has been kept intact by the fact that the outside world treats it as an entity. In his concluding remarks, Wirth reiterates two important points related to the understanding of all ghettos: (1) they must be viewed as sociopsychological as well as ecological (spatial), and (2) they are composed of heterogeneous cultural elements.

The heterogeneous nature of the ghetto is further emphasized in the next articles by Darden and Deskins. Darden, using census tract statistics for a Pittsburgh ghetto, observed that spatial variation exists within the ghetto according to the socioeconomic status of the residents. He concluded therefore that the ghetto is not homogeneous economically but is occupied by lower-, middle-, and upper-class residents, each class being residentially segregated in certain areas of the ghetto. Apparently the ghetto is a microcosm of the city as a whole.

The microcosm concept is further stressed by Deskins in his analysis of Detroit. Using city directories and census data as data sources and occupations as a variable, Deskins found that the internal structure of the black ghetto was similar to the internal structure in the nonghetto white community. In the white community, there is a direct relationship between residential neighborhoods defined by occupational level and distance from the center of the city, in that those in low-skilled occupations, e.g., laborers, will generally reside near the central business district and that those in high-skilled occupations, e.g., professionals, will live near the city's periphery and that all those in intervening occupations will be distributed spatially at distances from the central business district according to each group's level of occupational skill.

Within the context of ecological theory, Deskins argues that there exists in the black ghetto a pattern of residential neighborhoods defined by occupational level which is similar to that of the larger community—in other words, the black ghetto's internal structure is a microcosm of the city as a whole.

1

Joe T. Darden

DEFINITIONS OF GHETTO
Consensus versus Nonconsensus

It is characteristic of any discipline that its members are not always able unanimously to agree on the nature of the phenomena they examine. This lack of agreement is especially reflected in the formulation of concepts and definitions. The terminological confusion of phenomena probably occurs because too often a single term is used to symbolize a number of different concepts, just as the same concept is used to symbolize a number of different terms.

One of the crucial steps in the construction of functional theory is the analysis and clarification of concepts. Ambiguous concepts within any discipline can cause serious consequences since uncertainty about what is being referred to obstructs one from asking pertinent questions and thereby defining relevant problems for research.

Among urban social scientists who have focused their study on the ghetto, concepts of the ghetto have attained such a degree of heterogeneity that it is difficult to determine whether any one of the resulting definitions—or even any one group of definitions—affords an adequate description. To the extent that the degree of consensus is in doubt, one must remain uncertain as to whether different things are being described or whether the same thing is merely being viewed from different perspectives. This confusing situation calls for a reexamination of previous studies on the ghetto.

The term *ghetto* as used today is an oversimplification of both social and spatial relationships and conditions. It is therefore necessarily confusing. The students and social scientists now using the term not only risk being misunderstood; they may equally well be translating confusing impressions into assumptions. In this era of social consciousness, it would seem both appropriate and necessary to clarify terms, particularly when they are judgmental and have policy implications.

The objectives of this paper are therefore threefold: (1) to determine the extent of agreement on the meaning of the ghetto concept, (2) to explain the nature of any disagreement, and (3) to provide a framework within which an operational definition of ghetto may be derived.

SOURCES OF DATA AND METHODOLOGY

The sources of data for this paper consist of published and unpublished studies in which the term has been either explicitly or implicitly defined. Although the intention was to examine all the known definitions of ghetto, some have unavoidably been missed. The author however, believes that the definitions examined provides a representative sample. It is further believed that the present review of ghetto concepts is the most comprehensive ever conducted.

The method employed was a reference-by-reference search for every work incorporating the word "ghetto" in the title. Beginning with a single study, the author then examined the pertinent references given in the first study, the second study, and each study thereafter until total reference duplication was reached. Each work was then examined for an explicit definition of ghetto. When such a definition was found, it was recorded and labeled explicit. If no explicit definition was given, the examination continued in search of an implicit one. If such a definition was found, it was recorded and labeled implicit. If neither an explicit nor an implicit definition was found, the work was excluded from the analysis. Each usable definition was then examined to determine the characteristics or properties on which the concept was based. The characteristics and their contributing authors were listed for the purpose of analysis. The completed list was used to determine the extent of agreement between definitions and to group the authors according to their conceptualization. Several studies had to be discarded because no clearly formulated definition could be found, even though their subject matter was the ghetto. Thus, the final sample consisted of 103 definitions.

PRELIMINARY REVIEW OF GHETTO DEFINITIONS

Preliminary reviews of ghetto definitions revealed that the ghetto is probably the most misused and misunderstood spatial concept used by social scientists. There is not only disagreement concerning its meaning; there is also disagreement about the time and place of its origin.

It has been argued that the ghetto traces its ancestry back to medieval times; it has also been argued that the first ghetto was established in 139 B.C.—i.e., a date far earlier than the Middle Ages. There is also considerable disagreement on the location of the first ghetto. Some maintain that the first ghetto appeared in Western European cities; others maintain that the first ghetto appeared in Muslim cities and spread to Western Europe. Although the search for the origin of the ghetto is an interesting topic, it is beyond the scope of the present work. This study deals with the actual meaning of the word ghetto only in an attempt to find order among a plethora of definitions. Among such definitions are the following:

A ghetto is an area of the city characterized by poverty and acute social disorganization, and inhabited by members of a racial or ethnic group under conditions of involuntary segregation.

It is an area of the most deprived of all Americans in virtually every sense of the term.

It is an area of the marginally employed underclass, composed of people who lack the education and skills required to compete in the economy.

A number of scholars disagree with the above definitions. They argue that the ghetto is not necessarily an area of poverty, nor is it socially disorganized. The ghetto is not a homogeneous area of poor people or the marginally employed under class. Instead, it is inhabited by all incomes and social classes. The ghetto is merely ineffectually organized, not disorganized.

It is apparent from this preliminary review that consensus concerning the meaning of ghetto does not exist. A determination of the extent and nature of disagreement is the aim of the next section.

PERSPECTIVES ON THE GHETTO CONCEPT

As further review of ghetto definitions occurred, it became apparent that several social scientists were using the same variables to characterize ghettos as were used to characterize slums; i.e., the words ghettos and slums were being used interchangeably. The following definitions are typical:

The objective dimensions of the American urban ghettos are overcrowded and deteriorated housing, high infant mortality, crime and disease. The ghetto is an area of family disorganization, interpersonal distrust and suspicion, and high rates of social pathology.

The ghetto is a section of a city with the highest crime area, the largest proportion of uneducated and undereducated, and the largest proportion of unemployed.

The streets and sidewalks are often clustered with litter and garbage. Five-story tenements are flanked by shabby houses and wooden shacks; many are broken down and abandoned.

A ghetto has a high prevalence of social pathology, i.e., percentage of school dropouts, juvenile delinquency, illegitimacy, and dependency (percentage of the families in the area receiving aid to families with dependent children).

any dev. from norm. conditions

Social pathology is the common variable in the above definitions of ghetto. It is also well known that social pathology is the major variable likewise in the definition of slum. But are the terms ghetto and slum synonymous? This question is important because 77 or 75 percent of the 103 authors in the sample believe that ghetto and slum are synonymous and have thus used social pathology variables to define ghetto. If the two terms are, however, not interchangeable, then a large proportion of these scholars have incorrectly defined the ghetto and thereby may have at best added to the confusion and at worst contributed to the problem of the ghetto, rather than contributing to the solution. Whereas the former aspect has only academic implications, the latter has practical policy ones as well. In order to recommend effective policies for remedying the problems of the ghetto, there must first be cognitive clarity. Based on the present sample of 103 authors, only 26 or 25 percent, agree that the terms ghetto and slum are not synonymous. A number of authors have defended this position conceptually, theoretically, and logically.

Robert Forman wrote in *Black Ghettos, White Ghettos, and Slums* that although the terms slum and ghetto are frequently used interchangeably, they refer to different phenomena and should not be confused. Whereas residence in a ghetto is the result of racial or cultural characteristics, residence in a slum is primarily determined by economic factors. The typical slum resident lives in poor housing because he or she cannot afford to live in anything better. Whereas slum implies poverty, this is not necessarily true of ghetto. Forman recognizes, however, that there are slum ghettos; i.e., areas occupied by poor members of a racial, ethnic, or religious group whose location is the result not only of poverty but of there being segregation in housing, stemming from race, ethnicity, or religion. But Forman also recognizes that there are gilded ghettos, i.e., areas occupied by the nonpoor or middle and upperclass members of a racial, ethnic, or religious group caused by past and/or present discrimination in housing. Thus, social pathology is not a basic problem of the ghetto as a whole, just as it is not a problem of the city as a whole. Social pathology is only a problem of the slum portion. The ghetto as a whole includes successful families at both the working-class and middle-class levels.

Peter Labrie states in Chapter 14 of this volume that a ghetto is only a residential area inhabited by a common ethnic group. Economic poverty, for instance, is not a necessary characteristic of ghettos. Ghetto-slum areas constitute only one type of black residential area. Labrie is a firm believer in the work of E. Franklin Frazier, who demonstrated years ago in *The Negro Family in Chicago* that neighborhood differentiation by family organization and socioeconomic status tends to follow in broad outline the same general pattern within black residential areas as it does within white ones. The slum-ghetto is no more characteristic of black urban communities than skid row is of white urban communities. Karl Rasmussen in "The Multi-Ordered Urban Area: A Ghetto" has vociferously emphasized that the term ghetto cannot be interchanged with slum; they simply are not synonymous. The ghetto, unlike the slum, is not weak and hopeless. The ghetto derives its strength from consciousness of kind, social awareness, commitment and concern for betterment and change. The ghetto is not homogeneous nor is it as chronically pathological as people are often led to believe. The term refers to a wider area than the slum, and the ghetto spreads because of population growth, rather than because of deterioration. The spatial expansion of the black ghetto has been described by a number of social scientists. The center of the black belt is occupied by newcomers to the city who are often unskilled and unemployed. The more successful and better-educated residents tend to move farther out toward the periphery of the area. Occasionally they even move a short distance beyond the concentrated black area resulting in neighborhoods that are temporarily racially integrated, as the ghetto expands.

Empirical evidence that the ghetto is a microcosm of the city as a whole has also been presented by several sociological observers. E. Franklin Frazier was one of the first to use census statistics to test the concentric-zone pattern within subcommunities. According to this pattern, there is a residential distribution of the population by social classes. Growth of the city core and spatial expansion of the periphery set off waves in succession. New groups of immigrants, low in income, education, and occupational status settle close to the central business district; as these groups improve their socioeconomic status, they move out spatially toward the periphery, only to be succeeded by other more recent arrivals.

As long as this process continues, then, one would expect to find those with better incomes, more education, and higher occupational status living farther away from the central business district. Frazier examined 1920 census tract statistics for the black ghetto on the south side of Chicago. He found that the spatial expansion of the black community was, on the whole, similar to that of other racial and ethnic groups. The black population had gained a foothold in and near the center of the city, and as the city expanded, the segregation of the black population was part of the general process of segregation of different racial, economic, and ethnic groups. Moreover, as the black population moved farther southward toward the periphery of Chicago, a process of segregation of various elements in the black community on the basis of occupation occurred. Thus, it was possible to measure the process of segregation in the black community in 1920 by dividing the community into zones coinciding more or less with the expansion of the city as a whole.

Schnore in "Social Class Segregation Among Non-Whites in Metropolitan Centers" examined 1960 census tract statistics to determine if the pattern described by Frazier was also prevalent in other American cities. He selected only those tracts that (1) contained at least four hundred nonwhites and (2) were contiguous to the main areas of nonwhite concentration; i.e., the major ghettos. He found that nonwhite ghettos in the large Northern and border cities still tended to display the pattern observed earlier in Chicago—that is, as distance increases from the center of the city, the socioeconomic status of nonwhite neighborhoods goes up. Nonwhite family income is higher; nonwhite educational levels increase; and the relative number of nonwhite males in white collar employment is greater.

O. L. Edwards in "Patterns of Residential Segregation Within a Metropolitan Ghetto" used census data and the index of dissimilarity to analyze the spatial variation of social classes within the black ghetto of Milwaukee. He concluded that Milwaukee's black ghetto was not an undifferentiated mixture of elements of the nonwhite population. Within the area, nonwhite families of different income levels were segregated to a degree which was moderate in an absolute sense but approximated that of similar income groups in Milwaukee's white community.

Donald Deskins, whose paper is in Chapter 4 of this volume, used city directories to assess the residential mobility of blacks in Detroit. He found a strong correlation between social mobility and spatial mobility within Detroit's black ghetto. As distance from the center increased, there were increases in higher-status blacks, similar to the pattern found by E. Franklin Frazier. He therefore concluded that the black ghetto is a microcosm of the city as a whole.

In chapter 3 of this book, my own examination of 1970 census tract statistics for Pittsburgh's Hill District—the city's oldest black ghetto—revealed a similar pattern. The implications of the conceptual and empirical evidence are clear; that is, the black ghetto is a microcosm of the city as a whole (Figure 1.1). Yet most urban researchers of the ghetto have had an unfortunate tendency to speak and write about the black ghetto as if it were an indivisible entity, a slum, an area of social pathology where all blacks located in a central city area could be neatly fitted. Thus the myth, the misunderstanding and the confusions surrounding the ghetto have been created and perpetuated by a host of external ghetto researchers and writers. It has long been clear to blacks who live in ghettos that they, like other people, constitute different social groupings and that these separate social groups tend to congregate within the ghetto in different areas (Figure 1.1). Only a minority of authors in this book, however, hold this perspective; they apparently are able to recognize the fact that although some blacks live in slums, most do not. Most ghettos can be generalized as forming sectors emanating from a core in or near the central business district. In the inner part of the ghetto is the slum. But the outer portions are largely composed of middle- and upper-class families who are more similar economically to their white counterparts than to the residents of the inner-core slum. Yet the fact that the entire area remains black and is largely avoided by the white population is often because of erroneous information and negative perceptions of the character of the ghetto. The concept ghetto continues to evoke a mental picture of abandoned automobiles, garbage-filled vacant lots, dilapidated multi-family buildings, poverty, crime, disease, and hopelessness. Such a mental image has been shaped and perpetuated more by academicians and the popular media than by firsthand experience. There is reason to believe that the majority of Americans view the words *ghetto* and *slum* as one and the same thing and that they therefore use the concept interchangeably. It is still taken for granted that ghettos are by definition old, rat-infested, filthy central-city neighborhoods which should be avoided by the nonghetto population. Such a persistently negative image of the ghetto springing from the failure to distinguish between ghetto and slum has important policy implications.

DEFINITION OF GHETTO AND POLICY IMPLICATIONS

Unless cognitive clarity exists among policy makers concerning the meaning of ghetto and slum, and the consequent problems of each, no effective policies will be forthcoming. Once cognitive clarity is

Figure 1.1: Model of Ghetto as a Microcosm of the City

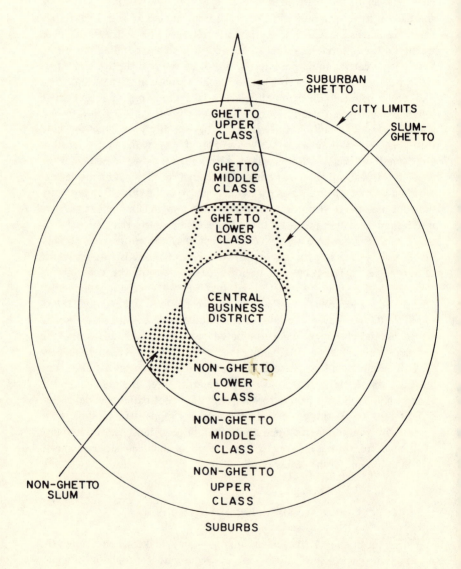

established, it will be obvious to policy makers that the problems of the ghetto and the problems of the slum are different. The problems of the ghetto are largely those stemming from discrimination in housing due to race, ethnicity, or religion, regardless of the socioeconomic status of the affected residents. On the other hand, the problems of the slum are economic, quite apart from discrimination in housing. A slum can be eliminated without spatial mobility or redistribution of the population. Elimination of the ghetto of necessity requires spatial mobility or a redistribution of the population. To eliminate a ghetto, deconcentration must occur. Thus the distinction between slum and ghetto is an important one.

There is reason to believe that much of the resistance to nonwhite entry into allwhite neighborhoods has been caused in part by the failure of the typical white resident to distinguish between ghetto and slum. Thus resistance to residential integration remains strong even against middle- and upper-class nonwhite residents. It therefore seems that nonwhite physical characteristics continue to be associated with slum characteristics. Such an association is prolonged by the fact that a high proportion of nonwhites in central cities do indeed live in ghettos. Take blacks, for example. It is apparent from the latest census that most blacks in cities live in ghettos. They do not however, live in slums. Nevertheless, the typical white resident's preoccupation with both color and social status appears to have encouraged him or her to make no distinctions within the ghetto population and thus to ascribe to *all* members of the ghetto the characteristics of those who live in the slum. The implications of this sort of outlook cannot be overemphasized. The nonslum dweller often associates the physical appearance and difficult living conditions of the slum with belief in the "natural inferiority" of those who live there: a slum is an inferior place; therefore those who live there must also be inferior. This image or mental picture which many, if not most, whites have of the ghetto, complete with all its undesirable characteristics, leads them to equate the "threat" of having a black neighbor on their block with that of having the slum spread right into their own street. Therefore, the movement of any black family into the neighborhood, regardless of socio- economic status, is usually resisted. This strong opposition has undoubtedly further hampered the already weak open-housing policies that exist in the United States.

TOWARD AN OPERATIONAL DEFINITION OF THE GHETTO

It is clear that the term ghetto has been used in various ways, leading to confusion and inaccuracies in defining its characteristics. What is needed is an operational definition of ghetto to eliminate the ambiguity. Such a definition should be based solely on racial, ethnic, or religious characteristics and not on housing quality, education, income, occupation, or other socioeconomic factors. Thus a ghetto is an area or contiguous areas of a city where more than 50 percent of a racial, ethnic, or religious group live due to past and/or present discrimination in housing. There can be micro ghettos that consist of a single city block and macro ghettos that consist of contiguous blocks, virtually encompassing the entire city. Most ghettos fall somewhere between these two extremes.

It has been demonstrated in this article that there is little agreement on the precise meaning of this concept *ghetto*. The nature of the disagreement centers on the perception by some social scientists that a ghetto is an area of social pathologies and the perception by others that the ghetto is a microcosm of the city as a whole. The former fail to distinguish between the difference in the characteristics of ghettos and slums. The latter make such a distinction and believe that such a distinction can be supported empirically. The confusion has implications for public policy by prolonging any solution to the problem of the ghetto. An operational definition of the ghetto based on racial, ethnic, or religious characteristics and not on characteristics that are socioeconomic in nature has therefore been presented to eliminate the persistent ambiguity.

2

Louis Wirth

THE GHETTO

For the past five hundred years the Jewish settlements in the Western world have been known as ghettos. The modern ghetto, some evidence of which is found in every city of even moderate size, traces its ancestry back to the medieval European urban institution by means of which the Jews were segregated from the rest of the population. In the East, until recently, the ghetto took the form of the "pale" of settlement, which represents a ghetto within a ghetto. The ghetto is no longer the place of officially regulated settlement of the Jews, but rather a local cultural area which has arisen quite informally. In American cities the name "ghetto" applies particularly to those areas where the poorest and most backward groups of the Jewish population, usually the recently arrived immigrants, find their home.

From the standpoint of the sociologist the ghetto as an institution is of interest first of all because it represents a prolonged case study in isolation. It may be regarded as a form of accommodation through which a minority has effectually been subordinated to a dominant group. The ghetto exhibits at least one historical form of dealing with a dissenting minority within a larger population, and as such has served as an instrument of control. At the same time the ghetto represents a form of toleration through which a *modus vivendi* is established between groups that are in conflict with each other on fundamental issues. Some

Reprinted from the *American Journal of Sociology*, Vol. 33 (July 1927), pp. 57–71, by permission of the publisher.

of these functions are still served by the modern ghetto, which, in other respects, has a character quite distinct from that of the medieval institution. In Western Europe and America, however, it is of primary interest because it shows the actual processes of distribution and grouping of the population in urban communities. It indicates the way in which cultural groups give expression to their heritages when transplanted to a strange habitat; it evidences the constant sifting and resifting that goes on in a population, the factors that are operative in assigning locations to each section, and the forces through which the community maintains its integrity and continuity. Finally, it demonstrates the subtle ways in which this cultural community is transformed by degrees until it blends with the larger community about it, meanwhile appearing in various altered guises of its old and unmistakable atmosphere.

This paper concerns itself, not with the history of the ghetto, but with its natural history. Viewed from this angle, the study of the ghetto is likely to throw light on a number of related phenomena, such as the origin of segregated areas and the development of local communities in general; for, while the ghetto is, strictly speaking, a Jewish institution, there are forms of ghettos that concern not merely Jews. Our cities contain Little Sicilies, Little Polands, Chinatowns, and Black Belts. There are Bohemians and Hobohemias, slums and Gold Coasts, vice areas and Rialtos in every metropolitan community. The forces that underlie the formation and development of these areas bear a close resemblance to those at work in the ghetto. These forms of community life are likely to become more intelligible if we know something of the Jewish ghetto.

The concentration of the Jews into segregated local areas in the medieval cities did not originate with any formal edict of church or state. The ghetto was not, as is sometimes mistakenly believed, the arbitrary creation of the authorities, designed to deal with an alien people. The ghetto was not the product of design on the part of anyone, but rather the unwitting crystallization of needs and practices rooted in the customs and heritages, religious and secular, of the Jews themselves. Long before it was made compulsory the Jews lived in separate parts of the cities in the Western lands of their own accord. The Jews drifted into separate cultural areas, not by external pressure or by deliberate design. The factors that operated toward the founding of locally separated communities by the Jews are to be sought in the character of Jewish traditions, in the habits and customs, not only of the Jews themselves, but of the medieval town-dweller in general. To the Jews the spatially separated and socially isolated community seemed to offer the best opportunity for following their religious precepts, their established ritual and diet, and the numerous functions which tied the individual to familial and communal institutions. In some instances it was the fear of the remainder of the population, no doubt, which induced them to seek each other's company, or the ruler under whose protection they stood found it desirable, for purposes of revenue and control, to grant them a separate quarter. The general tenor of medieval life no doubt played an important role, for it was customary for members of the same occupational group to live in the same locality, and the Jews, forming, as a whole, a separate vocational class and having a distinct economic status, were merely falling in line, therefore, with the framework of medieval society, in which everyone was tied to some locality. In addition, there were the numerous ties of kinship and acquaintanceship which developed an *esprit de corps* as a significant factor in community life. There was the item of a common language, of community of ideas and interests, and the mere congeniality that arises even between strangers who, coming from the same locality, meet in a strange place. Finally, the segregation of the Jews in ghettos is identical in many respects with the development of segregated areas in general. The tolerance that strange modes of life need and find in immigrant settlements, in Latin Quarters, in vice districts, and in racial colonies is a powerful factor in the sifting of the urban population and its allocation in separate local areas where one obtains freedom from hostile criticism and the backing of a group of kindred spirits.

Corresponding to the local separateness of the Jew from his Christian neighbors, there is to be noted the functional separation of the two groups. Just as the world beyond the ghetto wall was external to the life within the ghetto, so the personal relationships between Jews and non-Jews were those of externality and utility. The Jews supplemented the economic complex of medieval European life. They served a number of functions which the inhabitants of the town were incapable of exercising. The Jews were allowed to trade and engage in exchange, occupations which the church did not permit Christians to engage in. Besides, the Jews were valuable taxable property and could be relied on to furnish much-needed revenue. On the other hand, the Jews, too, regarded the Christian population as a means to an end, as utility. The Christians could perform functions such as eating the hindquarter of beef, and could purchase the commodities that the Jews had for sale; they could borrow money from the Jew, and pay interest; they could perform innumerable services for him which he could not perform himself. In the rigid structure of medieval life the Jews found a strategic place. The attitude of the medieval church had coupled trade and finance with sin. The Jews were free from this taboo, which made the occupation of merchant and banker seem undesirable to the Christian population. The Christian churchmen were not troubled about the "perils of the Jewish soul," for, so far as they knew, he had no soul to be saved. What made the trade relation possible, however, was not merely the fact that it was mutually advantageous, but the fact that trade relationships are possible when no other form of contact between two peoples can take place. The Jew, being a stranger and belonging, as he did, to a separate and distinct class, was admirably fitted to become the merchant and banker. He drifted to the towns and cities where trade was possible and profitable. Here he could utilize all the distant contacts that he had developed in the course of his wandering. His attachment to the community at large was slight, and when necessity demanded it, he could migrate to a locality where opportunities were greater. He owned no real property to which he was tied, nor was he the serf of a feudal lord. His mobility in turn developed versatility. He saw opportunities in places where no native could see them. While the ghetto was never more than a temporary stopping place, the Jew was never a hobo, for he had an aim, a destination, and his community went with him in his migrations.

While the Jew's contacts with the outside world were categorical and abstract, within his own community he was at home. Here he could relax from etiquette and formalism. His contacts with his fellow Jews were warm, intimate, and free. Especially was this true of his family life, within the inner circle of which he received the appreciation and sympathetic understanding which the larger world could not offer. In his own community, which was based upon the solidarity of the families that composed it, he was a person with status. Whenever he returned from a journey to a distant market, or from his daily work, he came back to the family fold, there to be recreated and reaffirmed as a man and as a Jew. Even when he was far removed from his kin, he lived his real inner life in his dreams and hopes with them. He could converse with his own kind in that familiar tongue which the rest of the world could not understand. He was bound by common troubles, by numerous ceremonies and sentiments to his small group that lived its own life oblivious of the world beyond the confines of the ghetto. Without the backing of his group, without the security that he enjoyed in his inner circle of friends and countrymen, life would have been intolerable.

Through the instrumentality of the ghetto there gradually developed that social distance which effectually isolated the Jew from the remainder of the population. These barriers did not completely inhibit contact, but they reduced it to the type of relationships which were of a secondary and formal nature. As these barriers crystallized and his life was lived more and more removed from the rest of the world, the solidarity of his own little community was enhanced until it became strictly divorced from the larger world without.

The forms of community life that had arisen naturally and spontaneously in the course of the attempt of the Jews to adapt themselves to their surroundings gradually became formalized in custom and precedent, and finally crystallized into legal enactment. What the Jews had sought as a privilege was soon to be imposed upon them by law. As the Jews had come to occupy a more important position in the medieval economy, and as the church at about the time of the Crusades became more militant, there set in a period of active regulation. The ghetto became compulsory. But the institution of the ghetto had by this time become firmly rooted in the habits and attitudes of the Jews. The historians of the ghetto are usually inclined to overemphasize the confining effect of the barriers that were set up around the Jew, and the provincial and stagnant character of ghetto existence. They forget that there was nevertheless a teeming life within the ghetto which was probably more active than life outside.

The laws that came to regulate the conduct of the Jews and Christians were merely the formal expressions of social distances that had already been ingrained in the people. While on the one hand the Jew was coming to be more and more a member of a class—an abstraction—on the other hand there persisted the tendency to react to him as a human being. The ghetto made the Jew self-conscious. Life in the ghetto was bearable only because there was a larger world outside, of which many Jews often got more than a passing glimpse. As a result they often lived on the fringe of two worlds. There was always some movement to get out of the ghetto on the part of those who were attracted by the wide world that lay beyond the horizon of the ghetto walls and who were cramped by the seemingly narrow life within. Sometimes a Jew would leave the ghetto and become converted; and sometimes these converts, broken and humiliated, would return to the ghetto to taste again of the warm, intimate, tribal life that was to be found nowhere but among their people. On such occasions the romance of the renegade would be told in the ghetto streets, and the whole community would thereby be welded into a solid mass amid the solemn ceremonies by which the stray member was reincorporated into the community.

The inner solidarity of the ghetto community always lay in the ties of family life, and through the organization in the synagogue these families gained status within a community. Confined as the province of the ghetto was, there was ample opportunity for the display of capacity for leadership. The ghetto community was minutely specialized and highly integrated. There were probably more distinct types of personality and institutions within the narrow ghetto streets than in the larger world outside.

The typical ghetto is a densely populated, walled-in area usually found near the arteries of commerce or in the vicinity of a market. The Jewish quarter, even before the days of the compulsory ghetto, seems to have grown up around the synagogue, which was the center of Jewish life, locally as well as religiously. A common feature of all ghettos was also the cemetery, which was a communal responsibility and to which unusual sentimental interest was attached. There were a number of educational, recreational, and hygienic institutions, such as a school for the young, a bath, a slaughterhouse, a bakehouse, and a dance hall. In the close life within the ghetto walls almost nothing was left to the devices of the individual. Life was well organized, and custom and ritual played an institutionalizing role which still accounts for the high degree of organization in Jewish communities, often verging on overorganization. These institutions did not arise ready-made. They represent what life always is, an adaptation to the physical and social needs of a people. In this case particularly, those institutions that had to deal with the conflict and disorder within the group and the pressure from without were the characteristic form of accommodation to the isolation which the ghetto symbolized and enforced. This holds good not merely for the institutions of the ghetto, but for the functionaries and personalities that center around them. The Jews as a race as we know them today are themselves a product of the ghetto.

The ghetto, from the standpoint of biology, was a closely inbreeding, self-perpetuating group to such an extent that it may properly be called a closed community. Not that there was no intermarriage, but these mixed marriages as a rule were lost to the ghetto. The Jews have frequently and rightly been pointed out as the classic example of the great force of religious and racial prejudices, of segregation and isolation, in giving rise to distinct physical and social types. These types persist roughly to the extent that ghetto life and its effects have continued relatively unchanged, which is most true of Eastern Europe and the Orient. The difference in community life accounts in large part for the differences between various local groupings within the Jewish population.

The Russian, Polish, and in part the Roumanian Jews differ from those of Western Europe—the German, French, Dutch, and English Jews—in several fundamental respects. For a long period the Jews of the East were merely a cultural dependency—an outpost—of Western Jewry. When an independent cultural life did develop in Russia, Poland, and Lithuania, it was self-sufficient and self-contained, set apart from the larger world. Not so with the Jews of Western Europe. They were never quite impervious to the currents of thought and the social changes that characterized the life of Europe since the Renaissance. While the Jews of the East lived in part in rural communities, in a village world, those of the West were predominantly a city people, in touch with the centers of trade and finance near and far, and in touch at least for some time with the pulsating intellectual life of the world. While the Jews of the Rhine cities were associating with men of thought and of affairs, their brethren in Russia were dealing with peasants and an uncultured, decadent, feudal nobility. When the Jewries of the West were already seething with modernist religious, political, and social movements, those of the East were still steeped in mysticism and medieval ritual. While the Western Jews were moving along with the tide of progress, those of the East were still sharing the backwardness and isolation of the Gentile world of villagers and peasants. Although until the middle of the last century the Jews of the East were never quite so confined in their physical movements as were the ghetto Jews of the West, the former lived in a smaller world, a world characterized by rigidity and stability; and when they were herded into cities, in which they constituted the preponderant bulk of the total population, they merely turned these cities into large villages that had little in common with the urban centers of the West. Many features of local life in the modern Jewish community bear the imprint of the successive waves of immigrants first from the West and then from the East.

The formal enactments that made the ghetto the legal dwelling place of the Jews were abolished toward the middle of the last century in most of the countries of the world. Strangely enough, the abolition of the legal ghetto was opposed by a great portion of Jews as late as a hundred years ago, for they had a premonition that the leveling of the ghetto walls would mean the wiping out of separate community life, which the formal ghetto rules merely symbolized. Those who saw in the new freedom the waning influence of the Jewish religion and the ultimate dissolution of Jewish life in separate communities had two things left to console them: (1) the formal equality decreed by law did not at once gain for the Jew ready acceptance and a parallel social status among his fellow citizens; and (2) although Western Jewry seemed to be crumbling, there were approximately six millions of Jews left on the other side of the Vistula who were still clinging to the old bonds that exclusion and oppression had fashioned. But since that time even Russia had been revolutionized, and the so-called last bulwark of Judaism threatens to disappear.

Just as the ghetto arose before formal decrees forced the Jews into segregated areas, so the ghetto persists after these decrees have been annulled. Israel Zangwill, in *Children of the Ghetto*, has said: "People who have been living in a ghetto for a couple of centuries are not able to step outside merely because the gates are thrown down, nor to efface the brands on their souls by putting off their yellow badges. The isolation from without will have come to seem the law of their being." The formal abolition of the ghetto and the granting of citizenship did for the Jews about what the Emancipation Proclamation did for the Negro. Slavery was more than a mere legal relationship, and the ghetto was more than a statute. It had become an institution. Though the physical walls of the ghetto have been torn down, an invisible wall of isolation still maintains the distance between the Jew and his neighbors.

Even in towns containing only a handful of Jews, there will be found in all parts of the world some more or less definitely organized community. The ecological factors that enter into its development are essentially those of the medieval ghetto. There are several items besides the continuity of traditions from within and prejudice from without that account for the persistence of the modern ghetto, particularly in American cities. One of these is the colonization movement among the Jews, by which Old World communities are sometimes kept intact in the New World. But even where no such organized effort exists, it is remarkable to what extent the Jewish community tends to perpetuate its old surroundings.

To a large extent the modern ghetto is necessitated by the precepts and practices of Orthodox Judaism, by the need of dwelling within easy reach of the synagogue, the schoolroom, and the ritual bath, the kosher butcher shop and the kosher dairy. But even for those who are indifferent to religious observances and ritual practices, residence in the ghetto is necessitated by social and economic circumstances. Ignorance of the language of the new country, of its labor conditions, and of its general habits and ways of thought, as well as the natural timidity of a fugitive from a land of persecution, compels the immigrant Jew to settle in the colony of his coreligionists. Among them he is perfectly at home; he finds the path of employment comparatively smooth, and if his efforts to attain it be delayed, he is helped in the interval by charity from a dozen hands.

In countries where the contact between Jew and non-Jew has been continued for a few generations, and where no new immigration from other countries in which the Jews retained their old status has taken place, the ghetto has to a large extent disintegrated. Under these circumstances, not only does the ghetto tend to disappear, but the race tends to disappear with it. Contact with the world through education, commerce, and the arts tends to bring about a substitution of the cultural values of the world at large for those of the ghetto. This contact, moreover, frequently brings about intermarriage, which is most frequent in those localities where intercourse between Jew and Gentile is least restricted. It is safe to say that the present fifteen and a half million Jews in the world constitute only a small portion of the living descendants of the original Jewish settlers in the Western world at the beginning of the Christian era. They are merely the residue of a much larger group whose Jewish identity has been lost in the general stream of population. What has happened in the case of the Jews is essentially what has happened to all minority groups in recent times. As the barriers of isolation have receded, social intercourse and interbreeding have decimated the size of the group and leveled its distinguishing characteristics to those of the milieu.

A Jewish community may in some respects be said to exist after the obstacles to ready intercourse with the world outside have been removed, but it tends to become a nondescript community. Where, however, as is the case in most large cities of Western Europe and especially the United States, a steady influx of new immigrants has replenished the disintegrating community, there a ghetto, with all the characteristic local color, has grown up and maintains itself. It is with such a community, as found in the Chicago ghetto, that this study has dealt.

Western ghettos differ from those of the East in that the former comprise at least two sections, the native and the foreign. The native section lives in some sort of concentration within convenient distance from the communal institutions. A rise in material prosperity is generally followed by a removal to a better district, where a new Jewish area is created, but one less distinguished from its environment by external tokens. The foreign section, however, lives in a state of dense concentration. Their poverty makes them settle in the poor quarter of the town, where they reproduce the social conditions in which they have been born and bred, so far as the new environment will allow. The ghetto in the East may be a symbol of political bondage; but in the West the only bondage that it typifies is that exercised by economic status, by sentiment and tradition.

If you would know what kind of Jew a man is, ask him where he lives; for no single factor indicates as much about the character of the Jew as the area in which he lives. It is an index not only to his economic status, his occupation, his religion, but to his politics and his outlook on life, and the stage in the assimilative process that he has reached.

West of the Chicago River, in the shadow of the central business district, lies a densely populated rectangle of crowded tenements representing the greater part of Chicago's immigrant colonies, among them the ghetto. It contains the most varied assortment of people to be found in any similar area of the world. This area has been the stamping ground of virtually every immigrant group that has come to Chicago. The occupation of this area by the Jews is, it seems, merely a passing phase of a long process of succession in which one population group has been crowded out by another. There is, however, an unmistakable regularity in this process. In the course of the growth of the city and the invasion of the slums by new groups of immigrants, there has resulted a constancy of association between Jews and other ethnic groups. Each racial and cultural group tends to settle in that part of the city which, from the point of view of rents, standards of living, accessibility, and tolerance, makes the reproduction of the Old World life easiest. In the course of the invasion of these tides of immigrants, the ghetto has become converted from the outskirts of an overgrown village to the slum of a great city in little more than one generation. The Jews have successively displaced the Germans, the Irish, and the Bohemians, and have themselves been displaced by the Poles, the Lithuanians, the Italians, the Greeks, the Turks, and finally the Negro. The Poles and Jews detest each other thoroughly, but they can trade with each other very successfully. They have transferred the accommodation to each other from the Old World to the New. The latest invasion of the ghetto by the Negro is of more than passing interest. The Negro, like the immigrant, is segregated in the city into a racial colony; economic factors, race prejudice, and cultural differences combine to set him apart. The Negro has drifted to the abandoned sections of the ghetto for precisely the same reasons that the Jews and the Italians came there. Unlike the white landlords and residents of former days in other parts of the city, the Jews have offered no appreciable resistance to the invasion of the Negroes. The Negroes pay good rent and spend their money readily. Many of the immigrants of the ghetto have not as yet discovered the color line.

The transition and deterioration of the ghetto has been proceeding at such speed that the complexion of the area changes from day to day. Dilapidated structures that a decade ago were Lutheran and Catholic churches have since become synagogues, and have now been turned into African M.E. churches. Under the latest coat of paint of a store-front colored mission, there are vestiges of signs reading "Kosher Butchershop" and "Deutsche Apotheke."

True to the ancient pattern, the most colorful and active section of the ghetto is the street market, which resembles a medieval fair more than the shopping district of a modern city. But this institution, together with the rest of ghetto culture, is fast declining. The life of the immigrants in the ghetto is so circumscribed and they are so integrally a part of it that they are unaware of its existence. It is the children of the immigrant who discover the ghetto and then ... flee. What a few years ago was a steady but slow outward movement has now developed into a veritable stampede to get out of the ghetto; for, with all its varied activities and its colorful atmosphere, the ghetto nevertheless is a small world. It throbs with a life which is provincial and sectarian. Its successes are measured on a small scale, and its range of expression is limited.

Not until the immigrant leaves the ghetto does he become fully conscious of himself and his status. He feels a sense of personal freedom and expansion as he takes up his residence in the more modern and less Jewish area of second settlement. As late as twenty years ago, when the first Jewish fugitives from the ghetto invaded Lawndale, an area about two miles west, which in Chicago represents the area of second settlement, they came into collision with the Irish and the Germans, who had turned what was recently a prairie into something like a park. It took the Jews about ten years to convert it into a densely settled apartment-house area. At first they could not rent. Experience in the ghetto from which the Irish and Germans had been displaced had given these residents a vision of what was in store for their homes. But this time the Jews could afford to buy, and they bought in blocks. By 1910 Lawndale had become a second ghetto. Its synagogues were a little more modern than those of Maxwell Street; the beards of the Lawndale Jews were a little trimmer, and their coats a little shorter, than in the original ghetto; but Lawndale had become Jewish. Those residents of the ghetto who stayed behind derisively called Lawndale "Deutschland," and its inhabitants "Deutschuks," because they were affecting German ways.

But the Lawndale Jews found little rest and satisfaction. Their erstwhile neighbors, impelled by identical motives—to flee from their fellow Jews, and be less Jewish—had given Lawndale a new complexion, unmistakably Jewish, though not quite as genuine as that of the ghetto itself.

In their attempt to flee from the ghetto, the partially assimilated Jews have found that the ghetto has followed them, and a new exodus sets in. The plans of those who fled from the ghetto in order to obtain status as human beings—as successful business or professional men, rather than as Jews—have been frustrated by the similar plans of others. So it is with the third settlement in the fashionable apartment hotels and the suburbs. As the area becomes predominantly Jewish, the non-Jewish settlers move, and the Jews begin the pursuit anew. Scarcely does the Jew get a glimpse of the freer world that looms beyond the ghetto when he becomes irritated by the presence of his fellow Jews, more Jewish than himself; he is bored, disgusted, and resumes his flight.

In the process he changes his character and his institutions. But what has held the community together in spite of all disintegrating forces from within and without is not only the replenishment of the ghetto by new immigrants—for this is a waning factor—but rather the return to the ghetto of those who have fled but have been disappointed and disillusioned about the results of their flight. They have found the outside world cold and unresponsive to their claims, and return to the warmth and the intimacy of the ghetto. Finally, the Jewish community has been kept intact by the fact that the outside world has treated it as an entity. The Jewish problem, if there be one, consists in the fact that the ghetto persists in spite of the attempt of so many to flee. As long as the nucleus remains, it will serve as a symbol of community life to which even those who are far removed in space and in sympathies belong and by which they are identified.

The Jews as individuals do not always find the way to assimilation blocked. They make friends as well as enemies. The contacts between cultural and racial groups inevitably produce harmony as well as friction; and the one cannot be promoted nor the other prevented by nostrums and ready-made programs and administrative devices. Interaction is life, and life is growth which defies attempts at control and direction, however rational they may be, that do not take account of this dynamic process. In the struggle for status, personality arises. The Jew, like every other human being, owes his unique character to this struggle, and that character will change and perhaps disappear as the struggle changes or subsides.

What makes the Jewish community—composed as it is of heterogeneous cultural elements and distributed in separate areas of our cities—a community is its capacity to act corporately. It is a cultural community and constitutes as near an approach to communal life as the modern city has to offer. The ghetto, be it Chinese, Negro, Sicilian, or Jewish, can be completely understood only if it is viewed as a sociopsychological, as well as an ecological, phenomenon; for it is not merely a physical fact, but also a state of mind.

3

Joe T. Darden

THE QUALITY OF LIFE
IN A BLACK GHETTO
A Geographic View

Since Friedrich Engels' study, *The Condition of the Working Class in England in 1844,* it has been generally agreed that the quality of life in an industrial city increases with distance from the central business district (CBD). The conclusions of Engels were reiterated by Ernest W. Burgess in 1924 in his classic study, *The Growth of the City.* According to Burgess, new groups of immigrants, low in income, education, and occupational standing, settled in and around the central business district; as these groups improved their social status or worked their way up in the social class structure, they moved out toward the periphery. As long as this process of social and spatial mobility continued, one would expect to find people with higher income, education, and occupational status living farther out from the center.

A few years later, E. Franklin Frazier, a student of Burgess', concluded in *The Negro Family in Chicago* that the social and spatial pattern described for the city of Chicago as a whole existed within subcommunities including the black ghetto. Recently Leo Schnore focused on the spatial variation of socioeconomic life within the black ghetto in his work, "Social Class Segregation Among Nonwhites in Metropolitan Centers." He used three measures of socioeconomic status; namely, income, education, and occupation. He concluded that, in general, nonwhite ghettos in large Northern and border cities still tend to display

Reprinted from the *Pennsylvania Geographer,* Vol. 12, No. 3 (November 1974), pp. 3–8, by permission of the publisher.

the spatial pattern observed earlier in the city of Chicago. In other words, as distance increases from the center of the city, the socioeconomic status of nonwhite neighborhoods goes up. Nonwhite family income and educational levels are higher, and the relative number of nonwhite males in "white-collar" employment increases.

Donald Deskins, Jr., in Chapter 4 of this volume, has used data from city directories and census tracts to conclude that "there exists within the black subcommunity a pattern of residential neighborhoods defined by occupational level which is similar to that of the larger community— in other words, the black subcommunity is a microcosm of the city as a whole." Taking Detroit as his study area, Deskins argues that the internal structure of the ghetto, which resembles the internal structure of an industrial city, continued unaltered from 1950 to 1970. Within this structure, Detroit's affluent blacks occupied residences on the edge of the ghetto as far removed from the CBD as circumstances permitted. Most of these upper-class black residences were concentrated in the northwestern part of the city, while those blacks with lower skills remained trapped in the inner city, next to the CBD.

None of these studies, however, focused on Pittsburgh, and most of their conclusions were based on data prior to 1970. Most of the antidiscriminatory housing legislation occurred in the decade from 1960 to 1970. Also during this decade, upper-class blacks made significant socioeconomic gains. Did such changes result from upper-class blacks moving out of the ghetto leaving behind a homogeneous population of low-income, poorly educated, poverty-stricken people? Or, in spite of the socioeconomic changes affecting blacks during the sixties, does the quality of life in the ghetto still continue to improve with distance from the CBD?

THE CONCEPT OF THE QUALITY OF LIFE AND METHOD OF ANALYSIS

The concept of the quality of life as used in this paper is very narrowly defined and merely refers to the level of socioeconomic well-being or standard of living. Thus it is not the intent of this paper to focus on the total quality of life in the ghetto. The aspects of the quality of life involving amenities and of how ghetto residents perceive the conditions under which they live are excluded. However, past evidence seems to show that at least one group of ghetto residents—namely, youth—have a negative perception of the quality of life in the ghetto, as indicated in Chapter 12 of this volume.

Data for this paper were obtained from 1970 census tract statistics for an area of Pittsburgh known as the Hill District. Most of the Hill District consists of the oldest black ghetto in Pittsburgh (Figure 3.1). Ghetto is here defined as an area of the city where blacks of diverse socioeconomic status have been forced to live because of past and present discrimination in housing. Census tracts were selected on the basis of (1) the percentage black and (2) location in reference to the CBD. A total of five tracts was chosen for intensive investigation. The tracts ranged

Figure 3.1

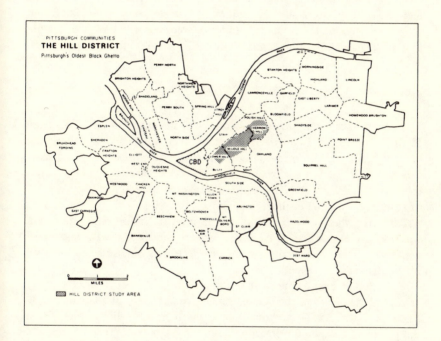

from 87.3 percent to 99.1 percent black. Each tract was placed into one-mile-distance zones from the center of the CBD. Three of the five tracts fell within the same zone. In order to reveal the intrazonal variation—that is, the differences from tract to tract within each zone—these three tracts have been listed in ascending distance from the CBD, and data have been presented on each tract along with the average figure for the zone. The following variables were chosen for investigation: income (including

the percentage of families on welfare), education, occupation (including unemployment), housing value, rent, room occupancy, and the percentage of housing units lacking some or all plumbing. Income here means median family income. Education refers to median school years completed by persons aged twenty-five and over. Occupation consists of the total number of employed persons sixteen years of age and over. Housing value refers to median value of owner-occupied one-family houses on less than ten acres, without a commercial establishment or medical office on the property. The value is determined by the resident's estimate of how much the property—house—would sell for if it were for sale. Rent means median contract rent, or monthly rent agreed to, or contracted for, even if the furnishings, utilities, or services are included. Room crowding refers to the percentage of households consisting of two or more persons living in dwelling units with 1.51 or more persons per room.

FINDINGS

Without exception, income increases with distance from the CBD from $2,087 to $7,000. Likewise, as distance from the CBD increases, the percentage of families on welfare declines. In both cases the spatial variation is not slight but major. As distance increases from the one- to two-mile zone, median family income more than doubles, and the percentage of families on welfare declines from 26 to 11 percent.

Although the spatial variation in the level of educational attainment was not as great as that of income, a pattern similar to the Burgess model was evident; i.e., as distance from the CBD increases, so does the level of educational attainment.

Perhaps the best evidence that the ghetto is a microcosm of the city as a whole is found in the occupational characteristics of the ghetto residents. A basic misunderstanding of the ghetto is the belief by many that the ghetto is composed primarily of unskilled laborers, private household workers, and the hard-core unemployed. Contrary to popular belief, the evidence reveals that all these groups are in the minority in the ghetto just as they are in the city as a whole. There are slightly less laborers (8 percent) and private household workers (5 percent) in the Hill District ghetto than professional, technical, and kindred workers (9 percent). Certainly unemployment is high in the ghetto, but it tends to be spatially confined to the area closest to the CBD. As the distance from the CBD increases, unemployment declines to about the level of the city as a whole. This spatial pattern of unemployment clearly reflects the Burgess model. Such a spatial pattern is also evident as the percentage of workers employed in white-collar jobs increases with distance from the CBD from 5 percent to 10.5 percent.

In spite of the antidiscriminatory housing legislation enacted during the sixties, black professionals have not left the ghetto. Their presence is very obvious as they rank fourth in number among all workers in the ghetto. More evidence that the ghetto is a microcosm of the city as a whole is reflected in the types of industries in which ghetto workers are employed. Ghetto workers are employed in every industrial category. Manufacturing ranks first, thus reflecting the industrial pattern of the city of Pittsburgh.

A final indication of the spatial variation in the quality of life in the ghetto is found in ghetto housing. As the distance from the CBD increases, housing values and rents also increase. However, room overcrowding and the percentage of units lacking some or all plumbing decline from 4.7 to 1.6 and from 27.2 to 8.3 respectively.

An analysis of a Pittsburgh ghetto has revealed that the quality of life is not the same throughout the ghetto, but increases with distance from the CBD. Thus the ghetto is a microcosm of the city as a whole; i.e., as distance from the CBD increases, the quality of life within the city as a whole increases. Therefore, the conclusions of E. Franklin Frazier on blacks in Chicago during the thirties and the conclusions of Donald R. Deskins, Jr., on blacks in Detroit also hold true for blacks in Pittsburgh during the seventies.

4

Donald R. Deskins, Jr.

THE BLACK SUBCOMMUNITY
A Microcosm

reality

Residential segregation of blacks is an obvious ~~phenomenon~~ in American cities, and although black segregation is particularly evident in contemporary urban America, it did not have its origin in this decade nor in this century. There is overwhelming evidence that the residential separation of blacks and whites in American cities has historical continuity. As early as 1899, W. E. B. Du Bois found Philadelphia's black population concentrated in that city's worst areas, and nearly thirty years later, in 1928, Ernest W. Burgess wrote that the "separation by residence of the Negro exists in some form in all American cities." Recent documentation of black residential segregation is presented in the monograph *Negroes in Cities* by Karl E. and Alma F. Taeuber in which they state that "residential segregation occupies a key position in patterns of race relations in urban United States." The reality is that residential segregation is increasing and urban blacks are more segregated today than they were a decade ago.

The objective of this paper, however, is not to dwell on either the historical documentation or definition of segregation. It is to gain insight concerning the ~~spatially manifested~~ effects of residential segregation by longitudinally comparing black and white residential patterns within the city of Detroit. To realize this ~~objective~~, the central focus is to examine

---

Reprinted from *Residential Mobility of Negroes in Detroit, 1837-1965*, Ann Arbor: Michigan Geographical Publication No. 5, 1972 (updated with 1970 data).

and analyze the change in the spatial patterns of residential neighborhoods defined by occupation and race (within the content of urban ecological theory.)

THEORIES ON CITY GROWTH AND STRUCTURE

The search for a ~~holistic~~ *encompassing* theory on growth and structure of cities is continuous and has never been the exclusive concern of geographers. In fact, this effort has always involved interested scholars from a wide range of disciplines. Traditionally sociologists, economists, geographers, and more recently historians have been actively engaged in this search.

Geographers' Contribution. Admittedly, geographers have not led this effort; however, geography as a discipline has long been engaged in studies which have contributed substantially to the better understanding of certain ecological aspects of city growth and structure. The works of Barrows, Colby, Whittlesey, and Ullman and Harris are representative of geography's contribution.

Barrows in his presidential address before the Association of American Geographers in 1922 called for an interpretation of city landscape by considering such factors as the location and distribution of residential, commercial, and manufacturing districts in a structural framework. Barrows' awareness of the urban environment's potential as a laboratory for geographic research is coincidential with similar developments in sociology.

On the other hand, Colby's contribution exceeds the call to urban research issued by Barrows. Colby's assertion that there are centrifugal and centripetal forces at work in the urban environment which together delineate its structure has had much more impact because he viewed the city as a dynamic organism constantly in the process of evolution. The true significance of Colby's contribution to urban studies may be more philosophical than substantive, but nevertheless is extremely important from either point of view. The emphasis on process and change may prove to be the single most important geographic contribution to urban ecological theory. Whittlesey's notion of "sequence occupance" also enriched the understanding of the process of growth and change in urban residential patterns.

These contributions were followed by that of Ullman and Harris in their theory on urban growth and structure presented in the widely referred-to paper, "The Nature of Cities." A detailed account of the Harris-Ullman contribution is made in the discussion entitled "Multiple-Nuclei Theory" [see below].

Toward a Holistic Theory. The processes of urban segregation and its effects on residential patterns can best be understood within the general context of urban ecological theory. Urban ecology, like urban geography, is concerned with the interrelationships between men and their spatial settings within cities. Although other social scientists have participated in ecological studies, sociologists in the early 1920s showed particular interest and leadership in developing human ecology as a research discipline. By pursuing scientific studies which integrated the ecological processes of (1) centralization, (2) decentralization, (3) segregation, and (4) invasion and succession, an ecological theory on urban growth and structure evolved. The stimulus which led to this development came in 1915 when Robert E. Park published his classic paper, "The City: Suggestions for the Investigation of Human Behavior in the Urban Environment."

Within the next three decades, in response to Park's stimulus, three theories on urban growth and structure emerged. The first of these theories is the "concentric-zone theory" on urban growth formulated by Ernest W. Burgess, a sociologist and colleague of Park at the University of Chicago. The second is the "sector theory" of urban growth which was first formulated by Richard M. Hurd and later developed by Homer Hoyt, a land economist trained at the University of Chicago. The third theory on urban growth to evolve is the "Multiple-Nuclei Theory" by geographers Chauncy D. Harris and Edward L. Ullman, also affiliated with the University of Chicago.

Concentric Zone Theory. Burgess' theory suggests that as the city grows it expands outward from its center, assuming a pattern approximating concentric zones, each with distinctive land use and socioeconomic characteristics. The respective zones from the city center to the periphery are (1) The Loop (central business district), (2) Zone in Transition, (3) Zone of Workingmen's Homes, (4) Residential Zone, and (5) Commuter Zone. The theory infers that as the city expands spatially the process of invasion and succession occurs where each inner zone has the tendency to extend its area by encroaching upon that of the next adjacent outer zone.

On the other hand, according to Hoyt, growth proceeds from the center of the city along radial transportation routes. The resulting pattern is a series of sectors or wedges which differ in land use and associated socioeconomic composition depending upon the tradition of past land use or occupancy in that area and the carrying capacity of the route. Hoyt's theory is based upon the findings of a real-property survey conducted in 147 American cities.

Multiple-Nuclei Theory. Harris and Ullman's theory is the most recent contribution to the theories on urban growth and structure. In this theory it is postulated that the city has not one but several centers, each of which has a specialized function or combination of functions. As the city expands, the resulting patterns are neither concentric nor wedge-shaped. The internal arrangement of land uses may assume any number of shapes depending on the particular city and the number and growth-generating capacity of its centers, some of which in the past may have been nearby small-town centers developed in a different era.

Each of these theories presents an abstract construct of a city's internal spatial structure, and empirical evidence has been found to support each of them. All of the theories, particularly Burgess', have been the center of controversy. However, Burgess' theory has the distinction of being the first to have been formulated, the most severely criticized, the most durable, as well as the most widely referred to.

Of the three theories, on city structure and growth, Burgess' concentric-zone theory also has the distinction of being the most explicit in its treatment of the ecological processes relative to the location of immigrant and racial groups in American cities. In his paper, "Residential Segregation in American Cities," he states:

This paper accordingly proposes to inquire into the residential separation of the Negro from the rest of the community in the setting in the larger process of urban segregation. From this perspective may perhaps be gained a clearer understanding of the interplay of the factors and forces which determine the location and movement of Negro neighborhoods within the larger community.

The implication derived from this statement is that any discussion of the location and change in black residential neighborhoods should be within the general context of ecological theory and specifically within the framework of the concentric-zone theory. Burgess also emphasizes that the ecological processes affecting the residential location of immigrant groups affect blacks similarly. In fact, both groups upon entry in the city occupy neighborhoods in zones I and II, which are collectively referred to as the "port of entry," and all expansion of immigrant or black residential neighborhoods is outward from the "port of entry."

Although the expansion of black residential neighborhoods may be met with legal or extralegal resistance, the same ecological processes are still operating.

E. Franklin Frazier in his study, *The Negro Family in Chicago,* observed that these ecological processes not only operate so that concentric patterns are revealed for the entire city, but these processes also show evidence of operating within the segregated black subcommunity. He found that there are zonal patterns within the black subcommunity that are similar to those described by Burgess for the city as a whole. This finding was later confirmed in Frazier's study of Harlem.

Although Burgess' theory has been criticized, it remains conceptually sound. It has not as yet been replaced by a better theoretical construct, and it is the only theory that has placed black residential neighborhoods and residential segregation into the overall scheme of city growth and structure. This reason alone amply justifies its use as the basic starting point for this paper.

HYPOTHESES AND ASSUMPTIONS

Before discussing the hypotheses to be tested, an exploration of the assumption that occupation is more closely related to area of residence than income or education has to be made.

It can be argued that income is the most important factor to consider when renting or purchasing a home is contemplated and therefore income is the determining factor in residential location. It is obvious that income strongly contributes to home-purchasing ability and should not be minimized. However, occupation appears to be the principal factor in determining an occupant's class position as well as being a very important factor in the establishment of a life-style pattern, and thus influences the residential-locational-choice decision. Occupation is the element which largely determines associations and interests, therefore defining the group in which the individual will participate. Interpreting this relationship spatially, it can be said that occupation defines the individual's interaction space. Taking all of these considerations into account, occupation then appears to be more closely related to the selection of a residential location than is income. Based upon the evidence to support this point found in the works of Arthur H. Wilkins and Albert J. Reiss, Jr., the assumption that occupation is the primary factor determining residential location is accepted in this paper. To expand this assumption to the group level, then it is assumed that residential neighborhoods are defined by occupation considering that occupation will largely determine the group's associations and interests, thus its interaction space. Since the associations and interests of occupational groups differ with skill level, occupational groups tend to separate themselves spatially.

Acknowledging these assumptions and that there exists a relationship between occupational levels and the types of residential neighborhoods described by Burgess, then it can be hypothesized that:

Figure 4.1: Relationship Between Burgess' & Frazier's Zones

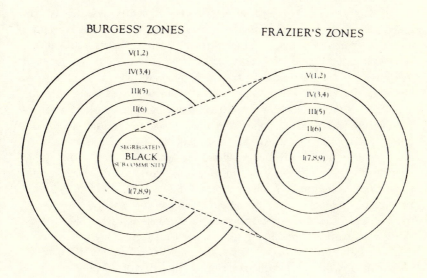

There is a direct relationship between residential neighborhoods defined by occupational level and distance from the center of the city, in that low-skilled occupations, e.g., *laborers*, will generally reside near the CBD, and high-skilled occupations, e.g., *professionals*, will locate near the city limits, and all intervening occupations will be arrayed at distances from the CBD according to each occupational group's level of skill.

A test of this hypothesis will reveal the pattern of residential neighborhoods for the city as a whole. Within the city, based upon theory and contemporary empirical evidence, it can be expected that the segregated black subcommunity will probably be located near the city's center.

Recognizing that black residential location is usually modified by the exercise of various constraints, and following Frazier's notions, it also can be hypothesized that:

There exists within the black subcommunity a pattern of residential neighborhoods defined by occupational level which is similar to that of the
larger community—in other words, the black subcommunity's internal
structure is a microcosm of the city as a whole.

The relationship suggested by Frazier is illustrated in Figure 4.1

DATA

Burgess and Frazier used land-use categories as the basis to establish
the intracity residential-area arrangements. Recently researchers have
relied heavily upon socioeconomic data as the basis for establishing intracity arrangements of residential areas. It is apparent that this substitution
is possible when Figure 4.2 is examined.

It is also obvious that data for this inquiry are drawn from, not one,
but several sources. The primary source from which data are extracted
is a series of city directories for Detroit covering approximately a ninety-
year period. All workers comprising the labor force residing in the city
during this period are listed in these volumes. For each worker listed,
name, occupation, and street address are available. In addition to re-
cording the above-mentioned information, the race of each worker
listed in the directories published between 1837 and 1924 is indicated.
For reasons which are not documented in the city directories reviewed,
the practice of identifying black workers terminated after 1924—at least,
this is the situation found in city directories for Detroit.

Data with similar characteristics are also found in the 1950 census
tract data for the city. Although census tract data yield only aggregates
of workers by race and occupation residing within each tract, these data
have utility because census tracts are relatively small units, nearly uni-
form in size, and the number of tracts found in the city is quite large and
through minor manipulations tract data can be easily transformed and
analyzed as point data. The procedure used to achieve this transformation
will be treated later in the discussion of analytical procedures. The information available in census tract form is none the less compatible with
city directory information in all categories used in this study. Census
tract data are also used as the major data source for 1960 and 1970.

To provide broader longitudinal coverage for the 133-year period
being examined two additional independently generated sources of information are also used, both generated by sample survey techniques.
The Detroit Metropolitan Area Traffic Study provides data for 1953
which supplement those drawn from the 1950 census. These data are

compatible with those drawn from city directories and census tracts. Similar data is also available from the report *Community Support for the Public Schools in a Large Metropolitan Area* for 1965.

Figure 4.2: Comparison of Burgess' Concentric Zones with Concentric Zones Defined by Major Occupational and Status Groups

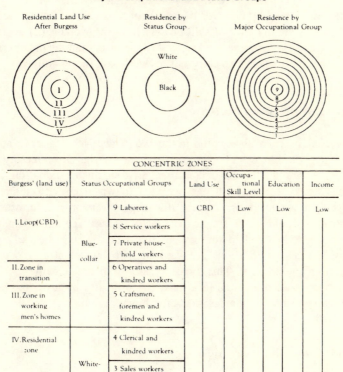

| Residential Land Use After Burgess | Residence by Status Group | Residence by Major Occupational Group |

CONCENTRIC ZONES						
Burgess' (land use)	Status	Occupational Groups	Land Use	Occupa- tional Skill Level	Education	Income
I. Loop (CBD)	Blue- collar	9 Laborers	CBD	Low	Low	Low
		8 Service workers				
		7 Private house- hold workers				
II. Zone in transition		6 Operatives and kindred workers				
III. Zone in working men's homes		5 Craftsmen, foremen and kindred workers				
IV. Residential zone	White- collar	4 Clerical and kindred workers				
		3 Sales workers				
V. Commuter zone		2 Managers, officials and proprietors				
		1 Professionals, technical and kindred workers	City limits	High	High	High

GROUPING OCCUPATIONS

Under normal circumstances the task of classifying occupations into major occupational groups is a challenge. The difficulty of this task is compounded when such a classification is attempted historically. In the samples drawn from city directories, 403 different occupations are identified. Using as a guide the *Alphabetical Index of Occupations and Industries,* prepared by Alba M. Edwards, which contains 451 occupations arranged into eleven occupational groups, the occupations identified in the data were classified into nine major occupational categories (professionals, managers, clerical workers, sales workers, craftsmen, operatives, private household workers, service workers, and laborers). All but 2 of the 403 occupations identified were found in Edwards' work.

The criteria used by Edwards to classify occupations into major occupational groups are (1) level of skill possessed by the worker, (2) degree of judgment exercised by the worker, and (3) level of training or experience necessary if the worker is to carry out his work task successfully.

ASSIGNMENT OF COORDINATES

Fortunately, each observation in the 1953 and 1965 data sets is accompanied by coordinates. This is not the case for the city-directory data sets, which are the major data source used in this examination. Since the addresses of nearly all the workers drawn from city directories are listed, it would at first appear that the conversion of addresses into coordinates would be a simple perfunctory task. The initial appraisal of this task is justified in the case of the data covering the early years because residential locations are described by sets of streets or street intersections references. This type of address listing greatly facilitates the conversion of residential locations to coordinates by using the period street map which accompanies most city directories.

STREET NUMBERING SYSTEMS

To further complicate matters, in 1870 the practice of describing a worker's residential location by referencing street intersection, etc., was discontinued, and a street number system was introduced. Early numbering systems were crude, nonsystematic, and continually changed without consistency from volume to volume. Only in 1920 did the street numbering system in Detroit become systematized and laid out along base lines; a system which has survived to the present. To resolve the problem of the inconsistency in street-numbering systems found between 1870 and 1919, period street maps of Detroit were used which had recorded on them at each intersection the corner building numbers. Without this documentation, accurate assignment of coordinates for this period would have been very difficult, if at all possible.

COORDINATE SYSTEM ADOPTED

The coordinate system adopted for use in the study has an interval of one-twentieth of a mile. The decision to adopt a coordinate system with this interval is somewhat arbitrary. Nevertheless there are several constraints which undoubtedly influenced the choice. First of all, the scale of maps available for the period are such that an interval less than one-twentieth of a mile would not facilitate the task of coordinate assignment. It is quite easy to determine the residential location of workers within the area of a cell defined by the one-twentieth of a mile grid interval. However, it is almost impossible with the materials available to establish locations which are more precise.

Conversion of Quadrant Data to Point Data. In some of the data sets, used coordinates are assigned to each worker's residential location. In census data sets the residential locations of workers residing in the tract are assigned the coordinates of the tract converting these data to the point data necessary for the statistical techniques to be used in the analysis. By taking the centroid of the tract using a grid system with an interval of one-twentieth of a mile, a point location can be established which then can be weighted by the number of observations located in the tract there by any analysis using point locations as input can be used.

METHOD OF ANALYSIS

Approximately 1.9 million observations have been generated on the residential locations of Detroit's black and white workers stratified by occupation spanning more than a century and a quarter. There are numerous ways by which these point data can be analyzed, however, centrographic methods are used in this study.

The Standard Deviational Ellipse. As a statistical technique, the standard deviational ellipse is particularly applicable to the analysis of dispersed point data. By employing this technique, large volumes of point data can be reduced and abstracted into summary measures. The ellipse and its associated set of measures are designed to describe a spatial population in terms of its location as well as its dispersion.

The following descriptive statistics are products of this technique: (1) the mean location of the distribution reported as the mean $\overline{X}$ and mean $\overline{Y}$ coordinates, (2) the degree of dispersion as a standard distance, (3) the directional orientation of the distribution as the length and the angle of inclination of the major axis, (4) the abstract shape of the distribution as the coefficient of circularity, and (5) the spread of the distribution as the area within the ellipse. When these statistical results are plotted graphically, the shape of the ellipse may vary between a circle and a bicircular quartic (Figure 4.3).

Figure 4.3: Standard Deviational Ellipse, Sample Occupational Group

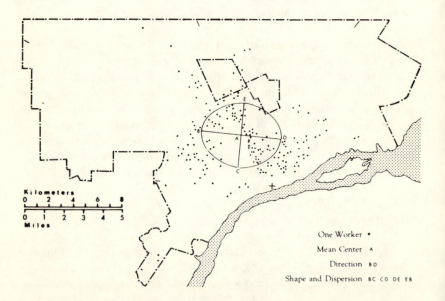

Although the standard deviational ellipse is an excellent technique to generate statistical measures which describe the central tendencies (summary measures) of an areal distribution, it has one major weakness when it is used primarily as a spatial rather than a purely statistical measure. This drawback is that it does not graphically show the actual expanse of the distribution. Therefore it is more a statistical than a graphical technique.

In order that the continuity and modality which are characteristics of a spatial distribution be properly interpreted, knowledge of the actual distribution is required. If the summary graphics of the ellipse are super-imposed over the actual distribution being measured, then the modality and continuity issues can be better identified and interpreted. Knowledge of the actual distribution will result in a much better analysis of the phenomena being described.

RESEARCH DESIGN

The graphics and statistics yielded by applying the standard deviational ellipse as an analytical technique are only descriptive. In order to proceed with this study, and give these statistics meaning, the summary measures yielded must be interpreted within the context of the hypotheses posed.

Hypothesis I—Internal Structure. By using the standard deviational ellipse, the mean centers of the residences of the nine major occupational groups by race can be calculated for each decade over the span of the study. In addition to this, the mean center of the residential locations of all black workers can also be calculated. Tests of the internal residential structure of the city involve primarily an assessment of how the mean centers of the various occupational groups are arrayed in relation to the CBD.

The major occupational groups have been classified by skill level. It is very difficult, if not impossible, to measure differences in skill levels between occupational groups by any measures resembling an interval scale. Therefore the occupational groups are ranked ordinally from high to low with professionals being the most skilled and laborers the least skilled. Based upon the argument made earlier, the residential locations stratified by the major occupational grouping are substituted for residential land uses identified in the concentric zone hypothesis. It has also been documented that blacks are generally segregated in cities and reside near the CBD and that the collective occupational skills of blacks are generally lower than those of whites. Within the context of city structure, Hypothesis I, where residentially white professionals are expected to be residing the farthest distance from the CBD and white laborers nearest but not as near as black workers is tested. This relationship is illustrated in Table 4.4.

Upon examination of Table 4.4 it is obvious that distances can also be treated as ordinal data based on the location of the residential center of each occupational group from the CBD. In this instance, white professionals would be the greatest distance from, and the black workers the nearest to the CBD.

By taking pairs of ordinal data, one for occupational level and the other for distance, a coefficient of rank-order correlation can be calculated. A result of -1.0 would indicate that there is a perfect inverse correlation between ordinally scaled occupational data and the ordinally scaled distances that occupational groups are located from the CBD. The perfect inverse coefficient of rank-order correlation indicates that the internal structure of the city according to Burgess' theory exists. If this test is administered for each decade, a statistic can be calculated describing the internal structure of the city. By using this technique, it is possible to describe all the coefficients of rank-order correlations possible from the

Table 4.4: Rank-Order Correlation Model Describing Internal Structure of a City

High Skill	(1)		(2)	
	1. Professionals		10	
	2 Managers		9	
	3 Clerical workers		8	
skill	4 Salesworkers		7	distance
level white	5 Craftsmen		6	ordinal
ordinal	6 Operatives		5	scale
scale	7 Private household workers		4	
	8 Service workers		3	
	9 Laborers		2	
Low-skill Negro	10 All black workers	CBD	1	

Rho coefficients of rank-order correlation between (1) ordinally scaled skill level of each occupational group and (2) ordinally scaled distance of mean residential centers to the CBD will range btweeen +1.0 and -1.0.

inverse (perfect disagreement) to the perfect relationship (perfect agreement) analogues to the description of the preindustrial city described by Sjoberg and others. According to Sjoberg's construct of the preindustrial city, there are several residential land-use patterns which contrast sharply with those found within the industrial city described by Burgess. The preindustrial city's central area is notable as the major residence of the upper class. Preeminence of the central area over the periphery is the dominant feature in the preindustrial city's structure—a feature which is particularly significant when the distribution of social or occupational groups are being considered. Within this framework the poorest groups in the city live farthest removed from the city center, a residential location which is inverse to the location of poor neighborhoods in the contemporary industrial cities found in the United States.

Spearman's Rho is used to calculate the coefficient of rank-ordered correlation which describes the city's internal structure. It is a satisfactory measure, particularly when numbers are small.

Hypothesis II—Microcosm. A test of the microcosm hypothesis is made by examining and describing at regular intervals the internal structure of the black community. Once calculated, then the results are compared with those of the white community to determine to what degree the internal structure of the segregated black community resembles that of the white community. Spearman's Rho is also used to provide the coefficients for the black community so that this hypothesis can be tested.

Test Results. All values calculated were positive between 1837 and 1864 (approximating +1.0), thus indicating that those workers with the highest skills resided nearest to the CBD. During this period white professionals lived nearest to the city center and occupied the best residential location in pedestrian Detroit. On the other hand (as skill level decreased), the remaining occupational groups resided farther from the business district. The mean residential center for all black workers was located on the city periphery, the greatest distance from the CBD.

The statistics describing the internal structure of Detroit between 1869 and 1910 indicate that the process of transforming the internal residential structure of the city from the preindustrial, pedestrian patterns to that of the industrial city with a street railway system was gradual. A structure resembling the pedestrian stage is suggested by the fluctuating Rho coefficients of rank-order correlations resulting from the test administered. In light of the fluctuation in Rho values, the structure leaned towards preindustrial until 1900. The impact of the street railway on residential structure of the city was not fully realized until 1910, nearly fifty years after their inception. The impact is reflected in a city structure where the upper class reside on the city fringes and the "have-nots" including blacks are mostly clustered about the CBD. The Rho values describing city structures for 1910 are negative .3, thus indicating a change in trend.

Rho coefficients of rank-order correlations for the years between 1920 and 1970 are all negative, indicating that there is an inverse relationship between the mean residential center of occupational groups defined by skill level and ordinal scaled distance to the CBD. The correlations describing the internal structure are particularly high for 1924 through to 1970. All correlations are greater than −.80, except 1965, and can be interpreted to indicate that the upper class (professionals) are residing in the outer city near the suburbs, the farthest from the CBD and the have-nots (laborers, service workers, etc., who are often black) are nearest to the CBD. These statistics confirm Burgess' hypothesis on the internal residential structure of an industrialized city.

INTERNAL STRUCTURAL CHANGE

Changes in the city's internal structure are undoubtedly manifestations of the industrial revolution which contributed to the transformation of Detroit from a commercial, pedestrian, preindustrial city to its present corporate, vehicular, industrial form. Specifically, technological advances in transportation, initially streetcar and eventually automotive developments, increased the mobility of Detroit's citizens—making all sections of the city readily accessible. Increased accessibility stimulated the upper class to search for residences on the city's edge, thus eroding the strong desire for central residential locations which was prevalent during most of the latter half of the nineteenth century. During this transition the have-nots, led by the city's black population, followed suit and reacted by filling the central residential areas vacated by the upper class, thus shifting the residential locations of the poorest groups from the periphery to the central city.

According to the coefficients of rank-order correlations, the transition was gradual and did not occur until 1900 when the internal structure of the city changed from preindustrial to industrial. It appears that Spearman's Rho (nonparametric techniques) are sensitive enough to provide an index that adequately documents internal structural change in the city which ranges between preindustrial and industrial constructs.

LOCATION OF THE BLACK SUBCOMMUNITY

The first distinctive black settlement in Detroit was found in the area east of Woodward and south of East Jefferson Street. There is evidence of the expansion of this black nucleus northward principally along John R., Brush and St. Antoine shortly after 1850. This northward expansion continued until 1950. After that time a northwesterly direction was assumed when the mean center of black residential location occurred west of Woodward Avenue for the first time. This northwestern trend continued and can be documented up to 1970.

Relative to white population, the mean centers of the black community have always been distinctly separate. During the period prior to the Civil War the mean locations of black residence were greater distances from the CBD than those for the white community, and mean black residential locations continued to be greater distances from the CBD than those for whites as late as 1900. After the turn of the century, for the first time white mean residential locations were farther from the CBD than those for blacks. As has been shown, this situation is the inverse of the relationships between respective white and black residential locations that existed in nineteenth-century Detroit. Furthermore, while the distances between respective white and black residential locations and the CBD have changed, the white and black communities continued to be separated.

THE BLACK SUBCOMMUNITY: A Microcosm?

In Detroit, as in New York, Chicago, and most other American cities, blacks are residentially concentrated in one or two districts commonly referred to today as black ghettos. Evidence of this is abundant and vividly illustrates the separation of Detroit's black community. It is now the aim of this paper to examine the internal patterns of the black community within the context of the "Microcosm Hypothesis."

Spearman's Rho is also used to test this hypothesis in the same manner that it was employed to test the "Internal Structure Hypothesis." In this case, however, the internal patterns of the respective white and black communities are generated separately and the results compared. The input data sets for the blacks are identical to those for whites. Once generated the fit between the resulting coefficients of rank-order correlations for the respective black and white communities are evaluated to determine whether or not the "Microcosm Hypothesis" is valid. It is convenient then to structure the examination of this hypothesis by periods similar in time frame to those used to examine the internal structure hypothesis. The comparable periods used are (1) Incipient Stage, 1837–1864—a period during which free blacks attempted to establish themselves as part of the Detroit community; (2) Transitional Period, 1865–1917—the era after emancipation when large numbers of European immigrants represented a large part of the city's population; and (3) Expanding Ghetto, 1918–1965—a period when large-scale European migration had terminated, only to be replaced by the great migration of southern blacks to the North.

INCIPIENT STAGE–1837-1864

Before the Civil War, relatively few blacks were found in Detroit. Although the U. S. Bureau of the Census reported 121 black inhabitants in 1840, the 1837 city directory listed only 10 blacks (half of whom were service workers). The remaining black workers listed in the city directory included one craftsman, one private household worker, and three operatives. It is quite apparent from the content of the 1840 census that the 1837 city directory did not adequately enumerate Detroit's black workers. Furthermore, it is significant to note that no black laborers were listed at the time. This omission perhaps reflects a policy of selective listing exercised by the directory editor. Nevertheless, the partial data contained in the Detroit city directory of 1837 and subsequent directories (1850 and 1859) are used to determine possible residential clustering by occupational level within the black subcommunity before the Civil War.

Black Neighborhoods Before the Civil War. In 1837, more than a decade before emancipation, only blue-collar black workers were listed in the city directory. The largest portion of the black workers were classified as service workers (namely barbers and hairdressers) residing near the town's commercial center. Those black workers remaining (one craftsman, one private household worker, and three operatives) did not share the same residential area as the service workers but instead were residentially situated on the edge of town. Although the service workers' residences were distinctly separate from those of all other black workers, the majority of the city's black workers lived east of Woodward Avenue and south of Gratiot.

By 1850, black workers were represented in seven of the nine major occupational groups with no workers categorized as clerical and private household. Thus in the short period from 1837 to 1850, black representation in the occupational groups had almost doubled. In 1859 still wider representation was achieved even though clerical workers as a category continued to be missing.

Given the wider representation of black workers among the major occupational groups in the 1850s, the geographical distribution of the black community did not show comparable signs of change. Even with the increased structural complexity of their community, due to the introduction of more black subgroups, most black workers continued to reside east of Woodward throughout the entire period prior to the Civil War.

Although nearly all of Detroit's blacks lived in one area, the residential structure of this subcommunity was at no time homogeneous. The well-to-do blacks comprised mainly of entrepreneurs (barbers, etc., who operated their own businesses) lived generally at the location where they earned their living. Barbers, for example, lived in the rear of their shops located in the commercial center of the city which had its foci at the junction of Woodward and Jefferson. Although this area was mainly commercial, the quality of the neighborhood relative to the area where the less skilled blacks resided was vastly superior. The remaining 80 percent of the city's black population resided on the east side south of Gratiot in small tenement-type dwellings. Although most of the houses occupied by the city's black majority were among the city's oldest, there was a differentiation in residential patterns of occupancy defined by occupation. It appears that the entrepreneurs who were also the leaders of the black community at the time tended to cluster together nearest to the city's commercial core (CBD) in contrast to the poorer black laborers and service workers who resided in the older quarters farther to the east. Although the internal residential patterns found within the black subcommunity were embryonic, residential differentiation by occupational group was well established prior to the Civil War. During this period, the internal neighborhood patterns clearly reveal that blacks with higher occupational skills lived nearest to the CBD. This generalization adequately describes the residential patterns of black workers in Detroit between 1837 and 1859.

Test Results. All of the coefficients of rank-order correlations resulting from applying Spearman's Rho to the mean residential centers of occupational groups and the respective distances from the CBD are positive for both black and white data. These results imply that the internal structure of the respective black and white communities in Detroit before the Civil War to varying degrees resembled that of a preindustrial city. Upon examination of the coefficients of rank-order correlations, it is obvious that the structural arrangement within the black community more closely approximate those found in the hypothetical model of a preindustrial city than do the structural patterns of the white community.

The coefficients calculated for the black community all approach 1.0, the coefficient of rank-order correlation which best fits the internal arrangement of Sjoberg's preindustrial city with upper-class residences situated about the city's center is in contrast to the poorest groups' residences on the city's periphery. Coefficients for the white community are also positive but are not as high as those for the black community and resemble the preindustrial construct to a lesser degree.

When comparing the resulting correlations for both groups, it is also apparent that differences in internal structure are not great, particularly in the years 1850 and 1859 when the differences in the correlations for blacks and whites barely exceed 0.1 (Figure 4.5). A much greater difference is noted in 1837, due to the fact that there were only four major occupational groups found among black workers as compared with nine for the white community.

Although blacks to a degree shared residential areas with whites before the Civil War, Detroit had yet to become the "promised land" for black migrants. Even though the black community was small and somewhat dispersed, it remained restricted to the east side and was in fact quite separate from the larger white community.

Figure 4.5: Comparative Internal Structures of Black and White Communities in Detroit, 1837-1970

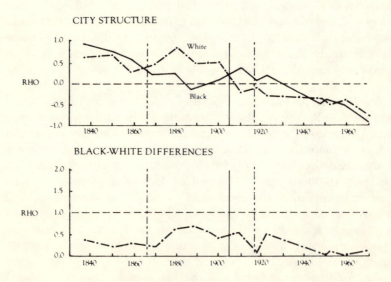

TRANSITIONAL PERIOD—1865–1917

After Appomattox, emancipated blacks came to Detroit, although not in significantly large numbers. Even though Detroit's black population increased by 59 percent between 1860 and 1870, in absolute numbers this increase barely exceeded 800 additional inhabitants. At no time between 1865 and 1917 did Detroit's black population exceed

6,000. Taking into consideration an increase in white population of more than 400,000 during the same period, the impact of emancipation on the growth of the city's black population was proportionately very small.

On the other hand, the foreign-born found in the city increased from 51,000 inhabitants in 1880 to 156,000 by 1910. The impact of these newcomers on the city's black population was devastating, for members of the newly arriving ethnic groups competed for many of the jobs which earlier were the exclusive domain of blacks—namely, those jobs in the service worker, private household worker, and laborer categories. For example, Detroit's Irish unlike other European immigrant groups—namely, the Germans—lacked skills. They worked as laborers on the roads and railroads as well as unskilled workers in the factories. Irish women could be found employed as domestics in the homes of the affluent while many of the men were coachmen for the rich. Others were grooms in the city's many livery stables. The impact of this foreign competition for the jobs usually identified with blacks was also felt in Philadelphia and Chicago.

The percentage of foreign-born in Detroit during this period ranged from the high of 44.4 percent in 1880 to a low of 33.5 percent in 1910. The portion of foreign-born found in Detroit is quite significant when compared to black portions which ranged from 2.4 percent in 1880 to 1.2 percent in 1910.

Black Residential Structure in the Ethnic City. For the most part Detroit's principal black community continued to be located on the lower east side. Woodward could still be identified as the western boundary of black Detroit.

In 1869, the only major occupational group without black representation continued to be clerical workers. Black clerical workers appeared for the first time in the 1880 directory. From that time on black workers were found in all the major occupational categories. Even with this wider representation, the majority of Detroit's black labor force was still disproportionately found in the blue-collar categories—with service workers and laborers forming the largest subgroups.

The residential patterns of the black subcommunity were less stable between 1869-1917 than it was in the period prior to the Civil War. During the latter half of the nineteenth century, Detroit evolved from a commercial town to a major industrial city. The technological changes in transportation which accompanied this transition transformed the community from a pedestrian city to a streetcar city. The transportation transformation increased the mobility of its inhabitants as well as facilitated city growth and consequently altered the internal residential structure.

Throughout this dynamic period the internal residential structure of the black subcommunity resembled that of a preindustrial city with white-collar black workers still found near the CBD and less skilled blue-collar black workers residing at greater distances from the city's business hub. However, the data for 1888 are anomalous and reveal a structure within the black community resembling that of an industrial city, the inverse of the preindustrial city common to this period. An explanation of this deviation will not be pursued at length for it is very likely due to irregularities in the data generated for that year.

At least one black lived in each of Detroit's political wards during the late nineteenth century. Nonetheless nearly 87 percent of the city's black residents were found in a contiguous area on the city's east side which since 1854 has been clearly identified as a black area. The principal north-south streets where the black majority lived during this period were Beaubien, St. Antoine, Hastings, Rivard, Ripoelle, and Prospect. Lafayette, Macomb, Clinton, Mullett, and Catherine, all located east of Woodward Avenue, were the principal east-west streets. The east side served the function of a "port of entry" for black newcomers just as it did for the many immigrant groups upon their initial entry to the city. With expansion the east-side black area extended its tentacles along Beaubien, St. Antoine, etc., north of Gratiot in the vicinity of Kentucky Street, commonly referred to as the Kentucky District because of the large number of Kentucky-born blacks residing there.

Detroit's east-side black community between 1865–1919 continued to be internally heterogeneous. For example, by 1910 well-to-do blacks in their quest for decent housing moved into the middle-class east-side residential area north of the Kentucky District. In this predominantly German area the quality of neighborhood was far superior to that of the south where the majority of the black population was trapped. Nearly all of the poorer blacks resided in the Kentucky District with its small frame houses with their postage-stamp-sized lots (averaging 2,914 square feet) located on Kentucky, Indiana, and Illinois streets between St. Antoine and Hastings. The high population density of this area contrasted sharply to lower densities and relatively large brick dwellings east of Russell with their spacious lots (averaging 7,130 square feet) and the fashionable residences of the upper class found on Woodward Avenue to the west. Contact between the black east side and the Woodward District was physically impaired during the latter half of the nineteenth century. Most of the east-west streets (Kentucky, Indiana, Illinois, occupied by blacks) located north of Adelaide did not extend to

Woodward, Detroit's most prestigious thoroughfare. This lack of through streets apparently did much to restrict Detroit's black population to the sector east of Woodward, a situation which continued until 1950.

Test Results. The coefficients of rank-order correlations resulting from applying Spearman's Rho to the data for the period 1865–1918 are generally positive. According to an interpretation of the correlations the preindustrial city structure continues to dominate the internal patterns of both black and white communities with few exceptions. Nevertheless, the first negative correlation found thus far appears in an analysis of the 1888 data for the black community. If the 1888 negative correlation were deleted, the trend within the black community would continue to strongly suggest that of the preindustrial stage (Figure 4.5). Generally the internal structure of the white community is quite stable as evidenced by continuous positive correlations for the years between 1869 and 1900. Only at the end of the period in 1910 does the appearance of a negative correlation first signal the emergence of an internal city structure similar to that hypothesized by Burgess.

The differences between the coefficients of rank-order correlations for the black and white communities are much greater for the Transitional Period than for those found in the Incipient Stage. The wider differences between correlations for this period may in fact be a function of the variance in population size that existed between the black and white communities. During the entire period, the black community never exceeded 5 percent of the city's total population. The respective internal structures perhaps would have exhibited greater similarity if the two populations had been more equal in size.

GHETTO EXPANSION–1918–1965

By 1918, when the United States was deeply involved in World War I, Detroit's population became fully mobilized to support the war effort. The automotive industry was producing enormous quantities of military goods. To meet the expanding war-production schedule, the need for additional labor became acute, particularly since the war and immigration restrictions effectively curtailed the arrival of European immigrants. To fill this need, the city's major industries looked towards an untapped domestic labor pool largely found in the South. In response to wartime labor shortages, industrial recruiters began to encourage Southern black workers to migrate northward to fill jobs which awaited them in the factories. As a result of this recruitment which was reinforced by vivid advertisements describing the opportunities to be found in the "promised land," thousands of generally unskilled blacks flocked to Detroit in search of better wages and a new and hopefully better way of life. Forty thousand blacks resided in Detroit by 1920, an increase of more than 600 percent over the city's 1910 black population. Detroit's black population became the fifteenth largest to be found in an American city, a far cry from its 1910 rank of sixty-eighth.

From then on Detroit's black population continued to increase in size until today it approaches nearly seven hundred thousand or 44 percent of the city's total population. Detroit's black community now ranks as third largest among U.S. cities. In fact, the growth of the Detroit black population is such that prospects of a black majority may be realized by 1980, if not sooner. Furthermore, since 1950, the city's black population has exceeded that of the foreign-born. Blacks now have numerical superiority over their traditional employment rivals.

RESIDENTIAL PATTERNS WITHIN THE BLACK GHETTO

The accretion of large numbers of blacks in Detroit since World War I has had a significant impact on the city's residential structure. In their search for shelter black newcomers poured into both the principal ghetto located east of Woodward and into a newly emerging black area on the westside. The latter community centers on West Grand Boulevard near Tireman, Warren, Livernois, and McGraw. Both areas rapidly expanded, and by 1960 enough blacks had entered the city to breach the barrier of Woodward Avenue. Thus, the east and west sides coalesced into a single massive black ghetto. With this expansion the long-established Woodward barrier on the western edge of the black settlement was replaced by a new barrier at Livernois. For the most part, blacks now occupy nearly all of an area which circumscribes the inner city within East and West Grand boulevards and its western boundary has reached the Southfield Expressway.

Within the ghetto, which is largely the inner city, the preindustrial structure continued to dominate until 1924. However, by 1950, it became obvious that the preindustrial structure was being transformed into a pattern similar to that of the industrial city described by the "Chicago School" of urban sociology. An internal structure of the ghetto which resembles the internal structure of an industrial city continued from that date until the present day. Within this structure Detroit's affluent blacks occupy residences on the edge of the ghetto as far removed from the CBD as circumstances permit. Most of these upper-class black residences are concentrated in the northwestern part of the city, while those blacks with lower skills remain trapped in the inner city next to the CBD.

The much publicized Russell Woods subdivision located on the city's northwest side documents the process of neighborhood change from a middle-class all-white neighborhood to a prestigious all-black area. The Russell Woods subdivision was on the edge of the city in 1919. Its natural wooded character identified it as a potential high-class residential site. Substantial brick homes with well-kept lawns and trees made the neighborhood appear serene and parklike. Even with the change in the neighborhood's racial composition which began in 1955 when the first black family bought in, Russell Woods remained a desirable residential area just as attractive to black professionals as the suburbs are to their white counterparts.

In contrast to the quality of the neighborhood found in Russell Woods and similar affluent black neighborhoods are the teeming inner-city slums where the majority of blacks—especially the less-skilled workers—continued to be hopelessly mired. In fact the concentration of blacks in the inner city was so pronounced in the decade 1940–1950 that two out of every three of Detroit's blacks lived in a five-square-mile area on the east side, an outgrowth of the infamous Kentucky District which contained the city's worst housing. The degree of overcrowding in this area, a consequence of segregation, was nearly twice that of the white population. No matter what phenomena indicating the quality of life were to be measured, this area would most likely produce the lowest indices.

Test Results. After applying Spearman's nonparametric techniques respectively to the data, only two positive correlations were found, both of which related to the black community in 1919 and 1924. As stated earlier, positive correlations are associated with preindustrial city structure. These negative values thus indicate that Detroit's black community for the years 1919 and 1924 continued to follow this pattern. All other correlations for the black data are positive and indicate that the black community from 1950 to the present has been similar to that identified in the studies by Burgess and Frazier. It is significant that the transformation of the black community structure from preindustrial to industrial first occurred after 1924 when Detroit's black population began to show a significant growth.

The results of the tests show that the white community retained one industrial structure as it had from the turn of the century. Again, the correlations describing the respective black and white internal structure are very similar with an average difference of less than 0.1. Even in 1965, when all values approach 0.0, perhaps due to the size of data sample input, the difference between the black and white community correlations still remains quite small.

The coefficients of rank-order correlations describing the respective black and white internal community structures provide ample verification of the Microcosm Hypothesis which states that the internal structure of the segregated black subcommunity is similar to the internal neighborhood arrangements found in the white community. The black and white structural correlations coincide more closely during the Incipient Stage, 1837–1864 and Ghetto Expansion, 1918–1970, than they do for the Transitional Period, 1865–1917. In the latter (transitional) stage the city was experiencing dynamic population growth, extensive areal expansion, and the technological transformation which changed it from preindustrial to industrial city. This transition occurred for the white community in 1900, but it was not until the late 1920s that the rapidly expanding black community experienced a similar transformation. Although the size of the population under analysis may perhaps affect the resulting coefficients of rank-order correlations, the results nonetheless provide support for the Microcosm Hypothesis.

The fact that the respective patterns of city structural change, implied by the Rho values for the black and white communities match so well throughout the 133-year period examined provides further support for Burgess' assertion that the same ecological processes that underlie city growth and structural dynamics affects each of these communities similarly. Although the city structure continuum for both black and white communities are very similar, it is obvious that it took longer for their effect to be noticed in the black community. If speculation is in order, then the ecological processes are not working at the same rate nor as unconstrained as they apparently are working in the white community. When the process of invasion and succession is viewed in terms of the degree to which black and white freely participate in the urban housing market, it is obvious that there is a differential level of participation.

Furthermore, the fact that the internal structure of both the black and white communities, a spatial manifestation of the ecological processes, is so similar suggests that the aspirations of these two groups, which are in fact, "Two societies, one black and one white—separate and unequal," according to the Kerner Report, are also similar. This implies that the goals of urban black Americans do not significantly differ from those of their white counterparts. They also want their share of the American dream and the accompanying amenities.

PART TWO

THE CHANGING COMPOSITION OF THE GHETTO POPULATION
Ethnic Ghetto versus Racial Ghetto

INTRODUCTION

The ghetto concept, although a medieval European urban institution, was diffused to American cities as the wave of ethnic European immigrants settled in urban areas. The first occupants of the ghetto in America, then, were white ethnics—Italians, Germans, Poles, Irish, Jews, to mention but a few. The racial ghetto occupied by blacks, Puerto Ricans, etc., emerged later.

It is the purpose of this section to present the basic similarities and differences between the ethnic ghetto and the racial ghetto. What was the nature of the spatial and social interaction between the two? Were the two types of ghettos in spatial proximity? If so, did this result in friendly and cooperative relationships or hostile and competitive ones? As immigrant areas began to change from ethnic ghettos to racial ghettos did the degree of resistance to such change vary by ethnic group?

Dennis Clark seeks to answer some of these questions by examining the relationship between selected ethnic ghettos and black ghettos. He argues that the two types of ghettos have usually been spatially contiguous and that such spatial proximity has been extremely important in shaping the relationship between the two areas. Residents of ethnic and racial ghettos, for example, often competed for the same poor housing, jobs, and other resources. Thus, as competitors for employment, space, and facilities, the black ghetto residents became a threat to be resisted by any means necessary, violence notwithstanding. Clark believes antagonism varied somewhat with each ethnic group's level of socioeconomic status. Using the Polish ghetto as an example, he maintains that because the

57

Poles have remained in a position near the bottom of the socioeconomic hierarchy, they are more likely to resist racial change and react violently to incursions by black residents into their Polish neighborhood. The Jews, on the other hand, who have enjoyed a top socioeconomic position among American ethnic groups have presented little resistance to black spatial mobility into Jewish ghettos.

As a final note, Clark emphasizes an important point, and one that cannot be overstated. He argues that the native white population had already set the tone for the reactions of ethnic ghetto residents toward nonwhites. The white citizenry had established a deep tradition of racial exclusion and restriction. In a sense, then, the social antagonism of the Poles and other ethnic groups was merely a demonstration of behavior in an area where racism had become the established norm.

This factor of race emerges as the primary distinction that separates ethnic ghettos from racial ghettos. Certainly, residents of both types of ghettos suffered from stereotypes by the native white population, and both groups experienced economic exploitation and poor-quality housing, but because the residents of ethnic ghettos were white in a white racist society, the barriers to escape from the ghetto were temporary. However, for the millions of urban blacks, the barriers are seemingly permanent, a permanence that has perpetuated the reiteration of an often-asked question, "Why have blacks been unable to escape from poverty and the ghetto, whereas the European immigrants did so?"

This question was answered comprehensively by the President's National Advisory Commission Report on Civil Disorders. The commission stated that four factors must be understood in order to understand the difference between the experience of immigrants and the experience of blacks in the ghetto. These factors were (1) the changing nature of the American economy, (2) racial discrimination, (3) differences in cultural experience, and (4) differences in political experience.

5

Dennis Clark

IMMIGRANT ENCLAVES IN OUR CITIES

The formation of the residential group was a response of newly arrived immigrants to the confusion and strangeness of the nineteenth-century city. This ethnic enclave based upon language difference or foreign origin became a fixture of American urban areas. It was a form of social protection and expression and a testimony to the pluralist character of our national life. Little Italy, Irishtown, Chinatown—dozens of such immigrant clusters dotted the cities. These neighborhoods provided the setting for the drama of ethnic group life. They also conditioned the common attitude and expectations with regard to the family and residential life of ethnic groups within the larger urban society. In the last century, the ethnic neighborhoods almost always established a picture in the public mind of poor living conditions and social disorganization. For over a century this picture was transmitted to a nation dominated by rural, native-born citizens, who prided themselves on their isolation from "foreign" influences and whose virtues of self-reliance and stability contrasted with the disorders of the struggling urban immigrant groups.

Eventually the dynamic quality of our urban life began to dissolve the ethnic communities which had partitioned the larger cities. Foreign immigration on a large scale ceased, and the influence of cultural media hastened the assimilation of the immigrant worlds which had flourished for decades. Physical and social mobility quickened this trend. But the experience of the immigration period and the concentration of ethnic

Reprinted from *The Ghetto Game: Racial Conflicts in the City* (New York: Sheed and Ward, Inc., 1962), pp. 4–6, 109–111, 113–118, 121–133, by permission of the author.

groups had left a strong imprint upon national opinion. The stereotypes with regard to the attitudes and practices of ethnic groups were a part of the general cultural outlook. They did not dissipate as the ethnic communities themselves waned in significance, for they were consecrated by tradition. They were given wider currency and more vivid outlines by their use in the mass media which grew up to serve the urban populations.

In addition, the fluidity of urban society created a great hunger for social status. Distinctions based on ethnic and racial characteristics became important instruments in the psychic game of status seeking. Thus, although rising educational levels have reduced the crudity of the prejudices and stereotypes inherited from the American immigration experience, that experience was too sustained and significant not to leave lasting impressions.

The persistence of racial and ethnic distinctions was helped by the fact that leadership in the industrial metropolis was not unitary but composed of a balance of contending groups reflecting the economic, ethnic, and religious affiliations of the citizens. A wide diveristy of leaders emerged in the political and civil life of the urban areas. In some an oligarchy of "old families" or political bosses became dominant, but their power was always conditioned by the presence of the disparate representatives of a variety of groups. Under these conditions, it was not wholly unnatural that racial groups should be set apart and cultivated as were the other urban population elements grouped around national origin, language or religion. . . .

The primary consideration of the relationship of foreign-language communities to nonwhite population is that the "immigrant" neighborhoods have usually been physically contiguous or in apposition to nonwhite concentrations. The Negro and the foreign-language immigrant shared the limitations of income that forced them both to accept the older housing in the areas close to the center of the city. For the Negro this condition was more enduring. He remained confined, often while a succession of foreign-born groups came and went through the old neighborhoods. This physical proximity is important. It meant that the two types of minority groups, racial and lingual, were often in competition for the same shabby tenements and back-street houses. The foreign-born groups were often accustomed from their European background to working within circumscribed physical conditions. Their diligence and ingenuity would be lavished upon tiny areas that, however poor they seemed by general American standards, still represented relative comfort and security for the immigrant. As the foreign-born groups thinned out, they tended to shrink their concentrations or yield territory to others.

The growing Negro population often filled the abandoned Irish, Italian, or Slavic areas. But in order for the Negro to gain access to the general channels of urban movement, he frequently had to overcome or somehow bypass a tradition-rooted core of immigrant residence. These immigrant communities served as barriers against Negro mobility for the rest of the city population.

Examples of such roadblocks to Negro movements could be seen in St. Louis around 1930, where Germans, Jews, Poles, and Italians bordered the Negro district west of the Mississippi. "The Polish Principality" of Hamtramck in Detroit has for years been impenetrable by Negroes. The ethnic ghettos along Franklin Street in North Philadelphia have long prevented the eastward movement of Negroes.

The physical confrontation of the Negro and the white minority groups has been fraught with social factors that bedeviled the relationship. The foreign-born were often not sure of themselves at all in their new urban environment. Many were unused to democracy and its concepts of social and racial equality. Upon achieving some status in this new country, they felt they could not afford to have it undermined by mixing with the stigmatized nonwhite group. Although at times sensitive to discrimination themselves, they were in too precarious a social position to let this permit a softening in their own attitude toward the nonwhites. The foreign-born groups were beset with many internal conflicts, and it was an easy response to direct hostility against the nonwhites. The social conflicts and tensions accompanying the process of adjustment of the foreign-born to urban life tended to produce crime and delinquency, which sometimes became a behavior pattern within the groups. This turbulence became exceedingly dangerous when racial incidents took place.

To the tightly knit foreign-born groups the Negro was often a strange and dreadful creature. They would have less knowledge of him than even the native white American. He would not be another European like the rest of the minorities. He would not have the elaborate rituals and customs of the Europeans, but would seem to defy any cultural defintion. As a competitor for jobs, space, and facilities, he was a threat.

It is evident, then, that among the group antagonisms in American cities, the relationship between the Negro and the foreign-born presented special difficulties. "But this is all in the past. It was acted out in the early part of the century," some would say. This is too facile a judgment. The foreign-born communities have become tenacious. Some have thrived for generations. In addition to the foreign-born persons in these groups, the second- and third-generation offspring are often strongly identified with ethnic ties.

Even where they have lost numbers and vitality, immigrant areas have imparted an identity to a section of the city. This identity is significant. People are often more impressed by reputations than by realities. Negroes may shun an area for a long while because of the area's reputation for hostility, despite opportunities to enter it. . . .

THE POLES

People with race-relations experience contend that Polish neighborhoods are particularly resistant to racial change and are likely to react violently to incursions by nonwhites. Areas of Polish immigrant or other Slavic concentration have been the scenes of some of the most notable outbursts of racial violence in Northern cities. Violence in Detroit is often ascribed to Polish elements, as were outbreaks in Cicero, Illinois, adjacent to Chicago.

The Poles are noted as a highly individualistic people, a people caught in historic contradictions. The history of the mother country may be very significant in explaining the Polish attitude toward group relations in this country. Poland's shifting borders and political life have embraced a number of traditionally hostile ethnic and nationality groups. Within Poland there have been in modern times a variety of populations coexisting in uneasy polity. Lithuanians, Estonians, German-speaking elements, Ukrainians, White Russians, Jews, and various Balkan strains have lived in Polish territory intermittently. The Poles have had a difficult time, to look at it from their viewpoint, with a long historical succession of fiery, separatist, unyielding, foreign-language and ethnic minorities. This accounts for some of the furious quality of Polish nationalism. With such a legacy of intergroup difficulty, it is not surprising that Poles did not come to the polyglot American city with a bland attitude toward minority neighbors in the New World. . . .

As a minority group the Poles have not fared as well in the American immigrant sweepstakes as others. . . . The second-generation Poles in the United States have actually a lower socioeconomic status than the first generation. Poles have also remained in a position near the bottom of the "social distance scale," a device drawn up by social scientists to reflect prevalent ethnic preferences.

In terms of educational attainment, the Poles rank low among immigrant groups in this country. The Jews and Irish do well in increasing the level of school years completed between the first and second generations. Italians and others complete fewer years in school. These factors would certainly have an influence upon the race relations of the group.

Deprivation of social status would heighten the likelihood that Poles would feel a need for a scapegoat. The Negro would be present, and often in a position to compete with the Pole for jobs and other opportunities. The lower educational achievement of the Pole would increase the possibility of unthinking and pugnacious responses to racial change.

Because the percentage of Polish-born persons in the population will decrease rapidly in coming years, and because residential mobility will continue to erode the old Polish-occupied neighborhoods, the acuteness of the racial problem with respect to this group is likely to diminish. Since the Poles are a predominantly Roman Catholic group, the gradual but pervasive Catholic moral concern for the elimination of racial inequities will have an effect as the educational level of people of Polish background rises.

THE ITALIANS

Of all immigrant groups the Italians are most symbolic for the twentieth century of the great American experience of immigration. Of the major immigration groups, they were the last great wave to arrive from Europe in the tens of thousands. Their arrival was the denouement of the tremendous Atlantic migration. They seemed to enact the drama of building an urban ethnic world in American cities with a zestful enthusiasm. Numerically, the Italian-born are our largest foreign-born group. Their concentrations in the "Little Italys" in the various cities are still very much with us. The Italian neighborhoods are some of our most striking examples of ethnic aggregation today, if we omit Negro neighborhoods from consideration.

The Italian neighborhoods with their accompanying churches, fraternal lodges, Italian food shops, and gregarious family life have not been confined to older large-city areas. Many smaller industrial towns in the East, fruit-growing areas on the West Coast, and food-processing centers have strong Italian communities. We are most concerned, however, with the Italian-occupied areas adjoining Negro districts. These older neighborhoods usually derived their Italian character from the first waves of immigration from Southern Italy. Beginning in the 1880s and reaching its height in the early years of this century, the tide ebbed after World War I. The exhaustion of the Sicilian sulphur mines, the demise of feudal estates with political change, the great disaster of the blight of the grapevines, and the hope for a better life in America brought tens of thousands of Italians to our urban areas. At times, the immigrants were recruited for American industry by agents in Italy. Employment was found in railroad construction, the garment trades, the building trades and food industries.

With some assurance of steady income the Italian immigrant turned, characteristically, to the domestic world, the family sphere focused on the neighborhood. He found himself in second-rate residential areas or outright slums. The cohesiveness and energy of the Italian families was turned to making the areas tolerable. The immigrant families seemed incurably horticultural. Gardens were ingeniously worked into backyards, onto balconies and rooftops. The houses were colorfully refurbished with a kind of casual Italian grace and flair. It is true that these improvements were often only a cosmetic treatment of basically inadequate neighborhoods, but the neighborhoods became familiar, distinctive, and alive. The vitality of the large Italian families was imparted to the neighborhoods in an informal but effective way. The Italian populations found their leaders in civic and political life and developed a morale and a distinct style of life which impregnated the local area.

One striking feature of the Italian residential blocks has been the housing improvements that have taken place under private initiative. The extensive engagement of Italians in the building trades meant that the families usually had valuable skills available. The men could cut stone, lay brick and cement, and do a great number of things by way of physical improvement of homes and shops. And, significantly, they could do these things themselves well enough to be proud of the results. Owing to the association of Negroes with shabby and deteriorated houses, the financial and emotional investment of the Italian householder was felt to be in jeopardy when Negroes encroached.

Also, the Italian neighborhood has been steadily replenished by second- and third-generation offspring. Strong family ties induce a number of the younger families to stay within walking distance of parents and grandparents. The beloved "nona," the winemaking grandfather, the generous uncle or godparent are just too well-accepted and compatible to desert.

Large families in small houses mean that the young will seek the outdoors. In cities this means the street corner or some familiar sandwich shop. In the Italian neighborhoods the "pizza" shops and the soda-fountain hangouts are the scenes for second- and third-generation street-corner society. It is in the relations of juvenile groups that antagonism between Negroes and white immigrant groups often flares up. . . . A further complication to the racial issue may be a Latin concept of personal honor which requires an injury to be avenged. This would increase the possibility of hostile exchange.

THE JEWS

Jewish people are wise in the ways of cities. They have for centuries been an urban people. Time after time they have seen racial antagonism mount in city streets. It is improbable, however, that they have ever encountered on such a large scale the kind of problem presented by the urbanization of the American Negro. The entire social life of the modern city is momentously different from that of the past. In the past, population movement was slow; today there is swift movement resulting in an almost random mixture of people from various backgrounds in metropolitan centers. In this setting the large Jewish populations of the major Northern cities are involved in a very distinctive way in the nation's struggle to resolve the "American Dilemma" of race relations.

One of the places in which Negroes confront Jews is the corner store. In many of the great segregated districts the last outposts of white residence are the groceries, small dry-goods stores, and pharmacies which are in many cases owned and operated as family businesses by modestly prosperous Jewish people. Because of their economic stake in these small businesses, the owners have frequently been reluctant to leave areas which have changed racially. In segregated neighborhoods where the earning power and standard of living are often depressed, these little stores fit intimately into neighborhood life. They are flexible enough to meet the irregular needs of informal, local, and family living. In overcrowded Negro districts the street-corner society which affords an outlet to the young centers around such small businesses.

In these circumstances the Jewish storekeeper is often the only white man many Negroes see on a regular basis. He is a person who gives service, but often he is also a family creditor to whom the grocery bill is owed. The amount of anti-Semitism that may grow out of this latter relationship is surprising. As the last white resident on the block in sections where existence is less than genteel, it is understandable that the small shopkeeper should at times feel the pressure of minority-group frustration and counterprejudice.

A second "sphere of influence" in which Negroes and Jews interact is in those heavily Jewish neighborhoods that have begun to change racially. The sequence of migrations of minority groups through our cities has often placed Negroes next in line to Jews in social status and home-buying ability. Neighborhoods once forbidden to Jews have received substantial influxes of Jewish home owners. Because of geographical convenience or economic accessibility, these same neighborhoods are now attractive to nonwhite home buyers. The aspiring Negro sees in these areas the same virtues of middle-class respectability that Jewish families, fresh from the immigrant "Jewtowns," saw in them a generation ago. Perhaps there is also some basis for supposing that the "liberal" opinion prominent in big-city Jewish circles and the traditionally nonviolent disposition of Jews exert an attraction on Negroes seeking a way out of segregated neighborhoods. . . .

The problem of a synagogue in a racially changing area should also be noted. Unlike many Christian denominations, the Jews do not proselytize. The synagogue congregation cannot absorb incoming Negro families the way a correctly oriented Roman Catholic or a Congregational or Methodist Church can, and reduction in the congregation due to the removal of a Jewish family is likely to be permanent. If a sufficient proportion of the congregation migrates, it may be economically mandatory for the temple to follow. This is one reason for the growth of the "echo ghetto" in the suburbs. The old downtown congregation re-forms in the new area.

The third sphere in which Negroes and Jews are particularly linked is not so much physical as it is one of social psychology. The Negro and Jew are both members of a minority group that experienced a sour tolerance or actual ill-treatment on the American scene. This fact has brought forth a sort of kinship or practical affinity between Jews and Negroes, based on their common concern for fair treatment and democratic rights. Hence Jewish and Negro organizations can usually be found working together for civil rights, fair employment, intergroup understanding, and racial integration. Many Jewish groups devote more effort to bettering race relations than to any other subject.

Opposite these factors facilitating contact between Negroes and Jews must be ranged certain social characteristics of each group which serve to produce a distressing tension between them. Despite the strong affinity that we have noted, there is a great cultural difference between the Jew and Negro. This is not just a difference between a group long urbanized and one of very recent agrarian background. It is a difference of cultural heritage and experience. Although the Negro folk culture had as a cardinal element a familiarity with and reverence for the Bible, and notably for the prophets and kings of Israel, there is a vast difference between the Jewish view of this heritage and the Negro folk view of it. The complexity of the unique Jewish tradition, heavy with history, stands in strong contrast to the youth and the directness of the American Negro orientation. This contrast is made most vivid when we compare the educational status of the two groups. American Jews have from the time of their immigration achieved an extraordinary educational eminence. In terms of formal schooling, they enjoy a top position among

American ethnic groups. Negroes, on the other hand, are still struggling under the educational disabilities inflicted upon them by segregation and exploitation. In education Negroes and Jews are further apart than any of the other groups in the mainstream of American life.

In family life and in the incidence of crime, Jew and Negro are also in vivid contrast. The ceremonial of the Jewish home has no parallel in highly variable Negro domestic life. The widely publicized crimes of some Negroes which glare from the pages of metropolitan newspapers have a bewildering effect on many Jewish citizens, who seem unable to comprehend that such things can exist. The American Jew, largely middle class in thought and demeanor, is out of touch with the world of rejection, privation, and violence to which the Negro has been assigned by current social forces.

The American Jew shares actively in the economic abundance that has been the nation's harvest for the last fifteen years. He walks with non-Jews as leader, organization man, and laborer in the economic activities of the day. He inhabits suburbia and plays a vigorous role both as producer and consumer. The Negro, by contrast, is just beginning to emerge from an economic limbo. His family income, job status, savings, and property ownership are all below the national average for whites, and nobody really knows how much of the recent progress of Negroes in these areas has been achieved at the expense of such sacrifices as the employment of mothers and the postponement of medical and educational needs.

In social organization we perceive once again a great disparity between Jew and Negro. Jews have an enviable apparatus of fraternal, charitable, and civic organizations manned by articulate and effective leaders. Negroes are still suffering from the paucity of leadership that has been a traditional characteristic of depressed ethnic groups arriving on the urban scene. Men like Martin Luther King were exceptional in any group. The ability of a group to train and consistently present skilled leadership is slow-growing. Leadership in effective force does not rise out of a vacuum; it must have preconditions of education, organized tradition, a degree of leisure and concourse with the elites of power and learning.

In addition to these social contrasts between Negro and Jew, there is the difference in the commitment each group bears to ideals of community life. Whatever our predictions about the future, we must recognize that at present Negroes do most emphatically exist as a social group. As such, they seem to have largely renounced the ideal of racial solidarity in favor of a rather loosely constructed racial affiliation permitting full integration, when possible, into the general community. In this respect nonwhites seem to have a somewhat unreserved commitment to the undifferentiated "liberal" egalitarian community. Jews, on the other hand, have a distinctive ideal of community life with deep religious implications. This historic ideal, which antedates by ages the "open community" concept, is operative today in the voluntary residential clustering around synagogues which produces heavily Jewish neighborhoods in our big cities. These two community ideals, that of the religiously based community and that of the open community based upon secular citizenship, are not mutually exclusive, but they can lead to divergent views on questions of intermarriage, community life, and education which are of mutual concern to both Jews and Negroes.

An examination of the relationship between the Negro and the Jew in the light of the social factors mentioned above indicates that there is a considerable social gap between the two groups in spite of the bond of sympathy they share. One of the practical effects of this situation is that Jews are often placed under extreme pressures when they face up to racial issues. Often Jewish people solidly supporting liberal race-relations practices and programs feel genuinely repelled by the social differences persisting in the Negro population when racial integration confronts them and they are brought face-to-face with the contrasts between the great bulk of the newly urbanized Negro population and their own established middle class. Thus Jews do seem to have a special problem with respect to racial change.

PUERTO RICANS

Although Puerto Rican migration to the mainland has not brought about a great dispersion of Spanish-speaking people generally through the Eastern cities, it has resulted in strong Puerto Rican concentrations in the old neighborhoods of Philadelphia, Chicago, Bridgeport, and above all, New York. The influx has thus placed the Puerto Ricans in some of the major urban centers which are today vast laboratories of social tension and racial change. Placed beside American Negroes or intermingled with them, the Puerto Ricans have been very confused in their racial attitudes. Their Hispanic background has endowed them with a rather casual attitude toward race. This attitude is subtle. In the mainland cities, the keen consciousness of race among the general population forces Puerto Ricans to question their own tradition in racial matters, and frequently to adopt a more decisive attitude toward racial differences in response to the mainland aberrations. But this is done with much inner confusion.

Racial distinctions in Puerto Rico are mild, but they are there. The Spanish terms of *el blanco* (white), *el indio* (dark skin with straight hair), *el grifo* (white coloring, but with hair or features of a Negroid cast), *el bien triguena* (a fairer Negro), and the use of the term *el Negro* as a word of opprobrium reflect the differing values ascribed to racial visibility on the island. Within the Puerto Rican group, however, particularly in Puerto Rico, color is inconsequential in social relations. In families there will sometimes be a subtle feeling of status difference based on color between siblings, but this is seldom serious. On the mainland, this attitude of casual acceptance can suddenly become starkly challenged, and the emotional impact on family life and personal awareness can be tremendous.

The acute in-group feeling and loyalty in the Puerto Rican communities induces the Hispanos to reject the American Negro on double grounds; first as an outsider, and second as a symbol of and a target for racial discrimination with which it would be unwise to be identified. The Spanish-speaking Puerto Rican of dark color is fraternally treated—except, perhaps, on the mainland where there is a question of intimate or permanent relationships—but the American Negro is an interloper, a threat, a puzzle. The fact that similar disabilities afflict both groups in many ways only heightens the Puerto Rican's resentment against the American Negro. Thus Puerto Ricans may resent appeals against prejudice and discrimination which link American Negroes and Hispanos.

Puerto Ricans in New York and elsewhere have been harbingers of racial change. In East Harlem, the Bronx, and Brooklyn they have preceded Negro entries. Having the Puerto Ricans in the role of precursors has not noticeably slowed the classic white response of withdrawal upon Negro influx. In the mainland cities, the relations between American Negroes and Puerto Ricans have commonly been strained, with juvenile fights the most frequent expression of this antagonism. The tension seems greatest with respect to newly arrived Puerto Ricans. There is some moderation of hostility as the groups reside in the same area over a period of time. Small groups will become friends and establish ties casually in the second or third generation, but the barrier to intimate association will usually remain.

There is the old area competition between the two groups for jobs and housing. The Negro resents the arrival of the Puerto Rican to work for lower pay. Puerto Ricans who open small shops and stores accuse Negroes of being stupid or lazy because they have in the main been slow to build such businesses. Any advances made by Hispanos are subject to criticism by Negroes because the Puerto Rican, not born on the mainland and speaking a foreign language, is successful "at the expense of Negroes."

While Hispanos and Negroes may resent one another, their residential association is constantly enforced. The Puerto Ricans are recently arrived in the cities, and so are many Southern Negroes. Landlords are seldom capable of according the groups separate status, although the language factor may make property rental more difficult for the Hispanos. The distinction and separation is made at the insistence of the Puerto Ricans, who tend to choose dwellings removed from Negro occupancy so far as this is possible in areas crowded by the adjacent groups.

Perhaps the chief factor separating the two groups, besides the consciousness of color, is a difference in attitudes about sex and the family. At the neighborhood level this is extremely important, for the residential world is a domestic one. The Hispano family is extended, proud, and has a careful code of behavior and relationships prescribed by long tradition. The Negro family is nuclear, weakened by many long-term influences, and informal in its relationships. In the Puerto Rican family, the male has high status. In the Negro family, the woman has so often been breadwinner that she is the main figure. Puerto Ricans resent the easy approach to women that mainland Negroes may exhibit. For Puerto Ricans the woman is guarded by a protective supervision of attitudes and customs. Hence there is a subtle strategy of withdrawal among the Spanish-speaking families which evades advances by American Negroes, even though life may be proceeding on a friendly basis. The Negro, who may have encountered promiscuous contacts between Puerto Rican males and American Negro women, sees no reason why the compliment shouldn't be returned by Puerto Rican women, especially since many may be just as dark as he is.

There are other divergences in churches and in recreation. Some commentators state that integration of the mainland Negroes and Puerto Ricans is far away. The two groups will continue to share the worst of the housing supply, with the Puerto Rican frequently unable to escape identification with the Negro, although residential segregation of necessity will operate less precisely in the case of some Spanish-speaking because they are not readily identifiable as colored. The Puerto Rican will continue to be the "alter ego" of the mainland Negro in residential matters.

The Negro neighborhoods adjoining the white minority communities have an ambiguous set of attitudes toward their "distant neighbors." On the one hand, the immigrants are subject to some discrimination, as is the Negro. In some ways relationships may be casual and unprejudiced. Negroes may shop in the curbside Italian markets, or go to school with Puerto Ricans, or realize that Jewish organizations are prointegration. On the other hand, there will be a recognition that the immigrants do constitute a group by themselves, with their own exclusive clubs and programs, and the Negro will know that acquiring a house in the immigrant area will mean trouble.

For the Negro population the significance of the white immigrant as a member of a minority group tends to be obscured by the simple fact that the immigrant is white, thereby sharing the negative characteristics of the stereotyped white person so common in the thinking of Negroes. It is frequently observed by native Negroes, with some bitterness, that they are denied opportunities which the foreign-born can easily obtain. The resettlement of Hungarian refugees after the disorders in that country in 1956 aroused resentment in Negro circles. As they saw it, persons who had made no contribution to this country were fussed over by the government and resettled in good houses in good neighborhoods. Negroes couldn't occupy those same houses without bringing the scorching wrath of their fellow citizens down on their heads.

On succeeding some immigrant population in an area, Negroes often find that the housing is owned by a number of absentee landlords of the previous immigrant group. The Negro families may face rent gouging and other forms of exploitation, and their attitude toward the group represented by the landlords may become hostile. The activities of immigrant savings-and-loan societies which control property to keep it out of the hands of Negroes produce the same kind of negative reaction.

The Muslim and Black Nationalist groups which have been widely publicized in recent years are not averse to singling out Jews and other groups for special indictment in race relations. These Negro extremist cults do not represent any large segment of Negro opinion, but their arguments in this matter will usually be listened to with care by a great number of Negroes, who may be familiar with the racial thinking of white ethnic groups.

As the inquirer proceeds to the more educated levels of Negro life, however, he finds that the commitment of Negroes to tolerance and interracial fellowship offsets bad experiences. The informed and intelligent Negro seldom singles out particular white ethnic groups for criticism in racial matters, but tends to argue in terms of the white population as a whole.

NATIVE WHITES

Although we have concentrated our attention upon foreign-born groups in this chapter, it should not be inferred that cohesive, native-born neighborhoods are not a frequent source of trouble. The problems arising from neighborhoods with a high percentage of Appalachian mountaineers have been of considerable concern in some cities. Cities with a high home-ownership rate, where neighborhoods are stable and the population relatively settled, produce the phenomenon of entrenched "burghers," with practically no immigrant ties, who yet vigorously oppose racial change. Such areas are not nearly so troublesome as immigrant locales, but they indicate that it is not so much immigrant peculiarities as the fundamental sense of group cohesion which threatens social harmony in racial situations.

The population elements deriving from "the old immigration" of the early nineteenth century have, of course, been deeply enmeshed in the traditions of racial exclusion and restriction. Whatever our estimate of the reactions of new immigrant groups, we must not forget that these groups have been entering into an American stream of social opinion in which racism was a strong current. The upper-class and middle-class neighborhoods of the successful "old immigration" elements were the models for the newer arrivals.

There are forces at work in native-born neighborhoods that on occasion can produce agitated waves of racial feeling, although such areas seldom hold the same violence potential as immigrant communities. The insecurity of the "junior executive" suburb is an example. In a suburb of "organization man" families, the corporations that control the jobs of the breadwinners may transfer a household head to another city on short notice. Hence the homeowners are extremely sensitive to anything which would make the selling of their houses more difficult. The presence of Negroes in the area is such a factor. This "junior executive" difficulty was thought to be one of the reasons why the suburban town of Deerfield, Illinois, reacted with hostility to a plan to erect a limited number of attractive homes for interracial occupancy nearby.

Another reaction in native-born "old immigration" areas in recent years has been the product of a decline in minority status on the part of formerly predominant groups. Old-line white Protestant communities in large cities, where the populations are increasingly Catholic and Negro, are beginning to display all the marks of minority psychology. They feel hemmed in, discriminated against, objects of the ill will of the growing Negro and Catholic elements. Security and self-possessed assurance are beginning to wane under the impact of metropolitan population mobility and changes in the urban power structure. Even though many of the old-line neighborhoods and suburbs are not yet confronted with racial change, they have had to admit Jews, Italians, and a variety of other formerly proscribed groups. Having been nudged this far, the old-line residents have begun to fear that the next step, racial change, is inevitable. This is a reaction that is not found among the hardier new immigrants, who are often ready to contest each street in their area.

The shifting population of the urban centers will alter the residential makeup in the central-city areas. Only vestiges of the immigrant communities will remain. For some years yet, however, these communities will have a special significance for race relations. In most of the larger cities the municipal intergroup-relations agencies have representation from the different ethnic groups on their boards or in staffs. This at least permits some communication with the groups so that when conflict situations or severe tensions arise, there can be consultation and the exertion of accepted leadership to avoid outbreaks or the continuation of hostility. Formal representation of ethnic groups on those civic bodies committed to peace and fair play increases the possibility that mutual respect will be maintained. The leadership of each group is loath to be stigmatized as irresponsible or incendiary in the eyes of the other group. Such a formula for civic peace in the diversified urban community can be effective if it is well administered and serviced with an adequate program of information, conference, and involvement of representative opinion leaders. But if the formula is mere window dressing, a coalition of ethnic leaders for mutual admiration and ego gratification or for the sake of political display, then the city that permits such fraud may find its peace broken and its minority group relations poisoned by antagonism.

The day of immigrant neighborhoods may be fading fast, but these areas have had a strategic significance in the last two decades in their effect upon nonwhite urban movement. They represent a notable interlude in intergroup relations. The lessons we can learn from them should not be readily forgotten.

6

The National Advisory Commission on Civil Disorders

COMPARING THE IMMIGRANT AND NEGRO EXPERIENCE

Here we address a fundamental question that many white Americans are asking today: Why has the Negro been unable to escape from poverty and the ghetto like the European immigrants?

THE MATURING ECONOMY

The changing nature of the American economy is one major reason. When the European immigrants were arriving in large numbers, America was becoming an urban-industrial society. To build its major cities and industries, America needed great pools of unskilled labor. The immigrants provided the labor, gained an economic foothold, and thereby enabled their children and grandchildren to move up to skilled, white-collar, and professional employment.

Since World War II, especially, America's urban-industrial society has matured; unskilled labor is far less essential than before, and blue-collar jobs of all kinds are decreasing in number and importance as a source of new employment. The Negroes who migrated to the great urban centers lacked the skills essential to the new economy; and the schools of the ghetto have been unable to provide the education that can qualify them for decent jobs. The Negro migrant, unlike the immigrant, found little opportunity in the city; he had arrived too late, and the unskilled labor he had to offer was no longer needed.

Reprinted from the *Report of the National Advisory Commission on Civil Disorders* (New York: E. P. Dutton and Co., 1968), Chapter 9, by permission of the publisher.

THE DISABILITY OF RACE

Racial discrimination is undoubtedly the second major reason why the Negro has been unable to escape from poverty. The structure of discrimination has persistently narrowed his opportunities and restricted his prospects. Well before the high tide of immigration from overseas, Negroes were already relegated to the poorly paid, low-status occupations. Had it not been for racial discrimination, the North might well have recruited Southern Negroes after the Civil War to provide the labor for building the burgeoning urban-industrial economy. Instead, Northern employers looked to Europe for their sources of unskilled labor. Upon the arrival of the immigrants, the Negroes were dislodged from the few urban occupations they had dominated. Not until World War II were Negroes generally hired for industrial jobs, and by that time the decline in the need for unskilled labor had already begun. European immigrants, too, suffered from discrimination, but never was it so pervasive as the prejudice against color in America, which has formed a bar to advancement, unlike any other.

ENTRY INTO THE POLITICAL SYSTEM

Political opportunities also played an important role in enabling the European immigrants to escape from poverty. The immigrants settled for the most part in rapidly growing cities that had powerful and expanding political machines, which gave them economic advantages in exchange for political support. The political machines were decentralized; and ward-level grievance machinery, as well as personal representation, enabled the immigrant to make his voice heard and his power felt. Since the local political organizations exercised considerable influence over public building in the cities, they provided employment in construction jobs for their immigrant voters. Ethnic groups often dominated one or more of the municipal services—police and fire protection, sanitation, and even public education.

By the time the Negroes arrived, the situation had altered dramatically. The great wave of public building had virtually come to an end; reform groups were beginning to attack the political machines; the machines were no longer so powerful or so well equipped to provide jobs and other favors.

Although the political machines retained their hold over the areas settled by Negroes, the scarcity of patronage jobs made them unwilling to share with the Negroes the political positions they had created in these neighborhoods. For example, Harlem was dominated by white politicians for many years after it had become a Negro ghetto; even today, New York's Lower East Side, which is now predominantly Puerto Rican, is strongly influenced by politicians of the older immigrant groups.

This pattern exists in many other American cities. Negroes are still underrepresented in city councils and in most city agencies.

Segregation played a role here too. The immigrants and their descendants felt threatened by the arrival of the Negro and prevented a Negro-immigrant coalition that might have saved the old political machines. Reform groups, nominally more liberal on the race issue, were often dominated by businessmen and middle-class city residents who usually opposed coalition with any low-income group, white or black.

CULTURAL FACTORS

Cultural factors also made it easier for the immigrants to escape from poverty. They came to America from much poorer societies, with a low standard of living, and they came at a time when job aspirations were low. When most jobs in the American economy were unskilled, they sensed little deprivation in being forced to take the dirty and poorly paid jobs. Moreover, their families were large, and many breadwinners, some of whom never married, contributed to the total family income. As a result family units managed to live even from the lowest-paid jobs and still put some money aside for savings or investment, for example, to purchase a house or tenement, or to open a store or factory. Since the immigrants spoke little English and had their own ethnic culture, they needed stores to supply them with ethnic foods and other services. Since their family structures were patriarchal, men found satisfactions in family life that helped compensate for the bad jobs they had to take and the hard work they had to endure.

Negroes came to the city under quite different circumstances. Generally relegated to jobs that others would not take, they were paid too little to be able to put money in savings for new enterprises. Since they spoke English, they had no need for their own stores; besides, the areas they occupied were already filled with stores. In addition, Negroes lacked the extended family characteristic of certain European groups—each household usually had only one or two breadwinners. Moreover, Negro men had fewer cultural incentives to work in a dirty job for the sake of the family. As a result of slavery and of long periods of male unemployment afterward, the Negro family structure had become matriarchal; the man played a secondary and marginal role in his family. For many

Negro men, then, there were few of the cultural and psychological rewards of family life. A marginal figure in the family, particularly when unemployed, Negro men were often rejected by their wives oʀ often abandoned their homes because they felt themselves useless to their families.

Although most Negro men worked as hard as the immigrants to support their families, their rewards were less. The jobs did not pay enough to enable them to support their families, for prices and living standards had risen since the immigrants had come, and the entrepreneurial opportunities that had allowed some immigrants to become independent, even rich, had vanished. Above all, Negroes suffered from segregation, which denied them access to the good jobs and the right unions, and which deprived them of the opportunity to buy real estate or obtain business loans or move out of the ghetto and bring up their children in middle-class neighborhoods. Immigrants were able to leave their ghettos as soon as they had the money; segregation has denied Negroes the opportunity to live elsewhere.

THE VITAL ELEMENT OF TIME

Finally, nostalgia makes it easy to exaggerate the ease of escape of the white immigrants from the ghettos. When the immigrants were immersed in poverty, they too lived in slums, and these neighborhoods exhibited fearfully high rates of alcoholism, desertion, illegitimacy, and the other pathologies associated with poverty. Just as some Negro men desert their families when they are unemployed and their wives can get jobs, so did the men of other ethnic groups, even though time and affluence has clouded white memories of the past.

Today whites tend to exaggerate how well and how quickly they escaped from poverty, and contrast their experience with poverty-stricken Negroes. The fact is, among many of the Southern and Eastern Europeans who came to America in the last great wave of immigration, those who came already urbanized were the first to escape from poverty. The others who came to America from rural backgrounds, as Negroes did, are only now, after three generations, in the final stages of escaping from poverty. Until the last ten years or so, most of these were employed in blue-collar jobs, and only a small proportion of their children were able or willing to attend college. In other words, only the third, and in many cases, only the fourth generation has been able to achieve the kind of middle-class income and status that allows it to send its children to college. Because of favorable economic and political conditions, these ethnic groups were able to escape from lower-class status to working-class and lower middle-class status, but it has taken them three generations.

Negroes have been concentrated in the city for only two generations, and they have been there under much less favorable conditions. Moreover, their escape from poverty has been blocked in part by the resistance of the European ethnic groups; they have been unable to enter some unions and to move into some neighborhoods outside the ghetto because descendants of the European immigrants who control these unions and neighborhoods have not yet abandoned them for middle-class occupations and areas.

Even so, some Negroes have escaped poverty, and they have done so in only two generations; their success is less visible than that of the immigrants in many cases, for residential segregation has forced them to remain in the ghetto. Still, the proportion of nonwhites employed in white-collar, technical, and professional jobs has risen from 10.2 percent in 1950 to 20.8 percent in 1966, and the proportion attending college has risen an equal amount. Indeed, the development of a small but steadily increasing Negro middle class while the greater part of the Negro population is stagnating economically is creating a growing gap between Negro haves and have-nots.

This gap, as well as the awareness of its existence by those left behind, undoubtedly adds to the feelings of desperation and anger which breed civil disorders. Low-income Negroes realize that segregation and lack of job opportunities have made it possible for only a small proportion of all Negroes to escape poverty and the summer disorders are at least in part a protest against being left behind and left out [see Chapter 14 of this volume].

The immigrant who labored long hours at hard and often menial work had the hope of a better future, if not for himself then for his children. This was the promise of the "American dream"—the society offered to all a future that was open-ended; with hard work and perseverance, a man and his family could in time achieve not only material well-being but "position" and status.

For the Negro family in the urban ghetto, there is a different vision—the future seems to lead only to a dead end.

What the American economy of the late nineteenth and early twentieth century was able to do to help the European immigrants escape from poverty is now largely impossible. New methods of escape must be found for the majority of today's poor.

PART THREE

THE SPATIAL EXPANSION
OF THE GHETTO

INTRODUCTION

Once a population is in a ghetto, there are two ways the members of the population may move. The first way is as individuals moving out of the ghetto into the city at large. The second is as part of a movement or expansion of the whole ghetto through ghetto boundary changes. The first way was a move many immigrants or white ethnic groups eventually took, but one which has been largely unavailable to blacks due to the persistence of racial discrimination in housing. Thus, blacks have moved largely through ghetto expansion.

Ghetto expansion is analyzed in two different ways in the two chapters which follow. One way, presented by C. R. Hansell and W. A. V. Clark is through the use of a spatial diffusion model. Their model goes beyond similar models to include the effect of an expanding central business district and the location of ethnic groups within the city. Hansell and Clark's spatial diffusion model is concerned with integrating the forces influencing land-use development in the city and the spatial expansion process of the ghetto. Although some overprediction in certain directions and underprediction in others did occur, Hansell and Clark have been able to replicate the direction, degree, and extent of the 1960 ghetto with some degree of success.

Gary Sands examines ghetto expansion through an analysis of newspaper advertising. Sands found that homes listed for sale in the black press indicated the spatial extent of the ghetto, since such homes were not listed in the papers serving the white or nonghetto population. On the other hand, neighborhoods undergoing racial change were listed in both types of papers. Sands concludes that the ghetto was reserved almost exclusively for the black press and that the black newspaper had little impact in all-white areas. Such a two-market situation based on race tends to promote the continuation of the existing pattern of ghetto expansion, according to Sands. Although ghetto boundaries may change rapidly, as long as black families are concentrated in a particular area due to a limited housing choice, the ghetto continues to exist. Both techniques are effective in predicting the ever-expanding black ghetto.

7

C. R. Hansell and W. A. V. Clark

THE EXPANSION OF THE NEGRO GHETTO IN MILWAUKEE
A Description and Simulation Model

The development of the black ghetto is one of the more spectacular spatial changes in modern American metropolitan areas. While the Negro population was 25 percent urban in 1910, by 1960 more than 65 percent of the Negro population was living in cities. Because the Negro was regarded by many residents as an unwelcome addition to the cities, he has been consistently contained in the older less desirable housing. In almost all cases the Negroes moving to Northern cities were forced to settle in separate areas, usually near the central business district (CBD). In addition, although sheer population growth has demanded areal expansion, the constraints on Negro movement have ensured that this expansion has occurred at locations close to the already established heart of the ghetto.

In an earlier study of the Negro ghetto, Richard Morrill in the article "The Negro Ghetto: Problems and Alternatives" developed a spatial simulation model to explain its spatial expansion. The model involved two steps. In the first step, Negro population was increased by 10 percent by in-migration to Seattle, and by natural increase. In the second step a change in residence of 20 percent of the Negro families was simulated using a probability field based on the observed migration distances of Negro families. In an attempt to incorporate other forces influencing the movements of Negroes, Morrill took into account the restraining or

Reprinted from *Tijdschrift Voor Economishe en Sociale Geografie* 61 (September-October 1970), pp. 267–277, by permission of the publisher.

barrier effect of a lack of Negro families in tracts near the ghetto, and the barrier effect of high-value housing.

One of Morrill's conclusions was that the effect of the restraining influence of housing values was not sufficiently taken into account in the model. In addition it appears that other forces influencing the development of the spatial pattern of land uses in a city should also be incorporated. Amongst the forces which warrant attention are the impact of segregation and centralization, invasion and succession, and public renewal and development. In the present paper an attempt is made to extend Morrill's study of the ghetto to include in addition to the value of housing, and locations of Negroes, the effect of an expanding CBD, and the location of ethnic groups within the city. To test the model of ghetto expansion, attention is focused on the Negro area in Milwaukee.

THE MILWAUKEE NEGRO GHETTO

In 1910, there were 980 Negroes living in Milwaukee, and although the number had increased to 21,772 by 1950, the greatest growth occurred between 1950 and 1960 when the Negro population reached 62,458. The Negroes have for the most part been confined to a concentrated area within the central city. In 1950, Negroes resided in twenty-six census tracts, but 79.3 percent of them lived in only six tracts. Between 1950 and 1960 the ghetto spread in a northern or northwestern direction, and by 1960 a significant number of Negroes lived in fifty tracts, although the original twenty-six tracts contained about 88 percent of all the Negroes in Milwaukee. Samples have shown that the majority of the in-migrants to Milwaukee, arriving from the Deep South, originally inhabited rented dwelling units in the older portion of the ghetto. The ghetto is not solidly inhabited by Negroes, for longtime white residents have remained in the area. It appears that under the influx of Negro in-migration, the majority of the white population moved out, leaving behind the older residents. Thus, 34 percent of the whites in the area are over 65 years of age, and about 80 percent have lived there for at least twenty-five years; on the other hand about 50 percent of the Negroes have lived in Milwaukee less than fifteen years. More Negroes than whites have incomes greater than $5,000, and more Negroes have incomes less than $3,000, possibly reflecting the presence of retired whites. Sixty-six percent of the whites are homeowners rather than renters, but only about 32 percent of the Negroes are owners. In addition, the ghetto shows an almost continuous progression in socioeconomic status from the lower older ghetto to the newer northern area. The lower ghetto is 61.8 percent female and has 62.5 percent of the population with incomes less than $5,000. Thirty-seven percent of the population is on relief. The larger number of females in the lower ghetto seems to be a reflection of the high number of separated Negro families. The upper ghetto shows an almost balanced sex and age structure and 26 percent of the population with incomes in excess of $8,000. About 80 percent of the Negroes in the lower ghetto are renters, while about 40 percent rent their homes in the upper ghetto.

A MODEL OF GHETTO EXPANSION

The Monte Carlo simulation model is a general model which can be used to examine the spread of ideas or of people, over space over time. The model has been applied to the diffusion of people as well as to the diffusion of innovations. The principle is the same—the distance a person moves or the probability of adopting a technique depends upon his social contacts or prior knowledge of the area. The probability of a person closer to the center of the source of the innovation already having adopted the innovation is greater because the knowledge about the innovation decreases as distance increases. It has also been shown that a population knows the immediate "home" area most intensively and the zones farther away less intensively. Barriers can be added to the models to simulate physical or cultural influences that might alter movement. A Mean Information Field expressing the relationship of probability of adopting versus distance, or the likelihood of moving versus distance, can be derived using some surrogate of social contact. In the present case the Mean Information Field is derived from studying the general field of movement of a group of people. The field can then be used to study individual movement, and any variation from the general field can be explained as a chance variant—the rationale being that the general field is derived from studying individual fields of movement. The present model is concerned with integrating the forces influencing land-use development in the city and the spatial expansion process of the ghetto. To do this it does not appear important to discuss the various models of land-use determination that have been proposed but only to extract from them the forces which might influence or control Negro residential mobility. Many studies examine land-use structure and land-use change, including William Alonso's *Location and Land Use* and F. Stuart Chapin, Jr.'s *Urban Land Use Planning*. Amongst the processes of urban structural change which appear particularly relevant to ghetto development and expansion are the forces of segregation and centralization, invasion and succession, and public renewal and development. One important way in which these forces influence the land-use structure is through the residence shifts of urban households. But land-use forces or determinants do not act independently but through a system of interactions. Thus, the ghetto can be thought of as a system seeking equilibrium with the other functional areas within the city and receiving energy from in-migration to the city, from inequality in living standards within the city, and from the changing social values of the population within the ghetto. The present model of the expansion of the ghetto seeks to integrate parameters specifying the broad land-use forces influencing the ghetto and the processes of population mobility. From studying the results of Morrill's investigation of the Seattle ghetto and from considering the forces influencing urban land use, several specific measures which seemed to influence the growth of the ghetto were operationalized in Milwaukee. The process of invasion and succession is difficult to measure but an approximation of areas which might first be invaded by Negroes can be made by the value of single-dwelling units. The suggestion is that Negroes would either only be able to afford lower-valued houses, or that other groups would be less likely to inhabit these units. The Negroes desire for centralization is reflected in the influence of already inhabited Negro blocks, and the influence of segregation is approximated by the barrier effect of other ethnic groups living within the city. The influence of renewal and development particularly the influence of public city development was approximated by envisioning the area falling near the CBD losing an increasing number of dwelling units each year through urban renewal or construction of public utilities or highways.

The resulting hypothesis is that the direction, extent, and degree of expansion of the Negro ghetto is proportional to the differential value of dwelling units, to the number of Negro dwelling units already in an area, to the location of ethnic groups within the city, and to the increasing area of influence of the CBD. The hypothesis was tested by simulating the movement of Negro-occupied dwelling units for the period 1950–1960.

The procedure used to operationally develop the model is as follows. The city of Milwaukee was gridded into a system of cells of .25 square miles each. With the use of census tracts and block data for 1950, the number of Negro dwelling units was entered into the appropriate grid cell to represent the distribution of generation-zone Negro dwelling units. The location of ethnic groups was entered by using an index derived from the ratio of the total number of foreign-born living in Milwaukee divided by the total white population. The ratio is approximately 1:10. Therefore, for every one foreign-born of an ethnic group in the city there will be ten inhabitants who will consider themselves members of that ethnic group. Analysis of the city showed that there were four clustered ethnic groups; Poles, Italians, Yugoslavians, and Jews. It was arbitrarily decided that areas which were homogeneous to the degree that 60 percent of the population was of one ethnic group would be considered as 100 percent barriers to Negro in-movement. Dense areas that already contained Negro dwelling units were considered no barrier to in-movement. This decision excluded the Yugoslavians and a portion of the Italians from acting as barriers.

The median single-dwelling-unit values for each census tract were mapped according to quartiles, and it was arbitrarily decided that values in the highest quartile would be 100 percent barriers, and those in the third quartile would act as 50 percent barriers. The first and second quartile would offer no barrier to Negro in-movement. An exception to this occurred in the northern portion of Milwaukee, where a few Negro dwelling units were found in 1950. An 80 percent barrier was incorporated here even though it was an area of the highest quartile value of dwelling units.

The area of expansion of the CBD was envisioned as a process whereby during each generation the CBD's influence expanded at a .25 miles per generation rate of expansion around the CBD. The number of dwelling units would be reduced two-thirds by this action, causing Negroes to be displaced. The amount of movement and displacement was empirically derived in an earlier pilot study. The Monte Carlo spatial model was operationalized with an existing computer routine. Because of the nature of the program several modifications had to be made. As it was not possible in the computer routine to allow for the expansion of the CBD, the total area falling under the influence of the CBD between 1950 and 1960 was determined and entered on the grid of Milwaukee. Prior to beginning the computer simulation, 1,000 Negro dwelling units were displaced from this area in a manual simulation operation. The 1,000 families to be displaced were selected in proportion to the number of units in a cell, relative to the number of units in the area as a whole. After the manual simulation, the boundary of the area of influence of the CBD was considered a 100 percent barrier with no movement across or within the CBD. The effect of this manipulation is to reduce the number of Negro-occupied dwelling units within the area into which the CBD was expanding. For the purposes of comparison a simulation was also run wherein the area near the CBD was not reduced by the 1,000 Negro families, but instead the number of dwelling units was held constant. In other words, the number of Negro dwelling units falling within the area is the same in 1960 and in 1950.

The simulations were run in five generations corresponding to the years 1952, '54, '56, '58, '60. In this program as the computer selects the location for a family to move, it does not remove the previous location of the family from the grid. Hence, instead of incorporating in-migration to Milwaukee, the prior locations of movers which were not removed were considered as occupied by an in-migrant. In conjunction with this, each family was offered the chance to move rather than only 20 percent each generation as in Morrill's study.

On the grid showing locations of recipient population and barrier values, the areas which were 100 percent barriers to movement were entered as zero recipient population instead of using barrier values (except in the area of the CBD). The mean information field was derived using observed moves of Negroes who were forced to relocate because of highway construction. The relationship between the frequency of moves and distances can be described with a pareto curve with the parameters $F = 15.6D - 2.61$, where F is the expected number of Negro household moves per square mile and D is distance.

TEST OF THE MODEL

The coefficient of correlation between the 1960 simulated and 1960 actual distribution is $r = .8785$, and $r^2 = .7718$. The model produces a greater extent of diffusion than reality, with a band of overprediction on the western edge. The errors in the spatial extent of the ghetto, can, for the most part, be explained by the modifications in the model necessary to use the available computer routine. If only 20 percent of the families had been offered a chance to move, certainly the cells with only a few families would not have diffused so quickly. In conjunction with this, allowing the model to grow first by in-migration to Milwaukee, with the families settling in tracts in proportion to their Negro density, would have caused more Negroes to settle in those areas which are greatly underpredicted. The band of overprediction along the eastern margin of the ghetto can also be explained as a result of the program used. This model weighs the probabilities from the mean information field by the recipient population in the cells. The model outlined in this study also argues that the probability should be weighed by the Negro population in each cell at each simulation time period rather than by the total recipient population if the process of centralization is in operation. This correction should result in the ghetto initially moving in the direction in which the greatest number of Negroes live and gaining momentum in this direction until a barrier of some sort is reached.

Simulated results also fail to show the beginning of the penetration into the eastern area of the city which was blocked by ethnic groups in 1950. The failure of the simulation model to explain this eastern movement can be partly explained by the locations of ethnic groups in 1960. The number of ethnic groups was calculated using an index as before and shows a ratio of 1:3, although in this case, the 1960 census does not list foreign-born but foreign stock. The index indicates that the only dominant ethnic group remaining is the Polish group. The Italians and Yugoslavians are diffused over the city with no significant grouping, and the Jewish group is greatly diminished. The result might indicate that the groups are decentralizing in the threat of invasion by the Negroes. The only group remaining along the eastern margin is the Polish group, which, although reduced in size, still acts as a barrier to Negro movement.

Analysis of the 1960 simulated distribution and error map with the Negro dwelling units near the CBD held constant reveals the same general errors. In addition, the more overpredicted original ghetto area and the related underpredicted areas to the west and northwest indicate the effect of the forced movement of Negroes from the area near the CBD.

The hypothesis around which the model is built seems to be basically sound and is not rejected. The direction, degree, and extent of the 1960 ghetto were replicated with some degree of success. Possible sources of error have been discussed. While the measures of land-use forces seem to be useful in determining the spatial pattern of the ghetto, the invasion and succession process was introduced only indirectly with the use of barriers. Although the method of measuring ethnic homogeneity used may be very crude, the results indicate that invasion and succession did occur. Analysis of dwelling-unit values indicates that invasion and succession may have caused values to drop in certain areas. It is not enough to reduce the barriers a limited amount to allow for invasion and succession in future models, but some method should be incorporated to move the barriers altogether once a certain degree of penetration is realized. The process of centralization, or that portion of the hypothesis that stated that the spread of the ghetto is proportional to the density of Negroes previously present in the cell, was used only for the initial time period.

Further research into the expansion of the ghetto might profitably return to a model where diffusion occurs in two steps—in-migration to the city, and movement within the city. However, the program should be such that the probabilities in the MIF are weighted for Negro population rather than recipient population, and both the model and the program should incorporate the nature of change of the total land-use pattern in the city itself, to see if a more rational approach to a decrease in the original 1950 ghetto near the CBD can be realized. Since the 1960 ghetto is actually composed of two different Negro socioeconomic groups, the study suggests it might be useful in future models of the ghetto to investigate different ghetto zones, each with different degrees of intensity. As in Morrill's analysis this study has described and replicated the process of ghetto expansion. Additional studies of this type will verify the nature of the expansion process, and possible policy decisions on a more desirable speed of ghetto expansion and hence dilution might be agreed upon and implemented.

8

Gary Sands

GHETTO DEVELOPMENT IN DETROIT

One of the dominant themes in twentieth-century America has been the increasing urbanization of the population. In 1920 America became more urban than rural. The urban proportion of the nation has continued to increase until it is now well over 70 percent. In the last quarter century it is possible to identify two distinct components in this trend—the urbanization of the black population and the suburbanization of the white population. Today the majority of black Americans live in urban ghettos. The consequences of this increasing separation of black and white populations have been manifest in riots and rhetoric.

Originally, the ghetto was the quarter of a city to which Jews were restricted. The first ghetto was built in Venice in the late sixteenth century. In fact, ghetto is the Italian word for "foundry," the dominant landmark in the area where Venetian Jews were forced to live. The Jews of Venice and other European cities were restricted to the ghetto because of their religion, not because of their social or economic status. Although crowding was characteristic of most ghettos, rich Jews lived alongside poor ones. No matter what material benefits could be provided, it was impossible for a Jew to "escape" from the ghetto since the ghetto was defined in terms of where Jews lived. The ghetto was first a concept of territory.

The popular conception of the ghetto in America has evolved in considerably different terms. The ghetto is frequently defined in terms of the

Reprinted from *Metropolitan America: Geographic Perspectives and Teaching Strategies,* ed., Robert Swartz et al. (Oak Park, Ill.: National Council for Geographic Education, 1972), pp. 175-197, by permission of the publisher.

social or economic characteristics of its inhabitants or the conditions and density of its housing. The ghetto, when defined in these terms, is a place which can be avoided by moving to a better neighborhood or by getting a better job. Although these objectives address themselves to serious problems for the ghetto dweller, they do not change the essential fact that the "better neighborhood" may still be in the ghetto. As long as a Negro household is limited in its choice of housing, it is only possible to trade one location in the ghetto for another. The ghetto may change in shape or extent, but there seems little prospect of its disappearance.

Current estimates place the black population of Detroit at approximately 640,000. This is a larger population than the total population of Boston or Pittsburgh. Although other cities may never attain this large a black population, some of the processes that can be observed in Detroit may occur in cities which are considerably smaller. This paper examines the growth of the Detroit ghetto and some of the forces which have influenced it.

GROWTH OF THE NONWHITE POPULATION OF DETROIT

The City of Detroit has experienced a pattern of growth in its nonwhite population which is typical of many Northern and Western American cities. Detroit did not acquire a significant nonwhite population until the twentieth century. Although Negroes lived in Detroit from the time of the first settlement, for nearly two hundred years they constituted only a small portion of the total population. Interestingly, the majority of slaves in Detroit were American Indians rather than Negroes. Nevertheless, the majority of blacks in Detroit were household servants or common laborers.

Until the beginning of the twentieth century, the overall growth of the city was not spectacular. In 1900, the total population of Detroit was approximately 286,000 (see Table 8.1). Of this total, only 4,100 (1.4 percent) were nonwhite. As Detroit grew, with the coming of the automobile age, the rate of population growth increased. By 1910 the total population of the city was approaching 500,000. During this period, the growth of the nonwhite population was much less dramatic, reaching a total of less than 6,000 in 1910.

The skills and capabilities of Detroit for large-scale industrial production set the stage for even more rapid growth during the next decade. While substantial increases were recorded in the white population, the nonwhite population growth was even greater. It was estimated that the black population of Detroit in 1925 was 82,000, a fourteenfold increase over the total of just fifteen years earlier. This rapid growth continued until the beginning of the Depression. During the twenties the white population of the city grew by almost 500,000. It was also during this period that the boundaries of the city reached their present limits and almost 125,000 new dwelling units were built to accommodate the expanding population.

Through the Depression years of the thirties, both white and non-white population growth slowed considerably. Natural increase declined and many families postponed marriage and children. Despite the proliferation of welfare programs, it was still less expensive to live in the country than in the city. Migration from rural areas slowed almost to a halt and many families left the cities. Detroit's population registered

Table 8.1: Detroit Population

Year	Total	White	Nonwhite	Percent Nonwhite
1900	285,704	281,575	4,129	1.4
1910	465,766	459,926	5,840	1.3
1920	993,678	952,065	41,613	4.2
1930	1,568,662	1,446,656	122,006	7.8
1940	1,623,452	1,472,662	150,790	9.3
1950	1,849,568	1,545,847	303,721	16.4
1960	1,670,144	1,182,970	487,174	29.8
1969	1,501,400	870,800	630,600	42.0

only modest gains during the thirties. The total growth of the city was only 55,000, almost equally divided between blacks and whites.

The year 1940 marked a significant turning point in the growth of Detroit's nonwhite population. When local industry began its conversion to war production, the migration to Detroit resumed. However, at this time the migration trends of the white and Negro populations began to diverge. The black population doubled during the decade while the white population increased by only 5 percent. In absolute numbers, the nonwhite increase was almost 100,000 more than that of the white population. By 1950, one Detroiter out of six was nonwhite.

The postwar period also marked the beginning of another important trend in Detroit's population—the migration of the white population to the suburbs. Eighty percent of the increase in the white population in the Detroit metropolitan area took place outside the city in the forties. (By contrast, only 10 percent of the nonwhite increase took place outside Detroit.) This suburbanization of the white population was a prerequisite for the continued growth of the nonwhite population within the city.

During the fifties the trends established in the previous decade continued at an accelerating pace. The black population grew by almost 190,000 persons, reaching 487,000 in 1960. The white population changed very little during the decade but began an absolute decline with the coming of the economic recession of the late fifties. By 1960 the white population had fallen to just under 1.2 million. It was during this period that the balance of population in the metropolitan area shifted from Detroit to the suburbs. Of the 3.76 million people living in the three-county Detroit metropolitan area, only 44 percent lived in the City of Detroit in 1960. However, the City of Detroit contained 86 percent of the area's black population.

Since 1960, the white population of Detroit has fallen by more than 300,000. At the same time, the nonwhite population of the city has increased by about 140,000. This slight decline in the growth rate of the nonwhite population can generally be attributed to the slowing of migration from the rural South (which in turn can be attributed to the fact that there were fewer people left in the rural areas) and a tendency toward a lower birth rate. It is expected that most of the growth of the nonwhite population in the future will be the result of natural increase rather than in-migration.

SPATIAL DIFFUSION OF THE GHETTO

Nonwhites have been consistently restricted in their choice of residential location in Detroit. Except for domestics and other "live-in" servants, there has been little integration of neighborhoods in the city. Particularly during the twenties (the first period of rapid expansion of the black population) nonwhites frequently encountered opposition in their efforts to move into white neighborhoods. Restrictive real-estate covenants and "Neighborhood Improvement Associations" were common devices used to maintain the all-white character of most of the city's neighborhoods. All too frequently the resistance to racial change took the form of violence. The most publicized instance of racial violence during this period was the killing of a white man outside the new home of Dr. Ossian Sweet, who had had the temerity to move two blocks away from the nearest black family. Although Dr. Sweet was judged innocent of the murder and remained in his home on Garland Avenue, the incident was typical of the climate of violence which prevailed.

By 1940, the black population of Detroit was large enough to have a ghetto which could be clearly defined by almost any definition. The area lay just east of Woodward Avenue, from the Detroit River to the Highland Park city limits. (See Figure 8.1 for the 1940 distribution of nonwhite population.) Seventy percent of the city's nonwhite population

Figure 8.1: Nonwhite Population, Detroit, 1940

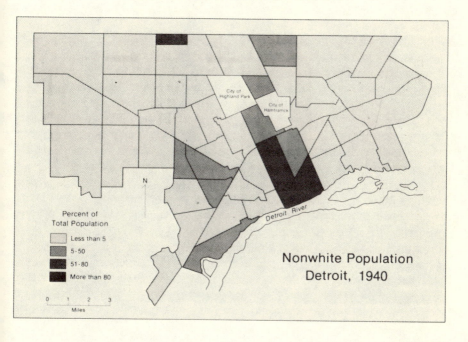

lived in this area. The area exhibited all of the pathology which has come to be associated with the American urban ghetto—overcrowded and dilapidated housing, high unemployment and low incomes, low educational attainment, and the like. Euphemistically termed "Paradise Valley," this was the area in which the Detroit race riot of 1943 took place. Two additional areas contained substantial numbers of nonwhites. The first of these was on the near west side of the city. The second was the Northlawn community, a semirural area at the northern boundary of the city and Wyoming Avenue. Although there were some nonwhites in every subcommunity, one-third had less than fifty nonwhite residents.

The doubling of the black population between 1940 and 1950 made the geographic expansion of the nonwhite areas inevitable. Figure 8.2 shows that the established ghetto areas in the John R and Oakland subcommunities were able to absorb some of the increase and the proportion of nonwhites in these areas increased. At the same time, these subcommunities formed the nucleus from which the black population ex-

Figure 8.2: Nonwhite Population, Detroit, 1950

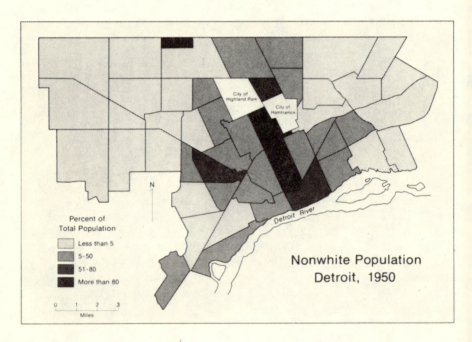

panded into adjacent areas which previously had only negligible black population. The Northlawn area is the only subcommunity where this extension of the black population into contiguous areas did not take place. This was largely the result of conscious efforts by white neighbors who went so far as to build an eight-foot-high wall to prevent the areal spread of the black population.

Despite this outward movement of the black population, segregation and separation were still the rule. Thirty percent of the subcommunities (an absolute change of only one) still had less than fifty black residents. The ghetto core contained just over 63 percent of the nonwhite population. Almost seven out of ten blacks lived in subcommunities where the majority of the residents were nonwhite (categories 3 and 4 in the accompanying figures). It is interesting to note that the black population was unable to make any inroads into the East European ethnic communities in the Ford, Springwells, and Baby Creek subcommunities. Rather, the nonwhite movement bypassed these areas and moved into the Oakwood subcommunity across the Rouge River.

Figure 8.3: Nonwhite Population, Detroit, 1960

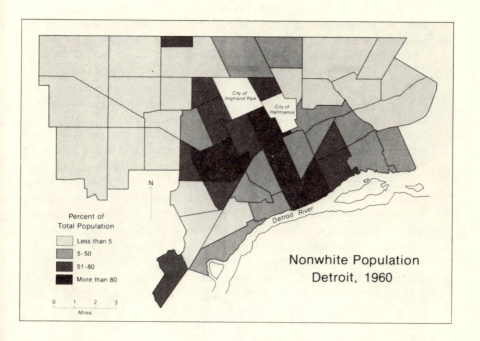

During the fifties, the diffusion of the nonwhite population was aided by several factors. One was the 1948 Supreme Court ruling that racially restrictive real-estate covenants were unenforceable. Another was the decision by Detroit Water Board to extend its service to residential customers outside the city. This permitted the construction of a large number of homes in the northern and western suburbs. The migration of the white population created a great many housing opportunities for black families in the city. A third factor was the general prosperity which prevailed throughout most of the decade. Many blacks shared in this prosperity, and rising incomes enabled them to move into housing which whites were leaving behind.

Figure 8.3 shows that several new areas were opened up to black families during the fifties. Three of these subcommunities were located on the lower east side while only one new area on the west side became integrated. However, the more common situation was an increase in the proportion of nonwhites in the existing ghetto areas. Eight subcommunities became predominantly black (category 3) and in two others the proportion of nonwhites exceeded 80 percent for the first time. Those subcommunities classified in category 4 contained 35 percent of the black population. Seventy-two percent of the nonwhite population lived in predominantly black areas. Although a residual white population remained in even the oldest areas, for three out of four nonwhites, social contact with the white population was limited.

Between 1960 and 1969, the black population of Detroit grew by some 140,000. This increase was accommodated again by increasing the densities in the established ghetto areas and by the opening up of new areas contiguous to the established nonwhite territory. Figure 8.4 shows that the movement of the nonwhite population during the sixties took a strong northwesterly trend. Every area between Grand River Avenue and Woodward, which was classified in category 3 in 1960, moved into category 4 by 1969. The three subcommunities at the northwest edge of the ghetto in 1960 each went from a negligible number of nonwhites in that year to more than half nonwhite in 1969. The Marygrove community went from a handful of nonwhites to more than 22,000 in nine years. To a somewhat lesser degree the black population continued to expand into the next tier of subcommunities. Data at the census-tract level illustrate this gradiant even more clearly.

The northwestward expansion of the ghetto areas is particularly significant in terms of the housing which is available to black families. After 1960 the black population had become so large that it could no longer be contained in the areas of .older housing. The farther to the northwest the black population moved, the better the overall quality of the housing became. Although the number of blacks living in poor-quality housing did not change substantially, the proportion living in good-quality housing did increase.

The proportion of nonwhites also increased in the established ghetto areas of the inner city and on the east side. However, there was virtually no change in the geographic extent of the ghetto in these areas. The stabilization of the eastern frontier of the ghetto was due in part to the fact that its movement had reached a natural barrier in terms of a major industrial corridor and in part because of the change in the quality of the housing to the east of the industrial area. Because of the strong resistance of the residents, blacks have largely been denied access to the better-quality housing in the northeast quadrant of the city.

Despite the appearance of a substantial areal diffusion of the non-white population during the sixties, by 1969 blacks in Detroit were in fact more segregated than before. Well over half (57 percent) of the

Figure 8.4: Nonwhite Population, Detroit, 1969

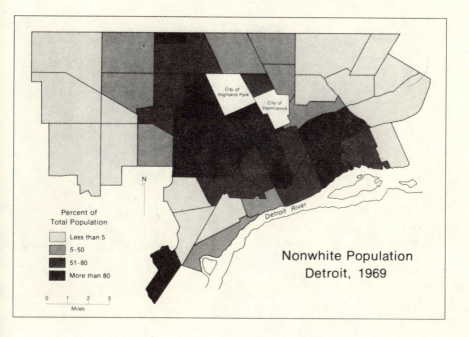

black population lived in subcommunities classified in category 4—more than 80 percent of the population nonwhite. In 1960, 35 percent of the black population lived in subcommunities in this category. During the decade there was also a 10 percent increase in the proportion of black families living in predominantly black areas. Fully four out of every five nonwhites lived in these areas in 1959.

Figure 8.5 provides an indication of the total change which has occurred in the proportion of nonwhites between 1940 and 1969. The areas which experienced only negligible change are those areas which remained predominantly white. However, once racial change began in a subcommunity, the change was likely to be extensive. Those areas experiencing moderate change are found at the edge of and in the heart of the ghetto. Little change took place in the John R and Cadillac subcommunities because their initially high proportion of blacks did not allow

Figure 8.5: Nonwhite Population Change, Detroit, 1940–1969

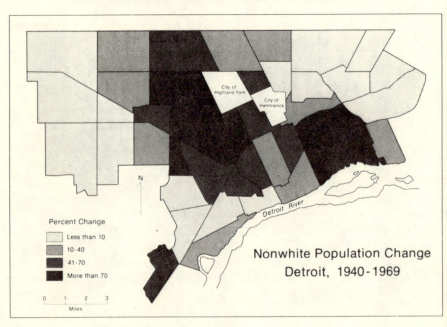

greater change. The areas at the fringe of the ghetto are just beginning their period of change. Those subcommunities which became "integrated" shortly after 1940 are the areas which have experienced the greatest change. Some have changed their racial character almost completely, and there is little indication that the process of change in the others will be halted before the areas have become all black. The gradient of change rises from the oldest ghetto areas; it then begins to slope downward toward those areas where there has been no change. The only areas of the city where the change has not proceeded at an extremely rapid pace are the Pershing and Cleveland subcommunities in the North End.

An important conclusion which may be drawn from this pattern of movement is that there has been little change in the essential nature of the ghetto in Detroit. A small number of pioneering black families at the edge of the ghetto may temporarily feel that they have left the ghetto. However, historical trends indicate that it is only a matter of time before they are once again surrounded by an area which is predominantly black and on its way to becoming all black. The continued growth of the black population means the continued expansion of the black territory. But change on a massive scale is required to prevent the exodus of the white population from the area into which the ghetto is expanding.

GHETTO EXPANSION AND THE REAL-ESTATE MARKET

The growth of the nonwhite population in Detroit may be expected to continue at only a slightly lower rate for the foreseeable future. When coupled with the observed trend toward smaller families, there is a clear demand for additional housing for nonwhite families beyond the boundaries of the existing ghetto. Local and federal laws guarantee that free access to housing opportunities shall be extended to all regardless of race. These guarantees have been in existence for a number of years. Yet the vast majority of nonwhites in Detroit still reside in an identifiable, relatively compact ghetto. To state the problem in a different way: A substantial number of nonwhite households in Detroit have the income and assets necessary to permit them to buy a home anywhere in Detroit or throughout the metropolitan area. But very few of these households move more than a few blocks from other nonwhite households. The perpetuation of the ghetto is not so much the result of legal or economic obstacles but rather social pressures.

Existing homes constitute the bulk of the sales market for housing in Detroit and most other metropolitan areas. In the Detroit metropolitan area, the number of existing homes sold in one year is approximately seven times the number of single-family homes built. Opportunities for changing current patterns of racial segregation are much more prevalent in the existing housing stock. Used houses being offered for sale are listed in a number of different newspapers, without any explicit or overt indication of the preferred race of the purchaser. A prospective home buyer, whether white or black, may avail himself of a choice of literally thousands of homes throughout the metropolitan area. Despite this remarkable potential knowledge of the market by the consumer, there has been little change in the established pattern of ghetto growth. Rather than contributing to the dissipation of the black population, the real-estate market tends to reinforce existing patterns of racial separation.

A comparison will now be made of the listings of homes for sale in four Detroit newspapers, each of which seeks the support of a different (although not necessarily mutually exclusive) client group. However, it should be noted that the decision as to which newspaper will carry a particular listing is frequently made by the real-estate broker, rather than the individual seller. For the broker, the overriding consideration in the decision of which paper will carry the advertising is the judgment as to which paper offers the best opportunity to sell the property.

Four papers were considered in this analysis. The first is the *Sunday News,* the Sunday edition of the daily *Detroit News.* The latest reported circulation of the *News* was approximately 850,000, the highest of any paper in the Detroit metropolitan area. For many years the Sunday edition of the *News* has been the traditional place to begin when looking for a new home. The classified real-estate section of the *News* is generally several times larger than that of the other metropolitan daily, the *Free Press.* In recent years, however, the *News* has fallen into increasing disfavor with the black and liberal white communities because of its strong stand in support of "law and order," which is interpreted as being anti-black. The circulation of the paper has dropped, particularly within the City of Detroit. The readership of the *News* is increasingly becoming a white audience.

The second paper included in the study was the *Michigan Chronicle.* The *Chronicle* is a weekly paper serving the black community. Despite the paper's name, the vast majority of the news and advertising it carries is limited to Detroit. The total circulation of the *Chronicle* is in excess of 50,000. The paper contains a substantial number of listings of homes for sale and is the primary advertising mode for black realtors.

The remaining newspapers are both "neighborhood" papers. This type of paper primarily provides news of local interest to the community. Advertising rates are generally less than in the higher-circulation metropolitan papers and space is provided for local school and club news. Each of the papers considered here is part of a small chain. The news portion of the papers is published in separate editions, usually with different names for each edition. However, all of the papers in the chain carry the same classified advertising. This not only simplifies the taking and listing of advertising, but also permits the charging of higher rates as a result of increased circulation.

The chain of neighborhood papers to which the *Redford Record* belongs serves the area of Detroit to the west of Wyoming Avenue, as well as some suburban areas. The total circulation of the chain is approximately 43,000. The area of Detroit east of Connor Avenue is· served by a chain of neighborhood papers which includes the *East Side Shopper*. The chain also serves the Grosse Pointe communities and southeastern Macomb County. The classified advertising section carried by the *East Side Shopper* has a circulation of just over 40,000.

The study of classified real-estate listings covered a period in the last half of August 1970. This time of the year is near the end of the home-buying season. The peak period for real-estate activity usually runs from spring through late summer, then slackens considerably when the school year begins. In fact, several of the listings suggested that an immediate purchase would permit the completion of moving before school started. Although this statement may have been something of an exaggeration, it is clear that the best time for purchasing a home was drawing to a close.

It was necessary to make several exclusions from data being considered. The first was to exclude all listings of homes in the suburbs. This was necessary primarily because the study's objective was to consider the Detroit ghetto. Suburban listings were considered simply as housing opportunities outside of the City of Detroit. No attempt was made to determine their precise location. A second category of listings which was excluded consisted of properties listed under headings other than single-family homes for sale. Flats, and similar types of properties were eliminated due to the likelihood that their purchase would represent an investment decision, rather than a strictly housing choice. In addition to these exclusions, it was not possible to identify the precise location of all houses listed for sale. The primary cause of this was the common practice of describing the location of a house in terms of nearby major thoroughfares, identifying the neighborhood but not the precise location. The streets commonly used for identification purposes are part of a one-mile grid system; considerable latitude in location is therefore possible. A random check of some of these listings indicated that the actual location might be as much as three-quarters of a mile from the intersection listed. Moreover, there was not a consistent pattern as to the direction in which the home lay from the intersection.

The four papers varied considerably in the number of listings which they carried. Table 8.2 shows the total number of listings of homes for sale in Detroit carried by each paper and the number of cases where it was possible to identify the location of the listing, either because an exact address was given or because a nearby intersection was identified.

Although there is substantial variation in the proportion of listings which could be located, there are a sufficient number of cases in each of the papers to permit a representative analysis.

A number of differences can be observed in the pattern of listings carried by the different papers. There are also some interesting similarities. For example, neither the *News* nor the *Chronicle* carry a significant number of ads for homes in the inner city despite the fact that both papers circulate throughout this area. Another part of the city which is neglected by all of the papers is the area south of Michigan Avenue. These two areas contain a large proportion of the city's older, less expensive housing stock.

With the exception of the absence of listings in these areas, the classified listings in the *Chronicle* provide a good approximation of the extent of the ghetto. Although a small number of the listings are in all-white

Table 8.2: Listing of Detroit Homes for Sale

Paper	Detroit Listings	Listings Number	Located Percent
Redford Record	209	164	78
East Side Shopper	201	106	53
Detroit News	1,011	780	77
East Side Listings	407	292	72
West Side Listings	604	488	81
Michigan Chronicle	882	522	59

neighborhoods, the vast majority are in areas with an already established black population. There is a considerable amount of listing activity in the one and one-half mile band north of McNichols Road and west of Meyers Avenue. As noted above, this is the area which has undergone extremely rapid racial change during the past decade, an indication of the continuing flight of white families from these neighborhoods.

It is interesting to note that on the west side there is a gradual tapering off in the density of listings, rather than a distinct edge. The bulk of the listings were found in the area east of Greenfield. However, there were sixteen listings to be found in the one-mile strip west from Greenfield to Southfield. In keeping with the northwesterly thrust of the ghetto expansion, thirteen of these listings were in the area north of McNichols. In the mile between Southfield and Evergreen, there were only four homes listed. For the remainder of the city to the west of Evergreen, the *Chronicle* carried no ads.

There is a noticeable difference in the listings on the east side of the city. Here the edge of the ghetto has been relatively sharp and stable for a number of years. In those areas which have recently opened up to blacks (such as the North End) there has been no large-scale turn-over of housing as on the west side. Throughout the east side, the *Chronicle* carried almost no listings of homes outside established black areas. There are only four listings in the *Chronicle* in the area north of Mack and east of Connor. All of these are in close proximity to the Parkside Homes public-housing project. It is also interesting to note that there is no perceptible increase in real-estate activity in the area just within the edge of the ghetto. This is in contrast with the situation of the west side where the movement of the ghetto edge seems to en-courage the clustering of activity.

The pattern of listings carried by the *News* presents a considerably different picture. The listings in the *News* are spread fairly evenly throughout the extreme eastern and western areas of the city. Virtually every neighborhood west of Meyers and east of Connor has at least one listing of a home for sale in the *News.* Although there is a slightly higher concentration of listings on the west side, there is still a significant number on the east side.

What is almost totally lacking from the *News* is any signficant num-ber of listings of homes in the established ghetto areas. The coverage in the *News* is almost the exact opposite of the distribution of listings found in the *Chronicle.* For example, in the predominantly black area bounded by the Lodge Freeway, Livernois, and Warren, the *News* carried only six listings. In the same area the *Chronicle* carried ads for seventy-seven homes. The same situation can be found on the east side. In a lower east-side ghetto area the *News* carried fifteen listings and the *Chronicle* sixty-six.

Perhaps the most interesting areas are those where there are a sub-stantial number of listings carried by both the *News* and *Chronicle.* Table 8.3 indicates three areas where the listings were fairly evenly divided. (See also Figure 8.6.) The areas of competition are also areas which are presently in the process of racial change. As the proportion of black families in these areas increases, it may be expected that the proportion of listings carried by the *News* will decline as it has in other black areas. When the white-oriented media, as represented by the *News* moves out of a neighborhood, it virtually assures that the housing offered for sale will be purchased by nonwhite families.

The two neighborhood papers appear to have been affected differently by the expansion of the ghetto into their circulation area. The *Redford Record* appears to have suffered a diminution of its market area as a result of the movement of the black population. Although the *Record* claims all of Detroit west of Wyoming Avenue as its circulation area, in the two miles immediately to the west of Wyoming the paper listed

Table 8.3: Areas Containing Listings in the
News and the *Chronicle*

| | Number of Listings | |
Area	*News*	*Chronicle*
Tireman–Eight Mile Meyers–Greenfield	133	101
McNichols–Eight Mile Dequindre–Chrysler	20	15
McNichols–Seven Mile Meyers–Palmer Park	26	39

only eleven homes for sale. In contrast, in the next mile to the west, forty-five homes were listed. The *Record* is a paper serving essentially a white audience. The sellers of housing in areas of racial transition evidently feel that there is no market among whites for their housing. This does not necessarily represent an individual act of discrimination but rather a recognition of the existence of distinct market areas.

Table 8.4: Comparison of City and Suburban Listings

Paper	Detroit	Suburb	Ratio
Redford Record	209	119	.57
East Side Shopper	201	131	.65
Sunday News	1,011	1,073	1.06
Michigan Chronicle	882	15	.02

The *East Side Shopper* circulates among a predominantly white audience. The paper contains listings of homes throughout its entire market area. It is interesting to note that the paper carried a substantially lower proportion of listings where it was possible to identify the exact location of the home from the ad. This may be interpreted as a device for ensuring the "acceptability" of the prospective purchaser. Although there are many reasons for not including a specific address in a real-estate listing, the fact that these omissions occur most frequently in the area of the city which has proven most resistant to racial change would seem to indicate that it is more than a simple coincidence.

Although the emphasis of this paper is on the market for existing housing in the City of Detroit, the suburban areas around Detroit do provide a complimentary market. Table 8.4 provides an indication of

Figure 8.6: Detroit Areas of Home Listings by Newspapers

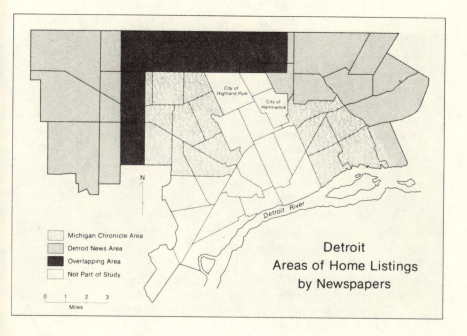

the relative importance of suburban listings in each of the papers. The neighborhood papers contain only a limited number of suburban listings, primarily in the areas close to the city. The lack of listings of suburban homes in the *Chronicle* indicates that there is little interest in offering black families the opportunity to purchase homes in the suburbs. Even the few suburban homes offered in the *Chronicle* were being sold by government agencies, the Federal Housing Administration and the Veterans Administration.

In summary, there is a clear distinction in the markets which each of the newspapers serve. These markets are not only distinct geographically but also racially. The ghetto area is reserved almost exclusively for the *Chronicle.* In areas of racial transition, there is a corresponding change in advertising patterns. The black newspaper has little impact in the all-white areas. This tends to promote the continuation of the existing pattern of ghetto expansion. Although these practices are not the cause of racial segregation, they are a manifestation of the existing situation.

This paper has examined some of the characteristics of the ghetto in the City of Detroit. Although the size of the nonwhite population in Detroit makes it somewhat unique, it would appear that the Detroit experience may be applicable to other Northern and Western American metropolitan areas which have growing nonwhite populations. The major findings are as follows:

1. The modern urban ghetto continues to be a specific territory. As long as the black population is not free to settle throughout a given metropolitan area, the territory in which black families are required to live is a ghetto. A rapidly growing black population makes the expansion of the areas inhabited by nonwhites almost inevitable. Ghetto boundaries may change rapidly, but as long as black families are concentrated in a particular area, the ghetto continues to exist.

This factor is extremely important as ghetto development progresses. In Detroit, the area occupied by nonwhites has outgrown the areas of old and deteriorating housing. For this reason, many black families are now living in better housing. These families are frequently considered to have escaped from the ghetto. However, despite these substantial gains in the quality of housing, most blacks remain in the ghetto because their housing choice is restricted.

2. The expansion of the ghetto territory is accomplished through the expansion of the black population into adjacent areas. As one proceeds farther from the oldest ghetto areas, the concentration of blacks declines. In some instances the growth of the ghetto may be diverted around a white neighborhood (as in the case of the ethnic areas on Detroit's southwest side). But, by and large, the ghetto expands by extending its frontiers outward in all directions, a little at a time.

3. An important characteristic of the ghetto is the apparent inability of most neighborhoods to maintain a stable integrated situation. Once racial change has begun in a neighborhood, it appears inevitable that it will continue until the neighborhood is virtually all black. In some areas of Detroit this change has been relatively slow, while others have

experienced a 90 percent turnover in less than twenty years. In neighborhoods where the change from white to black has begun, white purchasers seem to disappear from the market. The rate at which change takes place becomes dependent on how long it takes for all of the white homeowners to put their property up for sale, since the purchasers will inevitably be black.

4. These characteristics of the housing market in racially changing neighborhoods suggest a means of approximating the extent of the ghetto at a given point in time. The extent of the distribution of listings of homes for sale in the black press provides a fairly accurate idea of where black families currently live. The converse is also true, since the papers serving the white community generally do not carry listings of homes in black areas. Those neighborhoods which are currently undergoing racial change are represented by listings in both types of papers.

PART FOUR

THE GHETTO AS ANALOGOUS
TO AN INTERNAL COLONY

INTRODUCTION

In the first paper in this section, Robert Blauner is dealing with the political dimension of American ethnic relations. He rejects the assimilation model as a means of understanding the social and spatial mobility of blacks. Instead, Blauner has taken an alternative view to an understanding of the black experience in ghettos. His article takes the position that the assimilation model is inadequate when applied to nonwhites in general and to blacks in particular.

Blauner uses the concept of internal colonialism to characterize the position of blacks in United States ghettos. He views the internal colonial model as a conceptual framework for integrating caste, racism, ethnicity, culture, and economic exploitation. The colonial model consists of four components, namely, forced, involuntary entry; transformation or destruction of indigenous values, orientations, and ways of life; manipulation by outsiders; and racism.

According to Blauner, the crucial differences between black Americans and ethnic immigrant groups are that the latter have always been able to compete within that relatively open section of the social and economic order because these groups came voluntarily in search of a better life whereas blacks came involuntarily; ethnic immigrant groups' movements in society were not administratively controlled whereas the movements of blacks were; ethnic immigrant groups transformed their culture at their own pace, whereas the culture of blacks was forcefully transformed; the ghetto as a place of residence for ethnic immigrants tended to be temporary, i.e., a one- and two-generation phenomenon, whereas the ghetto has become a permanent place of residence for blacks and other nonwhites.

Blauner's basic thesis then is that the most important expressions of protest in the black ghettos in recent years reflect the colonized status *of Afro-America and that some violence is almost inevitable in the decolonization process.*

9

Robert Blauner

INTERNAL COLONIALISM AND GHETTO REVOLT

It is becoming almost fashionable to analyze American racial conflict today in terms of the colonial analogy. I shall argue in this paper that the utility of this perspective depends upon a distinction between colonization as a process and colonialism as a social, economic, and political system. It is the experience of colonization that Afro-Americans share with many of the nonwhite people of the world. But this subjugation has taken place in a societal context that differs in important respects from the situation of "classical colonialism." In the body of this essay I shall look at some major developments in black protest—the urban riots, cultural nationalism, and the movement for ghetto control—as collective responses to colonized status. Viewing our domestic situation as a special form of colonization outside the context of a colonial system will help explain some of the dilemmas and ambiguities within these movements.

The present crisis in American life has brought about changes in social perspectives and the questioning of long-accepted frameworks. Intellectuals and social scientists have been forced by the pressure of events to look at old definitions of the character of our society, the role of racism, and the workings of basic institutions. The depth and volatility of contemporary racial conflict challenge sociologists in particular to question the adequacy of the theoretical models by which we have explained American race relations in the past.

Reprinted from *Social Problems*, Vol. 16, (Spring 1969), pp. 393–408, by permission of the publisher and author.

For a long time the distinctiveness of the Negro situation among the ethnic minorities was placed in terms of color, and the systematic discrimination that follows from our deep-seated racial prejudices. This was sometimes called the caste theory, and while provocative, it missed essential and dynamic features of American race relations. In the past ten years there has been a tendency to view Afro-Americans as another ethnic group not basically different in experience from previous ethnics and whose "immigration" condition in the North would in time follow their upward course. The inadequacy of this model is now clear—even the Kerner Report devotes a chapter to criticizing this analogy. A more recent (though hardly new) approach views the essence of racial subordination in economic-class terms: black people as an under-class are to a degree specially exploited and to a degree economically dispensable in an automating society. Important as are economic factors, the power of race and racism in America cannot be sufficiently explained through class analysis. Into this theory vacuum steps the model of internal colonialism. Problematic and imprecise as it is, it gives hope of becoming a framework that can integrate the insights of caste and racism, ethnicity, culture, and economic exploitation into an overall conceptual scheme. At the same time, the danger of the colonial model is the imposition of an artificial analogy which might keep us from facing up to the fact that the American black and white social phenomenon is a uniquely New World thing.

During the late 1950s, identification with African nations and other colonial or formerly colonized peoples grew in importance among black militants. As a result, the United States was increasingly seen as a colonial power and the concept of domestic colonialism was introduced into the political analysis and rhetoric of militant nationalists. During the same period black social theorists began developing this frame of reference for explaining American realities. As early as 1962, race relations in this country were referred to as "domestic colonialism." Three years later in *Dark Ghetto*, Kenneth Clark demonstrated how the political, economic, and social structure of Harlem was essentially that of a colony. Finally in 1967, a full-blown elaboration of "internal colonialism" provided the theoretical framework for Stokely Carmichael and Charles V. Hamilton's widely read *Black Power*. The following year the colonial analogy gained currency and new "respectability" when Senator Eugene McCarthy habitually referred to black Americans as a colonized people during his campaign. While the rhetoric of internal colonialism was catching on, other social scientists began to raise questions about its appropriateness as a scheme of analysis.

The colonial analysis has been rejected as obscurantist and mis-leading by scholars who point to the significant differences in history and social-political conditions between our domestic patterns and what took place in Africa and India. Colonialism traditionally refers to the establishment of domination over a geographically external political unit, most often inhabited by people of a different race and culture, where this domination is political and economic, and the colony exists subordinated to and dependent upon the mother country. Typically the colonizers exploit the land, the raw materials, the labor, and other resources of the colonized nation; in addition a formal recognition is given to the difference in power, autonomy, and political status, and various agencies are set up to maintain this subordination. Seemingly the analogy must be stretched beyond usefulness if the American version is to be forced into this model. For here we are talking about group relations within a society; the mother country–colony separation in geography is absent. Though whites certainly colonized the territory of the original Americans, internal colonization of Afro-Americans did not involve the settlement of whites in any land that was unequivocally black. And unlike the colonial situation, there has been no formal recognition of differing power since slavery was abolished outside the South. Classic colonialism involved the control and exploitation of the majority of a nation by a minority of outsiders. Whereas in America the people who are oppressed were themselves originally outsiders and are a numerical minority.

This conventional critique of "internal colonialism" is useful in point-ing to the differences between our domestic patterns and the overseas situation. But in its bold attack it tends to lose sight of common ex-periences that have been historically shared by the most subjugated racial minorities in America and by nonwhite peoples in some other parts of the world. For understanding the most dramatic recent developments on the race scene, this common-core element—which I shall call coloniza-tion—may be more important than the undeniable divergencies between the two contexts.

The common features ultimately relate to the fact that the classical colonialism of the imperialist era and American racism developed out of the same historical situation and reflected a common world economic and power stratification. The slave trade for the most part preceded the imperialist partition and economic exploitation of Africa, and in fact may have been a necessary prerequisite for colonial conquest—since it helped deplete and pacify Africa, undermining the resistance to direct occupation. Slavery contributed one of the basic raw materials for the textile industry which provided much of the capital for the West's industrial development and need for economic expansionism. The essential condition for both American slavery and European colonialism was the power domination and the technological superiority of the Western world in its relation to peoples of non-Western and nonwhite origins. This objective supremacy in technology and military power buttressed the West's sense of cultural superiority, laying the basis for racist ideologies that were elaborated to justify control and exploitation of nonwhite people. Thus because classical colonialism and America's internal version developed out of a similar balance of technological, cultural, and power relations, a common *process* of social oppression characterized the racial patterns in the two contexts—despite the variation in political and social structure.

There appear to be four basic components in the colonization complex. The first refers to how the racial group enters into the dominant society (whether colonial power or not). Colonization begins with a forced, involuntary entry. Second, there is an impact on the culture and social organization of the colonized people which is more than just a result of such "natural" processes as contact and acculturation. The colonizing power carries out a policy which constrains, transforms, or destroys indigenous values, orientations, and ways of life. Third, colonization involves a relationship by which members of the colonized group tend to be administered to by representatives of the dominant power. There is an experience of being managed and manipulated by outsiders in terms of ethnic status.

A final fundament of colonization is racism. Racism is a principle of social domination by which a group seen as inferior or different in terms of alleged biological characteristics is exploited, controlled, and oppressed socially and psychically by a superordinate group. Except for the marginal case of Japanese imperialism, the major examples of colonialism have involved the subjugation of nonwhite Asian, African, and Latin American peoples by white European powers. Thus racism has generally accompanied colonialism. Race prejudice can exist without colonization—the experience of Asian-American minorities is a case in point—but racism as a system of domination is part of the complex of colonization.

The concept of colonization stresses the enormous fatefulness of the historical factor; namely, the manner in which a minority group becomes a part of the dominant society. The crucial difference between the colonized Americans and the ethnic immigrant minorities is that the latter have always been able to operate fairly competitively within that relatively open section of the social and economic order because these groups came voluntarily in search of a better life, because their movements in society were not administratively controlled, and because they transformed their culture at their own pace—giving up ethnic values and institutions when it was seen as a desirable exchange for improvements in social position.

In present-day America, a major device of black colonization is the powerless ghetto. As Kenneth Clark describes the situation in *Youth in the Ghetto:*

> Ghettoes are the consequence of the imposition of external power and the institutionalization of powerlessness. In this respect, they are in fact social, political, educational, and above all—economic colonies. Those confined within the ghetto walls are subject peoples. They are victims of the greed, cruelty, insensitivity, guilt and fear of their masters. . . .
>
> The community can best be described in terms of the analogy of a powerless colony. Its political leadership is divided, and all but one or two of its political leaders are shortsighted and dependent upon the larger political power structure. Its social agencies are financially precarious and dependent upon sources of support outside the community. Its churches are isolated or dependent. Its economy is dominated by small businesses which are largely owned by absentee owners, and its tenements and other real estate property are also owned by absentee landlords.
>
> Under a system of centralization, Harlem's schools are controlled by forces outside of the community. Programs and policies are supervised and determined by individuals who do not live in the community.

Of course many ethnic groups in America have lived in ghettos. What make the black ghettos an expression of colonized status are three special features. First, the ethnic ghettos arose more from voluntary choice, both in the sense of the choice to immigrate to America and the decision to live among one's fellow ethnics. Second, the immigrant ghettos tended to be a one- and two-generation phenomenon; they were actually way stations in the process of acculturation and assimilation. When they continue to persist as in the case of San Francisco's Chinatown, it is because they are big business for the ethnics themselves and there is a new stream of immigrants. The black ghetto on the other hand has been a more permanent phenomenon, although some individuals do escape it. But most relevant is the third point. European ethnic groups like the Poles, Italians, and Jews generally only experienced a brief period, often less than a generation, during which their residential buildings, commercial stores, and other enterprises were owned by outsiders. The Chinese and Japanese faced handicaps of color prejudice that were almost as strong as the blacks faced, but they very soon gained control of their internal communities, because their traditional ethnic culture and social organization had not been destroyed by slavery and internal colonization.

But Afro-Americans are distinct in the extent to which their segregated communities have remained controlled economically, politically, and administratively from the outside. One indicator of this difference is the estimate that the income of Chinese-Americans from Chinese-owned businesses is in proportion to their numbers forty-five times as great as the income of Negroes from Negro-owned businesses. But what is true of business is also true for the other social institutions that operate within the ghetto. The educators, policemen, social workers, politicians, and others who administer the affairs of ghetto residents are typically whites who live outside the black community. Thus the ghetto plays a strategic role as the focus for the administration by outsiders which is also essential to the structure of overseas colonialism.

The colonial status of the Negro community goes beyond the issue of ownership and decision making within black neighborhoods. The Afro-American population in most cities has very little influence on the power structure and institutions of the larger metropolis, despite the fact that in numerical terms, blacks tend to be the most sizable of the various interest groups. An analysis of policymaking in Chicago in 1968 estimated that blacks held less than 1 percent of the effective power in the Chicago metropolitan area. (Negroes were 20 percent of Cook County's population.) Realistically the power structure of Chicago was hardly less white than that of Mississippi.

Colonization outside of a traditional colonial structure has its own special conditions. The group culture and social structure of the colonized in America is less developed; it is also less autonomous. In addition, the colonized are a numerical minority, and furthermore they are ghettoized more totally and are more dispersed than people under classic colonialism. Though these realities affect the magnitude and direction of response, it is my basic thesis that the most important expressions of protest in the black community during the recent years reflect the colonized status of Afro-America. Riots, programs of separation, politics of community control, the black revolutionary movements, and cultural nationalism each represent a different strategy of attack on domestic colonialism in America. Let us now examine some of these movements.

RIOT OR REVOLT?

The so-called riots are being increasingly recognized as a preliminary if primitive form of mass rebellion against a colonial status. There is still a tendency to absorb their meaning within the conventional scope of assimilation-integration politics: some commentators stress the material motives involved in looting as a sign that the rioters want to join America's middle-class affluence just like everyone else. That motives are mixed and often unconscious, that black people want good furniture and television sets like whites is beside the point. The guiding impulse in most major outbreaks has not been integration with American society, but an attempt to stake out a sphere of control by moving against that society and destroying the symbols of its oppression.

The rioters were asserting a claim to territoriality, an unorganized and rather inchoate attempt to gain control over their community or "turf." In succeeding disorders also, the thrust of the action has been the attempt to clear out an alien presence, white men and officials, rather than a drive to kill whites as in a conventional race riot. The main attacks have been directed at the property of white businessmen and at the police who operate in the black community "like an army of occupation," protecting the interests of outside exploiters and maintaining the domination over the ghetto by the central metropolitan power structure. The Kerner Report misleads when it attempts to explain riots in terms of integration: The Kerner Report states that what the rioters appeared to be seeking was fuller participation in the social order and the material benefits enjoyed by the majority of American citizens. Rather than rejecting the American system, they were anxious to obtain a place for themselves in it. More accurately, the revolts pointed to alienation from this system on the part of many poor and also not-so-poor blacks. The sacredness of private property, that unconsciously accepted bulwark of our social arrangements, was rejected; people who looted apparently without guilt generally remarked that they were taking things that "really belonged" to them anyway. Obviously the society's bases of legitimacy and authority have been attacked. Law and order has long been viewed as the white man's law and order by Afro-Americans; but now this perspective characteristic of a colonized people is out in the open. And the Kerner Report's own data question how well ghetto rebels are buying the system: In Newark only 33 percent of self-reported rioters said they thought this country was worth fighting for in the event of a major war; in the Detroit sample the figure was 55 percent.

One of the most significant consequences of the process of colonization is a weakening of the colonized's individual and collective will to resist his oppression. It has been easier to contain and control black ghettos because communal bonds and group solidarity have been weakened through divisions among leadership, failures of organization, and a general dispiritment that accompanies social oppression. The riots are a signal that the will to resist has broken the mold of accommodation. In some cities as in Watts they also represented nascent movements toward community identity. In several riot-torn ghettos the outbursts have stimulated new organizations and movements. If it is true that the riot phenomenon of 1964–68 has passed its peak, its historical import may be more the "internal" organizing momentum generated than for any profound "external" response of the larger society facing up to underlying causes.

Despite the appeal of Frantz Fanon to young black revolutionaries, America is not Algeria. It is difficult to foresee how riots in our cities can play a role equivalent to rioting in the colonial situation as an integral phase in a movement for national liberation. In 1968 some militant groups (for example, the Black Panther party in Oakland) concluded that ghetto riots were self-defeating of the lives and interests of black people in the present balance of organization and gunpower, though they had served a role to stimulate both black consciousness and white awareness of the depths of racial crisis. Such militants have been influential in "cooling" their communities during periods of high riot potential. Theoretically oriented black radicals see riots as spontaneous mass behavior which must be replaced by a revolutionary organization and consciousness. But despite the differences in objective conditions, the violence of the 1960s seems to have served the same psychic function, assertions of dignity and manhood for young blacks in urban ghettos, as it did for the colonized of North Africa described by Fanon and Memmi in *Wretched of the Earth* and *The Colonizer and the Colonized*.

CULTURAL NATIONALISM

Cultural conflict is generic to the colonial relation because colonization involves the domination of Western technological values over the more communal cultures of non-Western peoples. Colonialism played havoc with the national integrity of the peoples it brought under its sway. Of course, all traditional cultures are threatened by industrialism, the city, and modernization in communication, transportation, health, and education. What is special are the political and administrative decisions of colonizers in managing and controlling colonized peoples. The boundaries of African colonies, for example, were drawn to suit the political conveniences of the European nations without regard to the social organization and cultures of African tribes and kingdoms. Thus Nigeria as blocked out by the British included the Yorubas and the Ibos whose civil war during the sixties was residuum of the colonialists' disrespect for the integrity of indigenous cultures.

The most total destruction of culture in the colonization process took place not in traditional colonialism but in America. As Frazier stressed, the integral cultures of the diverse African peoples who furnished the slave trade were destroyed because slaves from different tribes, kingdoms, and linguistic groups were purposely separated to maximize domination and control. Thus language, religion, and national loyalties were lost in North America much more completely than in the Caribbean and Brazil where slavery developed somewhat differently. Thus on this key point America's internal colonization has been more total and extreme than situations of classic colonialism. For the British in India and the European powers in Africa were not able, as outnumbered minorities, to destroy the national and tribal cultures of the colonized. Recall that American slavery lasted 250 years and its racist aftermath another 100. Colonial dependency in the case of British Kenya and French Algeria lasted only 77 and 125 years respectively. In the wake of this more drastic uprooting and destruction of culture and social organization, much more powerful agencies of social, political, and psychological domination developed in the American case.

Yet a similar cultural process unfolds in both contexts of colonialism. To the extent that they are involved in the larger society and economy, the colonized are caught up in a conflict between two cultures. Fanon has described in *Black Skins, White Masks* how the assimilation-oriented schools of Martinique taught him to reject his own culture and blackness in favor of Westernized, French and white values. Both the colonized elites under traditional colonialism and perhaps the majority of Afro-Americans today experience a parallel split in identity, cultural loyalty, and political orientation.

The colonizers use their culture to socialize the colonized elites (intellectuals, politicians, and middle class) into an identification with the colonial system. Because Western culture has the prestige, the power, and the key to open the limited opportunity that a minority of the colonized may achieve, the first reaction seems to be an acceptance of the dominant values. Call it brainwashing as the Black Muslims put it; call it identifying with the aggressor if you prefer Freudian terminology; call it natural response to the hope and belief that integration and democratization can really take place if you favor a more common-sense explanation, this initial acceptance in time crumbles on the realities of racism and colonialism. The colonized, seeing that his success within colonialism is at the expense of his group and his own inner identity, moves radically toward a rejection of the Western culture and develops a nationalist outlook that celebrates his people and their traditions. As Memmi described it in *The Colonizer and the Colonized:*

Assimilation being abandoned, the colonized's liberation must be carried out through a recovery of self and of autonomous dignity. Attempts at imitating the colonizer required self-denial; the colonizer's rejection is the indispensable prelude to self-discovery. That accusing and annihilating image must be shaken off; oppression must be attacked boldly since it is impossible to go around it. After having been rejected for so long by the colonizer, the day has come when it is the colonized who must refuse the colonizer.

Memmi's book, *The Colonizer and the Colonized*, is based on his experience as a Tunisian Jew in a marginal position between the French and the colonized Arab majority. The uncanny parallels between the North African situation he describes and the course of black-white relations in our society are the best impressionist argument I know for the thesis that we have a colonized group and a colonizing system in America. His discussion of why even the most radical French anticolonialist cannot participate in the struggle of the colonized is directly applicable to the situation of the white liberal and radical vis-à-vis the black movement. His portrait of the colonized is as good an analysis of the psychology behind black power and black nationalism as anything that has been written in the United States. Consider for example:

> Considered *en bloc* as *them, they,* or *those,* different from every point of view, homogeneous in a radical heterogeneity, the colonized reacts by rejecting all the colonizers *en bloc.* The distinction between deed and intent has no great significance in the colonial situation. In the eyes of the colonized, all Europeans in the colonies are de facto colonizers, and whether they want to be or not, they are colonizers in some ways. By their privileged economic position, by belonging to the political system of oppression, or by participating in an effectively negative complex toward the colonized, they are colonizers. . . . They are supporters or at least unconscious accomplices of that great collective aggression of Europe.
> The same passion which made him admire and absorb Europe shall make him assert his differences; since those differences, after all, are within him and correctly constitute his true self. The important thing now is to rebuild his people, whatever be their authentic nature; to reforge their unity, communicate with it, and to feel that they belong.

Cultural revitalization movements play a key role in anticolonial movements. They follow an inner necessity and logic of their own that comes from the consequences of colonialism on groups and personal identities; they are also essential to provide the solidarity which the political or military phase of the anticolonial revolution requires. In the United States an Afro-American culture has been developing since slavery out of the ingredients of African world views, the experience of bondage, Southern values and customs, migration and the Northern lower-class ghettos, and most importantly, the political history of the black population in its struggle against racism. That Afro-Americans are moving toward cultural nationalism in a period when ethnic loyalties tend to be weak (and perhaps on the decline) in this country is another confirmation of the unique colonized position of the black group. (A similar nationalism seems to be growing among American Indians and Mexican-Americans.)

THE MOVEMENT FOR GHETTO CONTROL

The call for black power unites a number of varied movements and tendencies. Though no clear-cut program has yet emerged, the most important emphasis seems to be the movement for control of the ghetto. Black leaders and organizations are increasingly concerned with owning and controlling those institutions that exist within or impinge upon their community. The colonial model provides a key to the understanding of this movement, and indeed ghetto-control advocates have increasingly invoked the language of colonialism in pressing for local home rule. The framework of anticolonialism explains why the struggle for poor people's or community control of poverty programs has been more central in many cities than the content of these programs and why it has been crucial to exclude whites from leadership positions in black organizations.

The key institutions that anticolonialists want to take over or control are business, social services, schools, and the police. Though many spokesmen have advocated the exclusion of white landlords and small businessmen from the ghetto, this program has evidently not struck fire with the black population and little concrete movement toward economic expropriation has yet developed. Welfare recipients have organized in many cities to protect their rights and gain a greater voice in the decisions that affect them, but whole communities have not yet been able to mount direct action against welfare colonialism. Thus schools and the police seem now to be the burning issues of ghetto-control politics.

During the sixties there was a dramatic shift from educational integration as the primary goal to that of community control of the schools. Afro-Americans were demanding their own school boards, with the power to hire and fire principals and teachers and to construct a curriculum which would be relevant to the special needs and culture style of ghetto youth. Especially active in high schools and colleges were black students whose protests were centered on the incorporation of black power and black culture into the educational system. Consider how similar is the spirit behind these developments to the attitude of the colonized North African toward European education. According to Memmi:

> He will prefer a long period of educational mistakes to the continuance of the colonizer's school organization. He will choose institutional disorder in order to destroy the institutions built by the colonizer as soon as possible. There we will see indeed a reactive drive of profound protest. He will no longer owe anything to the colonizer and will have definitely broken with him.

Protest and institutional disorder over the issue of school control came to a head in 1968 in New York City. The procrastination in the Albany state legislature, the several crippling strikes called by the teachers' union, and the almost frenzied response of Jewish organizations make it clear that the decolonization of education faces the resistance of powerful vested interests. The situation is too dynamic at present to assess probable future results. However, it can be safely predicted that some form of school decentralization will be institutionalized in New York, and the movement for community control of education will spread to more cities.

This movement reflects some of the problems and ambiguities that stem from the situation of colonization outside an immediate colonial context. The Afro-American community is not parallel in structure to the communities of colonized nations under traditional colonialism. The significant difference here is the lack of fully developed indigenous institutions besides the church. Outside of some areas of the South there is really no black economy, and most Afro-Americans are inevitably caught up in the larger society's structure of occupations, education, and mass communication. Thus the ethnic nationalist orientation which reflects the reality of colonization exists alongside an integrationist orientation which corresponds to the reality that the institutions of the larger society are much more developed than those of the incipient nation. As would be expected, the movement for school control reflects both tendencies. The militant leaders who spearheaded such local movements were primarily motivated by the desire to gain control over the community's institutions—they were anticolonialists first and foremost. Many parents who supported them shared this goal also, but the majority were probably more concerned about creating a new education to enable their children to "make it" in the society and the economy as a whole—they knew that the present school system fails ghetto children and does not prepare them for participation in American life.

There is a growing recognition that the police are the most crucial institution maintaining the colonized status of black Americans. And of all establishment institutions, police departments probably include the highest proportion of individual racists. This is no accident since central to the workings of racism (an essential component of colonization) are attacks on the humanity and dignity of the subject group. Through their normal routines the police constrict Afro-Americans to black neighborhoods by harassing and questioning them when found outside the ghetto; they break up groups of youth congregating on corners or in cars without any provocation; and they continue to use offensive and racist language no matter how many intergroup-understanding seminars have been built into the police academy. They also shoot to kill ghetto residents for alleged crimes such as car thefts and running from police officers.

Police are key agents in the power equation as well as the drama of dehumanization. In the final analysis they do the dirty work for the larger system by restricting the striking back of black rebels to skirmishes inside the ghetto, thus deflecting energies and attacks from the communities and institutions of the larger power structure. It has been noted that since the French Revolution, police and other authorities have killed large numbers of demonstrators and rioters; the rebellious "rabble" rarely destroys human life. The same pattern has been repeated in America's recent revolts. Journalists' accounts appearing in the press suggested that police see themselves as defending the interests of white people against a tide of black insurgence; furthermore the majority of whites appear to view "blue power" in this light. There is probably no other opinion on which the races are as far apart today as they are on the question of attitudes toward the police.

In many cases set off by a confrontation between a policeman and a black citizen, the ghetto uprisings have dramatized the role of law enforcement and the issue of police brutality. In their aftermath, movements have arisen to contain police activity. One of the first was the Community Alert Patrol in Los Angeles, a method of policing the police in order to keep them honest and constrain their violations of personal dignity. This was the first tactic of the Black Panther party which originated in Oakland, perhaps the most significant group to challenge the police role in maintaining the ghetto as a colony. The Panthers' later policy of openly carrying guns (a legally protected right) and their intention of defending themselves against police aggression brought on a series of confrontations with the Oakland Police Department. All indications were that the authorities intended to destroy the Panthers by shooting, framing up, or legally harassing their leadership—diverting the group's energies away from its primary purpose of self-defense and organization of the black community to that of legal defense and gaining support in the white community.

There are three major approaches to "police colonialism" that correspond to reformist and revolutionary readings of the situation. The most elementary and also superficial sees colonialism in the fact that ghettos are overwhelmingly patrolled by white rather than by black officers. The proposal—supported today by many police departments—to increase the number of blacks on local forces to something like their distribution in the city would then make it possible to reduce the use of white cops in the ghetto. This reform should be supported, for a variety of obvious reasons, but it does not get to the heart of the police role as agents of colonization.

The Kerner Report documents the fact that in some cases black policemen can be as brutal as their white counterparts. The report does not tell us who polices the ghetto, but they have compiled the proportion of Negroes on the forces of the major cities. In some cities during the late sixties, the disparity was so striking that white police inevitably dominated ghetto patrols. (In Oakland 31 percent of the population and only 4 percent of the police were black; in Detroit the figures were 39 percent and 5 percent; and in New Orleans, 41 and 4.) In other cities, however, the proportion of black cops was approaching the distribution in the city: Philadelphia, 29 percent and 20 percent; Chicago, 27 percent and 17 percent. These figures also suggest that both the extent and the pattern of colonization may vary from one city to another. It would be useful to study how black communities differ in degree of control over internal institutions as well as in economic and political power in the metropolitan area.

A second demand which gets more to the issue is that police should live in the communities they patrol. The idea here is that black cops who lived in the ghetto would have to be accountable to the community; if they came on like white cops, then "the brothers would take care of business" and make their lives miserable. The third or maximalist position is based on the premise that the police play no positive role in the ghettos. It calls for the withdrawal of metropolitan officers from black communities and the substitution of an autonomous indigenous force that would maintain order without oppressing the population. The precise relationship between such an independent police, the city and county law-enforcement agencies, the ghetto-governing body that would supervise and finance it, and especially the law itself is yet unclear. It is unlikely that we will soon face these problems directly as they have arisen in the case of New York's schools. Of all the programs of decolonization, police autonomy will be most resisted. It gets to the heart of how the state functions to control and contain the black community through delegating the legitimate use of violence to police authority.

The various "Black Power" programs that are aimed at gaining control of individual ghettos—buying up property and businesses, running the schools through community boards, taking over antipoverty programs and other social agencies, diminishing the arbitrary power of the police—can serve to revitalize the institutions of the ghetto and build up an economic, professional, and political power base. These programs seem limited; we do not know at present if they are enough in themselves to end colonized status. But they are certainly a necessary first step.

THE ROLE OF WHITES

What makes the Kerner Report a less-than-radical document is its superficial treatment of racism and its reluctance to confront the colonized relationship between black people and the larger society. The report emphasizes the attitudes and feelings that make up white racism, rather than the system of privilege and control which is the heart of the matter. With all its discussion of the ghetto and its problems, it never faces the question of the stake that white Americans have in racism and ghettoization.

This is not a simple question, but this paper should not end with the impression that the police are the major villains. All white Americans gain some privileges and advantage from the colonization of black communities. The majority of whites also lose something from this oppression and division in society. Serious research should be directed to the ways in which white individuals and institutions are tied into the ghetto. In closing let me suggest some possible parameters.

1. It is my guess that only a small minority of whites make a direct economic profit from ghetto colonization. This is hopeful in that the ouster of white businessmen may become politically feasible. Much more significant, however, are the private and corporate interests in the land and residential property of the black community; their holdings and influence on urban decision making must be exposed and combated.

2. A much larger minority have occupational and professional interests in the present arrangements. The Kerner Commission reports that 1.3

million nonwhite men would have to be upgraded occupationally in order to make the black job distribution roughly similar to the white. They advocate this without mentioning that 1.3 million specially privileged white workers would lose in the bargain. In addition there are those professionals who carry out the "dirty work" of administering the lives of the ghetto poor: the social workers, the schoolteachers, the urban-development people, and of course the police. The social problems of the black community will ultimately be solved only by people and organizations from that community; thus the emphasis within these professions must shift toward training such a cadre of minority personnel. Social scientists who teach and study problems of race and poverty likewise have an obligation to replace themselves by bringing into the graduate schools and college faculties men of color who will become the future experts in these areas. For cultural and intellectual imperialism is as real as welfare colonialism, though it is currently screened behind such unassailable shibboleths as universalism and the objectivity of scientific inquiry.

3. Without downgrading the vested interests of profit and profession, the real nitty-gritty elements of the white stake are political power and bureaucratic security. Whereas few whites have much understanding of the realities of race relations and ghetto life, I think most give tacit or at least subconscious support for the containment and control of the black population. Whereas most whites have extremely distorted images of Black Power, many—if not most—would still be frightened by actual black political power. Racial groups and identities are real in American life; white Americans sense they are on top, and they fear possible reprisals or disruptions were power to be more equalized. There seems to be a paranoid fear in the white psyche of black dominance; the belief that black autonomy would mean unbridled license is so ingrained that such reasonable outcomes as black political majorities and independent black police forces will be bitterly resisted.

On this level the major mass bulwark of colonization is the administrative need for bureaucratic security so that the middle classes can go about their life and business in peace and quiet. The black militant movement is a threat to the orderly procedures by which bureaucracies and suburbs manage their existence, and I think today there are more people who feel a stake in conventional procedures than there are those who gain directly from racism. For in their fight for institutional control, the colonized will not play by the white rules of the game. These administrative rules have kept them down and out of the system; therefore they have no necessary intention of running institutions in the image of the white middle class.

The liberal, humanist value that violence is the worst sin cannot be defended today if one is committed squarely against racism and for self-determination. For some violence is almost inevitable in the decolonization process; unfortunately racism in America has been so effective that the greatest power Afro-Americans (and perhaps also Mexican-Americans) wield today is the power to disrupt. If we are going to swing with these revolutionary times and at least respond positively to the anticolonial movement, we will have to learn to live with conflict, confrontation, constant change, and what may be real or apparent chaos and disorder.

A positive response from the white majority needs to be in two major directions at the same time. First, community liberation movements should be supported in every way by pulling out white instruments of direct control and exploitation and substituting technical assistance to the community when this is asked for. But it is not enough to relate affirmatively to the nationalist movement for ghetto control without at the same time radically opening doors for full participation in the institutions of the mainstream. Otherwise the liberal and radical position is little different than the traditional segregationist. Freedom in the special conditions of American colonization means that the colonized must have the choice between participation in the larger society and in their own independent structures.

PART FIVE

THE GHETTO ECONOMY

INTRODUCTION

Previous authors in this volume have demonstrated the socioeconomic heterogeneous structure of the ghetto (see Part One). The economic structure of the ghetto is now further examined by Daniel Fusfeld. Implicit in his analysis is the proposition that each sector of ghetto income follows a distinct spatial pattern and that it is the flow of income out of the ghetto that contributes to its continuous economic decline.

Although Fusfeld uses the words "ghetto," "urban poverty area," and "slum" interchangeably, he identifies four separate sources of ghetto income; namely, the high-wage sector, the low-wage sector, the irregular economy, and the welfare system. Within the context of ecological theory, one would expect the residents of the ghetto to be spatially distributed based on the income received. Fusfeld, however, does not address this aspect. He also does not indicate what percentage of the ghetto residents are receiving income from each of these four sources, or which sector or sectors of the ghetto economy are increasing or decreasing. These are important questions for further consideration if the ghetto economy is to be totally understood.

Nevertheless, Fusfeld does provide one of the most comprehensive assessments to date on the operation of the ghetto economy, especially the reasons for its lack of economic development due to the steady drain of resources to the wider society. Here Fusfeld, like Robert Blauner in the preceding chapter notes the striking similarities between the ghetto and the old-fashioned colonial economy. Income, according to Fusfeld, moves out of the ghetto in much the same way as capital and skilled human resources do, leaving the ghetto in a state of permanent economic depression where the highest unemployment rates in the metropolitan area occur.

Finally, Fusfeld views the ghetto as a residual subsystem, i.e., a place where society maintains its rejects. Such a perspective, he avers, has serious implications for public policy. Only within the context of transforming rejection mechanisms will programs to improve income maintenance, education, housing, and health be effective in making an impact on the ghetto.

Fusfeld endorses community self-determination as a promising, realistic, and practical movement when a group is victimized by semi-isolation, permanent economic depression and exploitation.

10

Daniel R. Fusfeld

THE ECONOMY OF THE URBAN GHETTO

The ghetto economy is in many ways a world apart. It differs markedly from that of the rest of the country in many ways. Perhaps its most important distinguishing characteristic is its backwardness, its lack of the dynamic, progressive changes that bring advancement to the rest of the economy. At the same time, there are points of contact through which the ghetto is influenced by economic activity in the rest of the nation.

SOURCES OF INCOME

The income of the urban poverty area comes from four major sources, only one of which represents a viable and continuing link with the forces of progress.

1. Some residents work in the high-wage, progressive sectors of the economy. In Detroit, for example, jobs in the automobile industry are held by a racially integrated work force, a number of whose members live in the urban ghettos. The industry is highly capital-intensive and oligopolistic, and has a strong union: labor productivity is high and wages correspond. Detroit, however, is something of an exception. Most large cities have a smaller portion of their central-city work force in such industries.

Reprinted from *Financing the Metropolis,* Urban Affairs Annual Reviews, Vol. 4, 1970, pp. 369–399, by permission of the publisher, Sage Publications, Inc. (Beverly Hills/London).

2. The economic base of the urban poverty area is the more backward sector of the economy, characterized by low wages, relatively wide cyclical variations, and exposure to all the debilitating forces of competition. A large portion of the workers who are employed full time in these industries earn wages around or below the poverty level.

3. This low-wage economy is supplemented by an irregular economy, partly legal and partly illegal, that provides further income for the residents of urban poverty areas, largely through provision of services to other residents.

4. Finally, income supplements from outside the urban poverty areas, some public and some private, provide the transfer payments without which the population could not survive. Welfare payments are probably th largest and certainly the most controversial of these transfers.

Although these four aspects of the economy of urban poverty areas can be relatively easily identified, the studies that would document their extent and significance have not been made. We do not know, for example, the proportion of the residents' income generated by these four sources. Nor do we know which are increasing and which are decreasing. Nor do we have much notion of how the four sectors have changed in recent years. Nevertheless, it is possible to look more closely at several of them.

The Low-Wage Industries and the Working Poor. A large number of ghetto residents work in low-wage industries. The jobs may be in manufacturing, service industries, or retail and wholesale trade. Their common characteristic is that many full-time employees who work steadily in these industries earn less than a poverty-level income. Table 10.1 gives some examples of industries in which a large portion of all employees falls in the category of the working poor.

The low-wage industries are not highly visible, and we do not look to them for examples of progress. Typically, the individual enterprise is small, requiring relatively little capital investment. The technology is labor-intensive. Both labor productivity and profits are low. Oligopolistic market control is generally absent, which means that employers are unprotected from the rigors of competition. Unions are largely absent, so that workers are subject to the wage-squeeze characteristic of labor-intensive, highly competitive industries. Sales in these industries are generally quite sensitive to prices, which means that even if competition were reduced, firms would have little chance of improving their revenues through price increases. Since profits are low, little is done in research or product development, which reinforces the technological backwardness of these industries.

The low-wage industries may well be subject to greater fluctuations than other sectors of the economy when aggregate demand falls. We know that labor turnover rates are high, which means that the incidence of unemployment in the labor force is also high. We also know that the bulk of the work force is relatively poorly educated and has relatively low levels of work skills. A large proportion of the jobs are dead ends; there are not many higher paying jobs which a worker can qualify for by his daily work on the job. There are relatively few ladders to better positions. Finally, workers who start out in the low-wage sector of the economy

Table 10.1: Selected Low-Wage Industries Employing Substantial Numbers of the Urban Poor

Industry	Year	Total Employ- ment	Average Hourly Earnings	Percent Earning Less than $1.60/hr.
Nursing Homes and Related Facilities	1965	172,637	1.19	86.3
Laundries and Cleaning Services	1966	397,715	1.44	72.5
Hospitals (excl. federal)	1966	1,781,300	1.86	41.2
Work Clothing	1964	57,669	1.43	72.8
Men's and Boys' Shirts	1964	96,935	1.45	70.4
Candy and Other Confectionery	1965	49,736	1.87	34.2
Limited-Price Variety Stores	1965	277,100	1.31	87.9
Eating and Drinking Places	1963	1,286,708	1.14	79.4
Hotels and Motels	1963	416,289	1.17	76.1
Department Stores	1965	1,019,300	1.75	59.6
Miscellaneous Retail Stores	1965	968,200	1.75	58.0
Retail Food Stores	1965	1,366,800	1.91	47.6

apparently tend to stay there rather than move into similar jobs in the high-wage sector (although more studies of this phenomenon are needed to determine how strong a tendency it is).

The low-wage industries are part of the unprotected economy. Workers are not unionized for the most part. Employers are not protected by the oligopolistic industrial structure that shields such firms as General Motors Corporation and the other industrial giants. Most protective legislation, such as minimum-wage laws, is only now being extended to low-wage jobs, and many are still not covered. Many federal programs that might have provided greater protection, such as the loan operations of the Small Business Administration, are only now beginning to provide services. The state employment services have left the area largely unserved. These industries are fully exposed to the "satanic mills" of supply and demand, which grind both workers and business firms exceedingly fine. The higher-income sectors of society have been protected while those needing it the most continue to be exposed.

The Irregular Economy. The urban poverty area supports an occupational structure and service economy that is quite unconventional and partly illegitimate. The need for it arises from the inability of residents to pay for the usual organized and commercially provided services used by higher-income areas, and by the lack of the business enterprises that normally provide them. To compensate for this lack, the ghetto economy has developed an irregular economy that involves: (a) informal work patterns that are often invisible to outside observers, (b) a network of occupational skills unique to ghetto life but which has little significance for jobs outside the ghetto, and (c) acquisition of skills and competences by workers in nontraditional ways, making their use in the larger society difficult if not impossible.

Louis Ferman has identified several occupational types in the irregular economy:

1. The artist. Entertainers, humorists, painters and craftsmen.

2. The hustler. The supersalesman who often operates on both sides of the law; for example, the casket salesman who retrieves coffins from the local cemetery, refurbishes them, and offers them for sale.

3. The fixer. The individual who receives cash income in exchange for information. Sometimes the information concerns the availability of stolen merchandise, sometimes job opportunities, sometimes the details of the welfare system.

4. The product developer. Products such as rum-raisin ice cream, sweet-potato pie, and barbecued spareribs enjoy a large sale in some ghettos. They are also produced there by ghetto residents.

Some of these irregular occupations are practiced full time, some part time, some almost as hobbies. They all fill needs not served through regular economic channels. Most are not illegal, although there is a substantial amount of illegal activity as well, carried out by fences, thieves, bookies, narcotics pushers, pimps and prostitutes.

The irregular economy's work has certain advantages over work in the regular economy. The worker is not accountable to any authority for his earnings, no records are kept, and taxes can be avoided. The work is individualistic in nature, and can give the worker a sense of competence and control over his existence that a regular job may not provide.

Entrepreneurship and risk give the activity some of the aspects of a game, yet the risks are usually not high. Finally, people who work either part or full time in the regular economy can supplement their incomes in the irregular economy, and vice versa.

The irregular economy has one major disadvantage, however. It encourages patterns of behavior and attitudes toward work which make it difficult for the worker accustomed to the irregularity, lax work standards, and high rates of labor turnover in the irregular economy to move easily into jobs in the regular economy, where work rules are more rigid, lost time and absenteeism is not tolerated to the same extent, and supervision is more rigorous. In some respects the work habits of the irregular economy are similar to those of the preindustrial work force that economic historians are familiar with, and some of the same difficulties are found in adapting workers in the irregular economy to jobs in the mainstream of a modern industrial society.

One more point: the irregular economy enables people to develop production skills, entrepreneurship, and sales ability that could be developed and put to use in more systematic ways for the economic development of the area. Its very existence indicates an unfortunate waste of ability and intelligence. Although the specific skills of the irregular economy may not be highly applicable in the regular economy, they indicate the presence of a high degree of initiative and entrepreneurship.

The Welfare System. When David Caplovitz surveyed a sample of residents of four low-income housing projects in 1960 in New York City for his book, *The Poor Pay More,* he found that 28 percent of the sample received incomes wholly or partly from welfare or pensions, and only 72 percent obtained their income exclusively from earnings. The proportion would certainly be higher today. In 1968, almost one million persons in New York City were receiving public-assistance payments alone, or about 12 percent of the population of the city as a whole. In 1960 the number receiving public assistance (not pensions) was around 375,000.

A November 1966 survey of slum areas in major U.S. cities showed that 47 percent of the families in the survey received transfer payments, including unemployment insurance (5.1 percent), welfare or aid for dependent children (18.1 percent), and other nonemployment income (24.6 percent). In the slums of Los Angeles, 30 percent of the population received welfare payments, and in Cleveland, 21 percent of the families received aid for dependent children (AFDC) payments. In all of the areas surveyed a very large proportion of the city's welfare cases were slum residents.

A substantial number of people received public assistance through the present federal-state system. In January 1968 the total was 9,057,000, divided as follows:

Persons in families receiving aid for dependent children	5,436,000
Old-age assistance	2,070,000
Aid to the blind	83,000
Aid to the disabled	651,000
General assistance	817,000
Total	9,057,000

The figure for 1968 was 23 percent greater than the 1961 total, in spite of economic growth and reduced unemployment over the intervening years.

Although the number of recipients was large and the amount disbursed was running at almost $5.7 billion annually in 1970, there was very little good information on the economic impact of the welfare economy. We did not know its effect on the mobility of labor, its effect on the tax base and financial structure of cities, its relationship to the rest of the ghetto economy, its impact on the structure of the community, its effect on property ownership and real-estate values, or its relationship to the incidence and nature of crime. Very few aspects of the welfare economy had been studied, including its place in the economy of the urban ghetto.

In one respect, the welfare economy is notorious. Administration of the welfare system has been blamed for a serious deterioration in the family structure. By withholding payments from families with an able-bodied male worker, the system encourages the unemployed to desert his family in order for them to receive assistance. The welfare system has undoubtedly had that effect, but other aspects of the ghetto economy work in the same direction, including low wages, erratic employment, and general conditions of poverty. Family stability is discouraged by the difficulties that poverty brings. Desertion has always been the poor man's divorce.

Another major question about the welfare economy concerns its effect on the supply of labor. It has been argued that many ghetto residents would rather be on welfare than keep a job. There may be something to this argument, but the extent of this effect is undetermined. It is true that welfare payments come regularly twice a month, while employment may be irregular. In such cases, welfare is less risky than employment. It is also true that many low-wage jobs open to persons on welfare are boring, dead-end jobs that don't provide adequate income anyway.

Why bother? The result appears to be that welfare payments reduce labor-force participation by a significant amount.

The welfare economy often does discourage people on welfare from working. Any earnings are usually deducted in full from the welfare payment. Since working also involves expenses (travel, clothes, and so forth), the welfare recipient who works often ends up worse off than if he didn't work. Some efforts are now being made to allow for work expenses, but they have not made much headway.

A family on welfare can avoid these effects only by breaking the law. Many do that, without avoiding family breakup and discouragement in the labor market. The result is a further disintegration of social controls and decreased respect for the institutions of organized society. Efforts to beat the system are generated by the system itself.

The welfare economy has a perverse effect on the ghetto economy. It encourages family disintegration, discourages work, and promotes a breakdown of social controls. These long-run effects may well be more costly than the short-run gains obtained be seeing that needy people receive the nominally necessary food, clothing, and shelter.

BUSINESS ENTERPRISE IN THE URBAN GHETTO

The retail business districts of central-city ghettos have an outward appearance much like any retail district, with the exception that they are usually a little shabbier and obviously cater primarily to a low-income clientele. There are important differences that are not obvious to the casual observer, however. Business practices are exploitive, and the customers often have few, if any, alternative sources of supply. In addition, the racial composition of the ghetto has tended to create a partially segregated, black retail market.

The underworld of shady and often unethical business enterprise which flourishes in the urban ghetto has been studied and described in depth by David Caplovitz, whose book illustrates the extent to which a distinct business way of life flourishes in the relatively isolated markets of central-city poverty areas.

Retail firms, particularly those selling consumer durables, flourish through provision of easy credit, selling high-priced and often shoddy merchandise by use of high-pressure tactics, and personal methods of attracting customers (peddling) and getting payment. This system of business enterprise is highly exploitive; high prices, high cost of credit, and shabby merchandise effectively strip the poor of whatever assets they may have and ensure their continuation in poverty. These practices are often supplemented by use of the law courts to get payment; repossession and garnishment of wages are devices used by furniture, appliance, and jewelry stores in particular.

Business practices of the ghetto perform an important function in the economy, however; they permit the poor to buy major durable goods that normal channels of trade do not provide. The poor pay more, but they obtain goods they would otherwise be unable to buy.

Caplovitz points out that one reason for the high prices and credit costs of ghetto retailing is the higher risks associated with selling to the poor. These risks cause businessmen in other retail areas to turn down such customers. Ghetto business establishments respond to this gap in the

Table 10.2: Nonwhite-Owned Business Enterprises, 1969

Industry	Number of Firms (000)	Percent of Nonwhite Business Enterprises
Retail Trade	71.0	45.0
Personal Services	33.0	20.9
Other Services	20.7	13.1
Construction	8.1	5.1
Wholesale Trade	5.8	3.7
Manufacturing	2.6	1.6
Other	16.8	10.6
Total	158.0	100.0

SOURCE: U. S. Small Business Administration (1969) *Quarterly Economic Digest* 2 (Winter): 26.

market by devising the business practices that enable them to sell to the poor and still make a profit.

A second feature of ghetto retailing is the fact that a very large portion of the customers are black. This has led to a racially segregated market in some areas of retailing which has enabled black business enterprise to develop.

The segregated market exists in part because of geographical considerations. Some types of retail stores stick close to a neighborhood simply because people don't want to travel far to buy food, personal-care products, and similar items. At the same time, business capital requirements and the size of the market make possible dispersal of many small retail units of neighborhood size.

A second reason for the segregated market is the historical unwillingness of enterprises catering to whites to serve blacks. Until World War II this included many substantial retail outlets such as department and furniture stores and, until very recently, restaurants, hotels, and similar establishments.

For example, in a segregated city like Washington, D.C., before the 1950s, Negroes who shopped in the downtown retail district could expect rude treatment designed to discourage their patronage, while inability to use eating places (and rest rooms) made shopping even more difficult.

Closely related pressures from the white community restricted the practice of most black lawyers, doctors, dentists, accountants, and other professionals to the urban ghetto and black clients.

Table 10.3: Location of Black-Owned and White-Owned Business Enterprises, 1969 (percent)

Location	Black-Owned[a]		White-Owned	
Urban, 50,000 and over	71.9		45.6	
Slum		33.3		3.4
Other Central City		35.1		30.3
Suburban		3.5		11.9
Urban, under 50,000 and rural	28.1		54.4	
	100.0		100.0	

SOURCE: U. S. Small Business Administration (1969) Fact Sheet (May 19, mimeo.).

[a]Does not include firms owned by other nonwhite minorities.

Finally, certain types of personal services such as haircutting and cosmetics have become black business specialties because of the special needs and fashions of black customers.

Black-owned business enterprise reflects the quasi-segregated nature of the ghetto market. Firms are centered in personal services and retail trade, with a scattering in other services and construction. Although very little precise information is available, the Small Business Administration has recently estimated that some 158,000 business enterprises were owned in 1969 by nonwhites, out of a national total of some 5,420,000, or 2.9 percent. The great bulk of the nonwhite owners were, of course, black people. The nonwhite-owned businesses were distributed among industries as shown in Table 10.2.

Most black-owned business enterprises were located in central-city areas, and especially in urban poverty areas, in contrast to white-owned businesses, which were not located in slum areas to any significant extent. The contrast in location is shown in Table 10.3

Although black-owned business enterprises were heavily concentrated in central-city areas and in slums, they did not comprise a majority of business enterprises, even in the urban ghettos. Even in New York's Harlem, a study of street-level businesses showed that only some 53 percent were black-owned. Studies of similar areas in other cities show nonwhite ownership varying from 20 to 40 percent. The Small Business Administration estimated that in central-city ghettos in the nation as a whole in 1969, nonwhites owned only 26 percent of business enterprises.

Table 10.4: Size Comparisons, White-Owned and Minority-Owned Business Enterprises

Number of Paid Employees	Minority-Owned (percent)	Other (percent)
0	32.5	26.0
1–9	61.0	55.0
10–49	5.0	13.2
50–99	1.2	2.7
100 and over	––	3.1
Gross Receipts ($000)		
0–9.9	33.4	18.7
10–19.9	14.8	12.5
20–49.9	18.5	19.4
50–99.9	11.1	14.7
100–999.9	19.8	25.8
1000–4999.9	1.2	6.2
5000 and over	1.2	2.7

SOURCE: U. S. Small Business Administration (1969) Fact Sheet (May 19, mimeo.).

Black-owned enterprises are small operations, often run by an individual or a small family, and have few employees. In most size dimensions, they are smaller than white-owned enterprises. Some relevant comparisons are show in Table 10.4

Although very heavily concentrated in small retail trade, food services, and personal-care services, black business enterprise has also developed a rudimentary network of manufacturing and wholesale trade to back up the black retail and service enterprises. For example, black-owned enterprises manufacture cosmetics for black-owned beauty parlors, and some of the distribution is in the hands of black-owned wholesale enterprises. Since the Negro markets are relatively small, however, the supporting production and distribution network is also relatively small.

Finally, there is an infrastructure of black-owned newspapers, banks, and insurance companies that is also relatively small, although highly significant for black business and the black community. Thus, in 1967 there were seventeen black-owned banks (out of a national total of some twelve thousand) with total assets of about $147 millions (0.039 percent of the national total). These banks were small, weak, and not highly profitable, although their growth record has been comparatively good in recent years.

Life-insurance companies owned by blacks have a similar record: twenty companies in 1962, which held almost all the assets of some fifty black-owned insurance companies, had 0.75 percent of industry sales while holding only about 0.25 percent of industry assets. This reflects both the growing demand for insurance by blacks and the tendency of smaller insurance companies to grow faster than the industry average. Nevertheless, their proportion of the business is very small, they tend to follow conservative investment policies, and have lagged in entering some of the newer areas of the industry.

The segregated nature of the market for the products and services of black business enterprise, together with its small size and concentration in retail and service industry, create some significant problems of economic development. Two conflicting trends can be observed.

The long-term trend until the mid-1960s was one of relative decline, black-owned business enterprise appeared as a decreasingly significant factor in the national economy, even within urban ghetto areas. Several developments lay behind this trend:

1. Small business enterprise in general, while growing in numbers, has been declining in relative importance. This is particularly true of retail trade, where large chain-store distribution has become the dominant pattern.

2. Urban renewal and low-cost housing projects have taken a heavy toll of the small enterprises located in urban ghetto areas.

3. As black incomes have risen, a growing proportion of black spending has gone into big ticket items such as automobiles, household appliances, furniture, and related purchases. These sectors of the retail market are not segregated, and are served almost exclusively by white-owned enterprises.

4. As the urban black population has increased, and the size of the Negro market has grown, it has been penetrated by white-owned enterprise taking advantage of larger opportunities for profits.

The situation is indeed paradoxical. A once highly segregated Negro market grew in both numbers of customers and in average income. The result was not a corresponding growth of the black business enterprise that grew up to serve this market, but a penetration of white enterprise. At the same time, the segregation of the black market tended to break down as blacks began to use the ordinary white channels of trade to a greater extent.

The second trend has been more recent. Following the uprisings of 1966 and 1967, white-owned business enterprises have tended to move out of ghetto areas or, if destroyed, to remain closed. This has opened the way for expansion of black-owned enterprise to replace them. How extensive this shift has been is a matter of conjecture, for hard data is lacking and the evidence is largely that of casual observation. The source of the shift has been dual. On the one hand, whites have moved out of ghetto businesses in large part as a result of uncertainty and fear. On the other hand, a growing awareness of black business by ghetto residents themselves—both a cause and a result of the uprisings—has stimulated black buying from black businessmen. This shift in consumer and community attitudes in the urban ghettos stimulated the movement to promote black business enterprise, community economic development, and expansion of black banks and other financial institutions.

It is too early to tell whether these recent developments will have a significant impact on the ghetto economy. The fact remains that most ghetto residents spend their incomes with business enterprises whose capital comes from outside the ghetto, whose ownership is outside the ghetto, whose sales and administrative personnel live outside the ghetto, and which sell products produced outside the ghetto. The flow of purchases, wage payments, profits, and other expenditures sets up a flow from the ghetto to the larger economy outside the ghetto. By contrast, the circular flow of spending within the ghetto, which runs from customer to enterprise to employment and payments back to customer, is meager. It is limited to a narrow and fragile segment of small retail and service enterprises which, until very recently, was declining in importance rather than growing.

THE DRAIN OF RESOURCES

One of the most striking characteristics of the urban poverty area is the continual drain of resources out of the area and into other sectors of the economy. Although largely unmeasured, and perhaps unmeasurable, the drain includes savings, physical capital, human resources, and incomes. As a result, urban poverty areas are left without the most important resources needed for development and improvement, and the economic infrastructure is seriously deficient.

The drain of resources can be seen most clearly in the process of transition as an area becomes part of the spreading urban ghetto. As migration and population growth spread the boundaries of the ghetto into neighboring parts of the city over the last two decades, middle-class whites moved out. With them went most of the professional personnel who provide personal and business services. Doctors, dentists, lawyers, accountants, insurance agents, and related professionals left and were not replaced.

Other human resources leave by way of the educational system and the high-wage economy. Drawn by opportunities outside the urban poverty area, many of the most intelligent, capable, and imaginative young people move into the progressive sectors where rewards are greater and opportunities wider. This drain of human resources leaves the economy of the ghetto—whose chief resource is manpower to begin with—without many of its best products.

The drain of capital is equally striking. A substantial portion of the savings of the urban ghetto goes into financial institutions such as banks and savings banks whose investment policies draw the funds out of the area and into business loans, mortgages, and other investments elsewhere. Little comes back to support the ghetto economy or promote its development. Even though the ownership of the original savings or thrift accounts remains with ghetto residents, the funds are generally used elsewhere.

Probably the largest flow of capital out of the urban poverty area, however, takes place in housing. Failure to maintain housing facilities enables the owner to withdraw his capital while at the same time maintaining his income. Ultimately the property will be worthless simply because of wear and tear, but while it is being used up, the owner has been getting his capital back and has been deriving a nice current income. Housing authorities in most major cities are quite aware of this process, and have found no way to stop it. Its basic causes lie in overcrowding and very high rates of deterioration through overuse, together with the failure of most cities to develop effective methods of preventing neighborhood decay.

Two aspects of the drain of capital out of housing should be noted. If one or two property owners take their capital out by refusing to replace depreciation, all of the surrounding owners have incentives to do likewise. One deteriorated building draws down the value of surrounding property. One house broken up into small apartments and crowded with numerous families makes it difficult to sell or rent to single families next door. These neighborhood effects cause the drain of capital to accumulate and accelerate once they begin, and are almost impossible to stop.

In addition, families owning their own homes may find themselves locked into the ghetto because of income, age, or race. Their investment in property either deteriorates or its value rises much more slowly than that of families outside the ghetto. A white suburban family discovers that economic growth creates a windfall gain in the form of rising property values. The effect on the ghetto family may be just the opposite; its house, located in a deteriorating urban ghetto, may well decline in value as the neighborhood deteriorates. At the very least, the ghetto resident discovers that over his lifetime the windfall gains from growth in property values is considerably below that of his white suburban counterpart.

Capital also flows out of urban poverty areas through public facilities. Local governments have allowed their capital investments to fall by not replacing depreciation of buildings and other investments. Schools and libraries have been allowed to deteriorate, parks to run down, streets and curbs to go unrepaired, fire and police stations and medical facilities to deteriorate. In part this process has been due to the added strains that a denser population has placed on public facilities. In part it has been the result of the financial problems that have prevented cities from increasing their expenditures for public services to meet expanding needs. In part it has been due to the traditional tendency of city governments to maintain facilities in the middle- and upper-income areas and to put the priorities of the slums last. But whatever the reasons, the process represents another drain of capital out of the urban poverty areas.

The transition to an urban ghetto also features the loss of many organized institutions. Hospitals have moved out. So have churches and other organized community groups. One of the striking features of today's urban poverty area is a deficiency of those groups and associations that have traditionally provided a community with stability and order and with a sense of continuity and participation. This gap in social needs has tended to be replaced by the development of those informal community groups present in every neighborhood. In the urban ghetto, however, much of this informal organization has been outside the law— juvenile gangs, for example. The lack of community groups, together with the strains inherent in poverty and the breakdown of family structures brought on by the system of welfare payments, contribute to and intensify the isolation and anomie inherent in urban life. The social and psychological problems of the urban ghetto add a further dimension to the urban and racial crisis, but it is important to realize that they are related to the fundamental economic problems of the area.

The net result of the drain of resources from the ghettoized slum is to create a backward, underdeveloped area in the midst of an otherwise progressive and expanding economy. Capital moves out, human resources move out, community structure is weakened, public services are inadequate, and the professional skills needed for improvement are largely lacking. The economic infrastructure required by development is primitive. The major resource of the area is its manpower, which is used by the rest of the economy as a pool of low-wage and relatively unskilled labor and, as the Vietnam war showed, by the armed forces for front-line infantry service. Although the charge of colonial exploitation may be an exaggeration, there are some striking similarities to the old-fashioned colonial economy.

The Drain of Income. Income flows out of the urban poverty area in much the same way as do capital and other resources. Earnings of residents are spent in retail markets through which purchasing power flows to the outside economy, where its multiplied growth-stimulating effects are dispersed without affecting the ghetto significantly. Products sold in the ghetto are imported from outside. The stores, particularly those selling higher-priced items, are owned by people who live outside the ghetto. Sales personnel and other employees live outside the ghetto, for the most part. Business services are obtained from banks and other firms outside the ghetto. A steady stream of payments—wholesale purchases, profits, wages, and so forth—moves outward from the ghetto residents to others. Instead of nurturing expansion of incomes and greater economic welfare within the ghetto, the money spent there promotes growth elsewhere. The ghetto is drained of the expansion-stimulating effect of its own purchasing power.

No community is self-sufficient. The goods purchased in any community are imported, except for a very small proportion of local products. In this respect the urban poverty area is like any other. But in other communities a significant portion of the retail and wholesale trades is owned locally, and most of the employees are local. The profits and wages earned by those people are spent locally, and serve to help support the local community. A chain of spending and respending is set up which adds strength and variety to the local economy.

These internal income flows are of growing importance in contemporary urban areas. Cities used to be noted for their export industries, such as steel in Pittsburgh, automobiles in Detroit, meat products in Chicago, and so on. Those industries formed the economic base around which retail and service industries developed. Although the economic-base industries are important, students of urban economics are coming increasingly to recognize that a very large portion of the economy of any metropolitan area is self-sustaining. Each sector of the city's economy strengthens and give support to the other sectors by means of the income flows that each generates. Cities still specialize in certain types of export products, but they are becoming increasingly general in their economic activities.

The urban poverty area lacks the highly developed internal income flows that might lead to a viable economic pattern. Aside from the irregular economy and relatively small enterprises requiring little capital, business enterprises are not owned by ghetto residents. Labor is the chief export, and the incomes earned are spent in chain supermarkets, outsider-owned furniture and appliance stores, and other enterprises with ownership, management, and many employees, almost always of non-ghetto origin. The profits and wages received by the outsiders do not come back into the ghetto to support other enterprises or employees. They flow, instead, into the economy of the progressive sector located elsewhere.

These patterns are exaggerated in urban poverty areas by the low incomes which prevail. Compared with the rest of the economy, relatively small amounts of ghetto incomes are spent on services. With a larger than usual amount spent on goods, the income drain which purchases of goods create in any community is proportionately larger for urban poverty areas than for others.

Low incomes also mean that housing costs are a larger proportion of family budgets than elsewhere. For many ghetto families the cost of housing ranges upward to 35 percent of family incomes. This means that a significant portion of ghetto income is transformed into withdrawals of capital by owners of rental property.

These patterns of income flow help to explain why the welfare economy is needed to stabilize the ghetto economy. Flows of income in the private sector are generally outward, requiring a compensating inward flow via the public economy. The outward flow of income also helps to explain why increased welfare payments may help the individuals or families who receive them, but have little or no impact on the ghetto economy as a whole. The bulk of the increased payments leaks out rapidly.

A word of caution about the drain of income is in order, however. Aside from general descriptive accounts, mostly of a nonscholarly nature, there are few firm data on which to estimate the income flow out of the ghettos. It is equally difficult to determine the extent to which urban poverty areas differ from other urban areas in this respect. At this stage the best we can do is sketch a noticeable, qualitative difference without being able to quantify it.

Table 10.5: Unemployment Rates in U. S. Urban Poverty Areas, 1966

Area	Unemployment as a Percent of the Labor Force
Boston (Roxbury)	6.9
Cleveland (Hough and surrounding neighborhood)	15.6
Detroit (central Woodward area)	10.1
Los Angeles (south Los Angeles)	12.0
New Orleans (several contiguous areas)	10.0
New York (Harlem)	8.1
(East Harlem)	9.0
(Bedford-Stuyvesant)	6.2
Oakland (Bayside)	13.0
Philadelphia (north Philadelphia)	11.0
Phoenix (Salt River Bed area)	13.2
St. Louis (north side)	12.9
San Antonio (east and west sides)	8.1
San Francisco (Mission-Filmore area)	11.1

PERMANENT DEPRESSION

One of the most striking economic characteristics of urban poverty areas is the condition of permanent depression that prevails. Even though the rest of the economy may be prosperous, even booming, and may feel the inflationary pressures of rising aggregate demand, unemployment in the urban ghettos will remain high. Ghetto unemployment rates stay at levels that would signal a serious depression if they prevailed in the economy as a whole (Table 10.5).

The unemployment figures in Table 10.5 include only those persons who were actively looking for work. They do not include those who should have been in the labor force but were not because they felt, rightly or wrongly, that they couldn't find a job (or for other reasons). This nonparticipation rate in urban poverty areas was 11 percent among men in the twenty-to-sixty-four-year age group, as compared with a 7 percent rate for men of that age in the economy as a whole.

The unemployment figures also exclude a substantial number of adult men that other statistical sources indicate should be part of the slum-area population. The November 1966 survey failed to find between a fifth and a third of the adult men of the slum areas. This parallels the census experience with the undercount problem.

Finally, the unemployment figures do not include persons who were working part time but wanted full-time jobs. The November 1966 survey showed that 6.9 percent of all employed persons in urban poverty areas fell into this category. The national figure was 2.3 percent.

These latter considerations indicate that the situation was worse than the figures on unemployment reveal. In particular, the contrast with the rest of the economy is sharp enough so that national unemployment rates become meaningless in describing conditions in the slums. This does not mean that when unemployment rates decline in the national economy the slums feel no impact. They do. The manpower resources of urban poverty areas are used by the larger economy, but they form a pool of workers, many of whom are unemployed or employed part time, which is always underutilized. Even when markets everywhere else are tight, and inflationary pressures in the progressive sectors of the economy are pushing up prices, wages, profits, and interest rates, unemployment in the urban slums is pulled down only to the levels that in the economy as a whole are characteristic of serious recessions. Charles Dickens' famous phrase, "It was the best of times, it was the worst of times," applies to this situation with something of an ironic twist; when the first part applies to the rest of the economy, the second part would be a good description of the urban poverty area.

Even the presence of inflationary pressures in the economy as a whole does not bring prosperity to the ghetto. In early 1969 the new Urban Unemployment Survey of the U.S. Department of Labor showed unemployment rates two and one-half times the national average in six slum areas, teen-age unemployment rates of 30 percent, and earnings of less than $65 per week for one-sixth of all employed workers living in slums.

CIRCULAR CAUSATION AND CUMULATIVE EFFECTS

The condition of the ghetto economy is a classic example of circular causation in social processes. The ghetto economy perpetuates its own poverty. Low incomes means low levels of living. This style of life has obvious deficiencies: poor food, bad housing, poor health, and bad sanitation. These conditions lead back to low labor productivity and a perpetuation of low incomes.

The drain of resources out of urban poverty areas—manpower, capital, income—serves to reinforce the poverty. Social overhead capital is inadequate. The public services that might overcome part of the deficiencies in private incomes are insufficient. In particular, deficiencies in the educational system lead to inadequate training, low skill levels, and low productivity.

Employment patterns, especially in the low-wage industries and the irregular economy, reinforce the pattern of poverty and create barriers to movement of workers into the high-wage sectors outside the urban poverty area. At the same time, those ghetto residents who do move up and out take with them much of the entrepreneurship that development of the ghetto economy requires.

Economic development is further retarded by ineffective instruments for local control; the destinies of urban poverty areas have been largely in the hands of outsiders. Weak political representation and control of local governments by an establishment power structure have kept the poor out of power. The result is a weak infrastructure of voluntary organizations and a low level of popular participation in the decision-making process. This, in turn, retards the development of decision-making and entrepreneural abilities. This dual lack of entrepreneurship and effective power means that decisions which affect the ghetto economy will be made largely by the outsiders who dominate the decision-making process.

One result has been that many policies and programs have hurt, rather than helped, the ghetto. Welfare payments have tended to weaken attachment to the labor market. Urban renewal has increased the overcrowding of housing rather than diminished it. Highway construction has had the same effect. Educational programs have been unable to prevent a serious deterioration of the schools. Even the benefits of low-cost housing have been relatively small compared with the incomes generated for nonghetto residents.

In this context, the racial attitudes of whites and the long heritage of black repression take on key significance. Together they have kept the great majority of blacks in the ghetto, unable to move out of the vicious circle of self-generating poverty that prevails there.

The pattern of the ghetto economy, then, presents a series of self-reinforcing influences:

1. Poverty breeds a style of life which reinforces the conditions that lead to poverty.

2. Resources that might lead to betterment and development are drained out.

3. Lack of political power has brought public programs that are often harmful to the ghetto economy.

4. White attitudes toward race have kept most of the ghetto residents from moving out.

A social system in which a pattern of circular causation operates will generally reach an equilibrium in which causative factors balance each other. It may be a moving equilibrium if growth processes operate. If outside forces impinge on the equilibrium, and if they set up secondary effects moving in the same direction, a self-sustaining process of growth can be established, particularly if the social system can move beyond the position, or threshold, from which the old equilibrium can no longer be reestablished. These basic propositions from the theory of growth and economic development embody the concept of cumulative effects; circular causation can lead to maintenance of the existing equilibrium, but it can also lead to cumulative movements toward either growth or retrogression.

Economic growth is particularly difficult for the ghetto economy. Its weak infrastructure, the lack of local initiative and entrepreneurship, and the shortage of capital make it difficult to get a growth process started. This is part of the self-reinforcing process by which poverty creates the conditions that preserve poverty. More important, the tendency for resources and income to drain out of the ghetto economy means that even if the forces of development were to appear, much of their strength would be dissipated before they had a significant impact on the ghetto itself. Any program (or programs) that seeks to improve the economy of urban poverty areas must reverse the drain of skilled manpower, capital, and income if a cumulative process of growth is to be established.

Rather than growth, a cumulative process of retrogression has been the fate of urban poverty areas over the last twenty years. The key outside influence was the migration of the 1950s and the ensuing population explosion. These demographic changes both expanded the size of problems and worsened the condition of a social and economic system already suffering from permanent depression and a self-reinforcing pattern of underdevelopment. Retrogressive forces were set in motion which worsened the poverty, speeded up the drain of resources, and further weakened the social and economic infrastructure. Only massive increases in transfer payments and large increases in public expenditure programs have been able to stem the tide and re-create (perhaps) a new equilibrium.

Conditions may still be getting worse rather than better. The incomes of blacks appear to be rising more slowly than those of whites, creating a widening income gap between races. There appears to be a tendency for the gap between the high- and low-wage industries to widen. Recent studies of the interim and special censuses indicate that housing segregation is growing rather than decreasing. As the second wave of the urban-ghetto population explosion starts—the children who comprised the first wave in the early 1950s are now entering young adulthood—a second lost generation is about to appear in the cities. The current picture is one of continuation of ghetto conditions and the circular causation of poverty and deprivation.

THE URBAN GHETTO AS A RESIDUAL SUBSYSTEM

Although it is a world apart, the urban ghetto also serves an essential need of our society as a repository for people for whom the larger social and economic system has little or no use.

Every social system rejects individuals who do not meet the standards established for membership in the various subsystems that make up the larger social order. For example, the requirements for acceptance into the northeastern suburbs of Detroit—one of the subsystems that make up the whole—include the income required to buy or, rent an expensive home. Those families unable to meet that requirement are rejected, and find residences in less expensive Detroit suburbs—one of the other subsystems. Other family characteristics, such as race, religion, and national background, have also been important for acceptance or rejection, and at one time were formalized into a point system operated by realtors to determine a family's eligibility for the wealthy northeastern suburbs.

Rejection mechanisms are many and varied. Test scores and grades are important for admission to college. Certain requirements must be met to obtain a civil service job. Formal or informal restrictions keep some country clubs and fraternal organizations free of Jews or blacks. A middle-class pattern of behavior is necessary for acceptance in the typical suburban community. Examples can be multiplied, but the principle is clear; each of the subsystems into which the social system divides itself accepts or rejects individuals according to its own formal or informal criteria. One of the most unfortunate aspects of our society is that race is one of the major criteria for acceptance or rejection.

Rejection from one subsystem does not mean rejection from all, in most cases. The individual or family unable to find a place in one will usually find another. For example, the scholar whose work is unacceptable for employment at Harvard or Yale takes a job at a university a little down the ladder of academic prestige, or at a small liberal arts college, a former teachers college in the Southwest, a community college. There may be frustrations and disappointments, but a place is usually found. Most people are not rejected from the social system as a whole.

But some are. Dangerous or particularly bizarre (irrational) behavior takes some to mental hospitals. Crimes draw others to prisons. Others gravitate to the urban ghetto, often because of a syndrome of characteristics such as race, poor education, low skill, and lack of adaptability to the behavior patterns of the more successful sectors of the social order. Mental hospitals, jails, and slums—these are the chief depositories our society has created for those who cannot fit, or be fitted into, the dominant way of life. They make up the residual subsystems into which society's rejects congregate.

An example will show how the mechanisms works. The black sharecropper, poor, almost uneducated, lacking in skills, who found employment in agriculture in the Mississippi Delta region in 1950 found that he was redundant there in 1955. He was rejected from the economic system in which he had formerly been able to subsist, even though he was at the bottom of the economic and social order. Cast out there, he made his way to the ghetto of a Southern city or a Northern city. He moved by a process which we do not understand, to the place where other economic rejects also had moved. Partly by choice, and partly because there was no other place to go, he ended up in the urban ghetto.

People rejected from the social-economic system are not scattered at random. They do not stay in the suburbs, or in Southern agriculture, or in the universities, if they are caught up in the rejection mechanisms. The residuals tend to collect or be collected at specific points in the system as a whole. The best analogue is physical-refuse trash dumps, auto graveyards, and so forth, although cemeteries also qualify. This tendency for residuals to congregate in specific areas is characteristic of humans, too, and we have our jails, mental institutions, and slums.

Residual subsystems are usually separated from the functioning central sectors of the social order by barriers of various types. Mental hospitals and jails are walled or fenced, and entry is by a formal process of legal commitment. The urban ghetto is different. There are no physical barriers between the ghetto and the rest of society, and no formal methods by which individuals are committed to life in the ghetto. The barriers are economic and social rather than physical, and the selection process is informal.

The barriers between the urban ghetto and the rest of the economic and social system do not cut off the ghetto completely. A substantial number of individuals move out and up into other sectors of society. Others move down and into the ghetto. Individuals are always moving from one subsystem to another in our highly mobile society. The process is not that simple, however. The urban ghetto has three characteristics which make it different:

1. Mobility outward for many people is not based on merit, or even income, which often acts as a proxy for merit. Race is an important criterion for movement out. It is a barrier for blacks and Puerto Ricans that is not present for whites.

2. The culture of the ghetto creates and fosters a way of life that makes it difficult for individuals to be accepted in other sectors of the economy and society. This includes such factors as work habits and attitudes toward work developed in the irregular economy, and patterns of behavior fostered by the welfare economy.

3. The fact that the urban ghetto is a depository for people rejected from society influences the attitudes of the rest of society toward the ghetto. These attitudes are reflected in inadequate provision of public services, such as education and health, which tend to preserve ghettoization and reduce the upward mobility of ghetto residents.

These informal and unseen barriers show up in the economic statistics of inordinately high levels of unemployment, relatively low income levels, relatively low residential mobility, and many other distinctive features of the ghetto. More important, they tend to keep within the ghetto a large number of people whose native abilities and potential for development are largely wasted. This waste of human resources is particularly tragic in the case of young people whose opportunities are restricted and whose futures are bleak simply because of the environment into which they are born and in which they are raised.

The national economy is not a seamless web of relationships that make up a unified, articulated whole. Rather, the urban ghetto is a quasi enclave. It is part of the national economy and is affected by what goes on in the national economy, but the connecting links are seriously deficient. Barriers exist which prevent, for example, an increase in gross national product from having the same effects in the ghetto that it has in the rest of the economy. Barriers prevent the rising living standards due to economic growth from having the same effects in the urban ghetto that they have elsewhere.

The quasi enclave of the ghetto has developed its own characteristic system of relationships within which its inhabitants function. We have described some of the economic aspects of this social subsystem: the low-wage sector, the irregular economy, and the welfare economy. We have noted some of the results: poverty, permanent depression, and under-development. We have also identified some of the relationships between the ghetto subsystem and the larger social system: the flow of transfer payments into the ghetto which serves to stabilize and helps to support it, and the outward flow of capital, income, and human skills. And we have emphasized the fact that the ghetto subsystem tends to preserve the conditions that lead to ghettoization, generates the attitudes that keep people ghettoized, and largely prevents a process of economic development from getting started. The ghetto subsystem, in short, tends to preserve itself in a relatively static position, and reproduce itself from generation to generation. It may also grow in size, as it has done in the last fifteen years.

This concept of the urban ghetto as a residual subsystem—a place where society maintains its outcasts and semioutcasts—is essential to the development of policy and programs. In this context the welfare system or other forms of income maintenance are not solutions, but ameliorative devices. Improved education and training programs may help individuals, but they will not transform the ghetto unless they operate on a scale large enough to enable more people to overcome the barriers to outward and upward mobility than are moving inward and downward to the ghetto. Better housing may improve living conditions but will not necessarily make an impact on ghettoization—our experience with public low-cost housing confirms that view. Better health services and other public facilities, while also needed and desirable in themselves, likewise fail to attack the basic causes of ghettoization.

This is not to say that concerted and large-scale programs to improve incomes, education and training, housing and health, and to provide jobs are doomed to failure. If they are large enough and if they are sustained long enough, they can make an important contribution to a solution of the problem, but, in essence, they are addressed to symptoms rather than basic causes.

The causes of the urban and racial crisis are the rejection mechanisms of our society which turn people into residuals. And the crisis will be with us until those social processes are changed.

1. The rejection mechanisms must be identified and their operation modified or ended. In particular, the relationship of blacks to the larger opportunity system must be drastically transformed.

2. Better feedback mechanisms must be developed to bring society's rejects back into the mainstream. The greatest potential lies in employment and job training, but they have never been used on the massive scale required.

It is in connection with programs to transform the rejection mechanisms and generate better feedbacks that programs for income maintenance, education, housing, health, and all the rest begin to make sense. Standing by themselves, or even used together, they can have little effect, because they do not change the fundamental workings of a social system that continually creates residuals. However, they can be useful when developed in conjunction with policies and programs directed toward significant changes in some of the more dysfunctional aspects of our economic and social system.

One promising development is the movement for community self-determination. It takes such varied forms as community control of schools and programs for community-oriented economic development. This movement is a realistic and practical reaction to the semi-isolation, permanent depression, and exploitation of the ghetto, on the part of people who realize that they themselves are the only ones who can move their little subsection of society toward a more desirable condition. It is an effort to reconstruct the relationships between their world and the larger world outside on more favorable terms. These new relationships are yet to be defined, but the community self-determination movement promises for the first time to give ghetto dwellers a degree of control over their own destiny. If it can be combined with a thoroughgoing effort to reconstruct those elements in our social and economic order which create and preserve ghetto conditions, some real progress may ultimately be made.

PART SIX

ATTITUDES TOWARD THE QUALITY OF SOCIAL SERVICES IN THE GHETTO

INTRODUCTION

Are ghetto residents satisfied or dissatisfied with the delivery of social services? Do they have a positive or negative attitude toward the quality of social services? These questions are examined in the next two studies. In the first article, Howard Schuman and Barry Gruenberg present the results of randomly surveying blacks and whites in fifteen cities in order to determine differences in satisfaction with the quality of four essential municipal services; namely, schools, parks and playgrounds, police protection, and garbage collection. They concluded that racial differences in dissatisfaction do indeed exist and that such differences are associated with variations by neighborhood within cities.

More important, however, are the reasons for such dissatisfaction. The authors associated the reasons not with the race of the individual per se but with the racial composition of the neighborhood. Black dissatisfaction was highest in all-black neighborhoods and lowest in mostly white neighborhoods. Logically then, blacks are more dissatisfied than whites with the delivery of social services because most of them live in largely black areas, i.e., ghettos, and differential treatment (perceived and actual) exists in the delivery of such social services to black ghetto areas. Such dissatisfaction was most pronounced in the low-income or slum ghetto.

The second article focuses on one city, Pittsburgh, and one subgroup, black ghetto teen-agers. Based on interviews with ghetto high school seniors, Darden's data revealed that most seniors in the school believed that their environment was of bad quality. If the attitudes of seniors in the Pittsburgh ghetto high school are typical, such subjective evaluations on a broader scale could serve as indicators of potential violence.

What the two articles have in common is that both link the riots of the 1960s to dissatisfaction with social services and the perception that the city administration discriminates against ghetto neighborhoods in the provision of such services. These two articles strongly imply that "perception of differential treatment combined with dissatisfaction is a very important factor in the causes of civil disorders by ghetto residents."

11

Howard Schuman and Barry Gruenberg

DISSATISFACTION WITH CITY SERVICES
Is Race an Important Factor?

The adequacy of the services a city provides its citizens cannot be judged accurately by the amount of money expended or the number of persons paid to provide the services. High levels of either may simply indicate inefficiency, excessive patronage, or some other feature of urban life irrelevant to satisfactory services. More appropriate criteria of adequacy are objective indices of performance and results: frequency of garbage collection, low crime and high arrest rates, reading levels of school children. This article examines still a third measure of civic adequacy: subjective reports by random samples of citizens about their satisfaction with four essential city services.

Subjective evaluations are of fundamental importance insofar as we regard citizen satisfaction both as the ultimate goal of city services and in the form of dissatisfaction as a major factor prompting change in the delivery of services. But such reports are also, as we know from much experience, ambiguous in nature and origin since they may be influenced not only by objective reality, but also by expectations, ideology, and a host of other individual and group characteristics. We deal here with a crucial perspective on municipal functioning, but one which, like data on expenditures, cannot be taken at face value.

Four apparently straightforward questions about "satisfaction" with specific neighborhood services were posed at the beginning of a lengthy

Reprinted from *People and Politics in Urban Society,* Urban Affairs Annual Review, Vol. 6, 1972, pp. 369–392, by permission of the publisher, Sage Publications, Inc. (Beverly Hills/London).

interview in 1968 with cross sections of black (n = 2809) and white (n = 2584) citizens in fifteen American cities. The four services covered are "quality of public schools," "parks and playgrounds for children," "police protection," and "garbage collection." Table 11.1 presents the percentage of respondents of each race showing different degrees of satisfaction with each service. Each item was scored on a three-point scale (where 3 = very dissatisfied), and means and standard deviations based on such scoring are presented as well. A related question on the sense of relative deprivation in these services felt by respondents is also shown in the table.

Although all the questions are rather abstract in phrasing, follow-up inquiries to a random subsample of one hundred respondents indicate that most people answered the questions within the intended frame of reference. For example, the following are typical explanations by two respondents about their initial answers on "police protection":

Generally satisfied: Whenever anything happens they are here right away. If there is an accident or anything. Nothing else happens.

Very dissatisfied: Police are of little use to call here. Rapes, robberies, and murders are committed. Police give no service to citizens in this area. I feel that there is no concern by the law-enforcement people for those who live here.

The main finding of interest in Table 11.1 is that blacks are more dissatisfied with each service than whites. The differences are not pronounced, but they are clear-cut and consistent. We take their explanation as the main task of this article. In the course of pursuing it, we will also account for some of the variation in levels of satisfaction within each race, that is, for urban inhabitants as such, regardless of the color of their skin.

We may note initially two quite different lines of explanation for racial differences in dissatisfactions with city services. One possibility is simply that blacks experience objectively worse services than whites. For example, blacks could live disproportionately in cities that have poorer services, or in areas within cities that have poorer services. The problem with such an explanation is the assumption that objective reality is perceived without distortion and that these perceptions in turn are transformed directly into levels of satisfaction. Concepts like "relative deprivation" have sensitized social scientists to the problematic nature of the link between the social world as seen by the detached observer and the same world as experienced by the actors in it. For example, satisfaction with a service may be based on limited past personal experience or on ideological beliefs, rather than on broad observation of the current state of things.

Table 11.1

1. "First, I'd like to ask how satisfied you are with some of the main services the city is supposed to provide for your neighborhood. A. What about the quality of the public schools in this neighborhood—are you generally satisfied, somewhat dissatisfied, or very dissatisfied?" [Repeat question for B, C, and D] (in percentages)

	A. Quality of Public Schools		B. Parks and Playgrounds for Children		C. Police Protection		D. Garbage Collection	
	Black	White	Black	White	Black	White	Black	White
1. Generally satisfied	53	68	36	56	51	71	70	82
2. Somewhat dissatisfied	28	20	30	23	21	18	14	9
3. Very dissatisfied	19	13	34	21	28	10	15	8
Total	100	101	100	100	100	99	99	99
n	(2,265)	(1,837)	(2,386)	(2,226)	(2,553)	(2,468)	(2,733)	(2,492)
Mean score	1.64	1.46	1.97	1.65	1.77	1.40	1.46	1.25
Standard deviation	0.77	0.71	0.84	0.80	0.86	0.67	0.75	0.59

2. "Thinking about city services like schools, parks, and garbage collection, do you think your neighborhood gets better, about the same, or worse service than most other parts of the city?" (in percentages)

	Black	White
Better	11	19
About the same	65	71
Worse	24	10
Total	100	100
n	(2,581)	(2,312)
Mean score	2.12	1.89
Standard deviation	0.57	0.52

Such reflections raise the possibility that blacks show more dissatisfaction with city services than whites for reasons unrelated to the objective character of the services themselves. We are often told that blacks are alienated from American institutions generally, and there is some evidence to support such claims. Questions about city services may simply furnish a convenient screen onto which a disillusioned racial group projects its dissatisfactions with life in America. This reasoning would lead us to look for the causes and correlates of dissatisfaction with services among ideological rather than ecological variables, and to focus on the way politics affects personality rather than on the way politics affects city streets.

The two perspectives just outlined provide some broad hearings for our search, but do not exhaust or even clearly identify specific variables. We turn to these, and to the evidence, after noting two other features of Table 11.1. The reader may have noted that the ordering of dissatisfactions by service is not exactly what one would expect. The greatest dissatisfaction is not over police protection or schools, which dominate the newspapers as sources of complaint, but with "Parks and Playgrounds for Children." We are unable to illuminate this ordering very much, since the four services are objectively incommensurable and relative "satisfaction" from one to another involves intrinsically subjective factors. The primacy of parks is real enough, however, for it holds for each race and for most of the fifteen cities. Perhaps overall citizen satisfaction could be increased substantially by municipal emphasis on park construction and management. One thinks of the abandoned commercial areas in cities that suffered rioting in the late 1960s; reclaiming some of these central city areas for park land might be well received.

At the other end of the scale, it is no great surprise that dissatisfaction is lowest for garbage collection for both races. In the middle are schools and police, rather close together but with the ordering for blacks the reverse of that for whites. We will be able to throw some light on this reversal at a later point.

The ordering of the four services leads to the related question of how much respondents distinguish among them. In one sense the items in Table 11.1 could be treated simply as four indicators of an underlying construct about general dissatisfaction with city services. Indeed, the format of the questions encouraged such a "set," since the items were grouped together and asked in exactly the same ways. Yet the quite different levels of dissatisfaction across the four services indicate that considerable differentiation did in fact occur. It is noteworthy that such differentiation seems to be greater for blacks than for whites. For example, the gap between satisfaction with garbage collection and with parks is 36 percent for blacks and only 26 percent for whites. This does not fit the hypothesis that blacks are responding with a more ideological set of attitudes toward all city services than are whites.

CITY DIFFERENCES IN DISSATISFACTION LEVELS

The presentation of our analysis will move from a social structural to an individual level, and from larger to smaller units. We begin with major cities as units of analysis. Then we look within cities at areas defined in terms of racial and economic proportions. Finally we shift to individuals and their characteristics, starting with demographic and socioeconomic attributes, and ending with personal attitudes and ideology.

Our total sample actually comprised fifteen city samples of each race. City of residence is a particularly relevant level of analysis because the city is the governmental unit responsible for the four services. It is possible, for example, that cities differ sharply in the services they provide, and that racial differences in dissatisfaction result from the differing distribution of the races across the fifteen cities. Thus our black sample (when properly weighted) came more from Washington than Milwaukee, while the reverse was true for our white sample. If services are poorer in Washington than Milwaukee, this would tend to produce the racial differences in dissatisfaction in Table 11.1.

On the question first of whether racial differences in dissatisfaction can be reduced to city of residence, the answer is clearly no. A racial comparison was possible for each city on each of the four services: a total of sixty comparisons, not all independent, of course. With the exception of five scattered small reversals, blacks were more dissatisfied than whites on each service in each city. On the whole, when city of residence was controlled, racial differences in dissatisfaction appeared larger than in the aggregated data presented earlier in Table 11.1.

A second question is whether cities vary in levels of dissatisfaction. "City of residence" accounts for from 2.5 to 6.8 percent of the variance in satisfaction levels, depending on the particular race and service. These are all significant proportions, and indeed somewhat greater in magnitude than the variance in satisfaction levels explained by race. We can also be reasonably confident that variation in dissatisfaction levels by city of residence is not merely a reflection of socioeconomic or demographic differences among city populations.

The fact that city and race produce independent variation in dissatisfaction provides some perspective on the aggregate racial differences reported in Table 11.1. While blacks are almost always less satisfied than whites when city is held constant, blacks in one city are often more satisfied than whites in another city. To take a concrete and extreme illustration, the average black person in Boston could reduce his dissatisfaction with parks from 2.30 to 1.78 by moving to San Francisco (assuming he becomes an "average black person" in the latter city), while he could reduce it only to 1.96 by remaining in Boston but "becoming" white. We are not suggesting cross-continental busing as a way to solve the problem of parks, but the example does remind us that racial differences are only one component in dissatisfaction with city services.

Having shown that cities differ markedly in levels of satisfaction with services, can we discover what causes these differences? The ordering of black and white city means was somewhat similar for three of the services and strikingly so for the fourth (police protection), indicating that a city tends to appear similar to both its black and its white inhabitants. This suggests some objective reality to overall city differences in services. We found additional evidence for interpreting satisfaction scores as representing objective reality when we compared city whites with suburban whites. Comparisons were available for Cleveland and Detroit, where suburban as well as central-city white samples were obtained. The data revealed greater suburban satisfaction with each of the four services, although most notably with police protection. A cross-section survey allowed no firm conclusion about causal direction, but the most reasonable assumption is that services are indeed better in suburbs than in central cities, and that this fact is the source of the difference in satisfaction levels. If people move to suburbs partly because they desire improved municipal services, our data indicate that they are not disappointed.

With these two indications that satisfaction does reflect objective differences in services, we expected variations in satisfaction among the fifteen central cities to be associated with differences in objective measures of the four services. We expected a *negative* correlation between the number of parks in a city and the degree of dissatisfaction about parks which we found. Indeed, all the correlations were in the direction one would predict if satisfaction reflects the objective character of city services. However, the correlations were all modest in size and some were trivial. Apart from their lack of statistical significance, to be expected with only fifteen cases, we are reluctant to make much of such small associations. The consistency over five tests in both racial samples suggests that dissatisfaction is related at least slightly to measurable aspects of city services, but the relation is either very small or it is seriously attenuated by measurement problems with the indicators used. Perhaps if we had direct observations on regularity of garbage collection, rather than an indirect measure such as number of sanitation employees, we would find stronger associations. Future research in this area could usefully obtain direct observational data on the quality of such services in order to test its correspondence with attitudes measured at the same time through survey interviewing.

We also examined the ordering of cities inductively to allow for the possibility that other city characteristics might emerge as possible causes of dissatisfaction levels. Boston turned out to be the locus of greatest dissatisfaction on all four services for blacks and on three of the four services for whites. Newark and Gary also tended to be high in dissatisfaction. Since these three cities are among the smaller ones in our sample, there is a negative correlation between city size and dissatisfaction. For blacks, there is also a positive association between northern location and dissatisfaction, with the above-mentioned cities high, while Baltimore, St. Louis, and Washington (the only "Southern" cities in our sample) were all relatively low. We have no interpretation of either of these results; until they are confirmed with a larger set of cities, we mention them mainly as suggestions for checking in future research. It is difficult to explain why Boston is at the top of the dissatisfaction list; we are less inclined to regard it as a sign of a newly discovered dimension of urbanism than as the product of a unique constellation of factors located in the city on Massachusetts Bay.

AREAS WITHIN CITIES

Although cities differ considerably in levels of dissatisfaction, these variations have not helped us account for racial differences. We turn now to look *within* cities but still with an areal emphasis. All four services can be thought of as distributed over neighborhoods: parks and schools in the most visible sense, police protection and garbage collection somewhat less so. Our inquiry concerns the extent to which racial differences can be reduced to neighborhood differences.

We begin with residential segregation, perhaps the most salient social fact of life today in most American cities. A question in our interview schedule asked each respondent to define his own neighborhood in this regard:

In this block and the two or three blocks right around here, are all the families (Negro/white), most (Negro/white), about half Negro and half white, or are most of them (white/Negro)?

(The first term in parentheses was used when the respondent was black, the second when white.) Answers to the question allowed us to characterize neighborhoods as all-black, most-black, about half and half, most-white, or all-white. Mean dissatisfaction scores for respondents in each of these types of neighborhoods are given in Table 11.2. The results are striking: with few exceptions, black dissatisfaction declines each step of the way from all-black to mostly white areas, while white dissatisfaction rises each step of the way from all-white to mostly black areas.

Table 11.2: Mean Dissatisfaction Scores for Each Race by Degree of Residential Integration (integration areas)[a]

Racial Mix of Residential Area

	All-Black	Most-Black	Half and Half	Most-White	All White	Variance Explained (percent)
Schools						
Black respondents	1.75	1.61	1.66	1.51	—	0.7
White respondents	—	1.70	1.86	1.52	1.37	3.2
Parks						
Black respondents	2.00	2.00	1.87	1.72	—	0.8
White respondents	—	1.91	1.84	1.74	1.55	2.0
Police						
Black respondents	1.87	1.81	1.54	1.51	—	1.9
White respondents	—	1.69	1.62	1.46	1.32	2.3
Garbage						
Black respondents	1.52	1.50	1.30	1.28	—	1.2
White respondents	—	1.29	1.30	1.28	1.23	0.2
Neighborhood Worse Off						
Black respondents	2.21	2.16	1.96	1.70	—	5.0
White respondents	—	2.18	2.05	1.89	1.85	1.9
Minimum black sample sizes	(556)	(1,256)	(332)	(87)	—	
Minimum white sample sizes	—	(65)	(104)	(703)	(950)	

[a]The higher the score, the greater the dissatisfaction.

There are inversions in the case of schools and garbage, but even these items continue to show the overall trends portrayed more clearly by parks, police, and the relative deprivation question. Degree of neighborhood "whiteness" can be thought of as an important source of satisfaction levels for both blacks and whites.

An even more direct comparison can be made between black and white dissatisfaction levels in terms of segregation of area. The largest racial difference for each question occurs when we subtract the scores of whites in all-white areas from blacks in all-black areas:

	Difference
Schools	.38
Parks	.45
Police	.55
Garbage	.29
Relative Deprivation	.36

The differences are roughly twice the size of those obtainable from Table 11.2 for the total black and white samples. We now ask what happens when we compare blacks and whites who live in areas with the *same* degree of integration. The most precise comparison possible is for "half and half" neighborhoods:

	Difference
Schools	-.20
Parks	.03
Police	-.08
Garbage	.00
Relative Deprivation	-.09

For this comparison, with area of integration held constant, the black/white difference not only vanishes, but tends to be slightly reversed, with whites more dissatisfied than blacks. Thus we have in an important sense completely solved the problem we posed initially: blacks are more dissatisfied than whites because most of them live in largely black areas. It is not color of skin, but color of area that is associated with dissatisfaction.

Moreover, black and white differences on the four services disappear even more completely in mostly white areas, with the added advantage that absolute dissatisfaction is generally low for both races in such areas. Projecting these results in a purely hypothetical fashion, if the black population were dispersed into outlying areas so as to create a smaller proportion of blacks than whites in each area, racial differences in dissatisfaction should disappear, with only a slight rise in white dissatisfaction. Indeed, comparing white dissatisfaction in all-white suburbs with white levels in all-white parts of cities, we saw that *area* continued to be important even when color was controlled. Hence both black and white levels of dissatisfaction could theoretically be "adjusted downward" still further by moving both racial groups from city to suburban towns. The end point of this exercise is to suggest—only half seriously, to be sure—that a dispersal of blacks (and whites) from central cities to suburbs, with care to keep the white middle-class proportion high everywhere, would not only eliminate racial differences in dissatisfaction with services, but considerably reduce the overall level of such dissatisfaction in the metropolitan area. This would, fo course, leave central cities vacant, but a creative metropolitan administration could no doubt come up with imaginative uses for so much well-located space. Central cities might become giant airports servicing surrounding areas! Or perhaps they could be turned back into agricultural production, reversing the age-old direction of flow between center and hinterland.

If we have solved our original problem in one sense, there are two important senses in which it remains. First, there is the question of giving a clear causal interpretation to the association between the racial mix of an area and its dissatisfaction with services. One interpretation that suggests itself immediately is differential treatment of neighborhoods, as was indeed indicated explicitly by at least one black respondent: "This is a partially white neighborhood and they give better service in a mixed neighborhood than they give in an all-colored neighborhood." Our findings would occur if in black neighborhoods garbage is collected less frequently, police come less quickly or act less concerned, parks are fewer or less cared for, teachers are less qualified or less interested. These interpretations all assume that the racial character of the neighborhood leads to differential treatment by the city government, which in turn leads to differences in satisfaction.

An alternate interpretation exists, however, which points to a direct causal link between the racial mix of an area and the level of dissatisfaction there, without differential treatment by city administrations being involved. A school that is "half and half" may seem less attractive to white parents than an all-white school, even though it may be more attractive to some black parents than an all-black school. Likewise, "street crime" rates (and thus a sense of lack of police protection) are probably correlated inversely with the "whiteness" of the neighborhood; hence, blacks in mixed neighborhoods may feel safer, but whites less safe, than comparable blacks and whites in completely segregated neighborhoods. More generally, respondents may be reacting directly to the effects of racial mixture, rather than to the nature of services provided by the city.

It is difficult to locate decisive evidence bearing on these two radically different interpretations, but several considerations suggest that the first, differential treatment, has at least some importance. First, garbage collection seems clearly the responsibility of city administration, yet it shows much the same trend as the other services, at least on the black side. (However, the disappearance of a trend on the white side may well be significant.) Second, the white suburbs show even greater satisfaction than the all-white areas of the city; thus where racial composition is controlled, "administration" makes a difference in each service. Finally, citizens themselves perceive the problem as one of differential treatment. The relative deprivation item at the bottom of Table 11.2 shows the same trends by neighborhood as the other items, if anything a bit more sharply.

Indeed, the item presents a noteworthy reversal, with white respondents in mixed areas especially likely to cry foul with respect to the provision of services by the city. All these considerations suggest that the relation of dissatisfaction with services to areas of the city reflects at least in part differential treatment by city administrations and not merely racial composition as such.

A second basic question involves the nature of the areal units we have been considering. The degree of integration of an area correlates with other characteristics of the area, notably its socioeconomic level. What appears to be discrimination (or composition) in terms of the racial character of the area may actually be discrimination (or composition) on the basis of social class. Some respondents spoke explicitly of economic level, rather than of race: "The city officials think this is a poor neighborhood and they don't care and think that people who live here don't care either. So they pick up garbage just whenever they get around to it."

In order to determine more specifically the nature of the areal unit, it is necessary to look at dissatisfactions with services both by areal integration of neighborhoods and by economic levels of neighborhoods, with each controlled for the other. We did so by computing mean dissatisfaction scores for both "integration areas" and "income areas," with each adjusted to remove the effects of the other (as well as the effects of city of residence) by means of multiple classification analysis.

In general, integration areas continued to be associated with dissatisfaction scores after this adjustment. The distinction between all-black and most-black areas proved to be of little importance, which is not surprising if we assume that the latter category would be better characterized as "almost all black." From the standpoint of both racial composition and the view from city hall, the distinction between the two categories is probably slight. On the other hand, the difference in means between most-black and half and half is sharply as predicted for all but one question (schools). The results were equally consistent for half and half versus most-white, despite the small number of cases in the latter category. It is also instructive to compare the all-black and most-white area means: the differences are consistent and large in each case, about as large as the differences between black and white means in Table 11.1.

Clear trends also appear to income areas, with level of integration controlled, although the differences are not quite as consistent. Schools no longer show any difference and parks only a slight one. But the overall finding is that both the color and the income of one's neighborhood count when it comes to perceived quality of services. We must think of a more general dimension of status, which includes race, class, and perhaps other attributes, all of which affect satisfaction with city services.

So far as we can tell, these attributes are additive, so that living in a neighborhood which is high in "whiteness" and high in income leads to the greatest satisfaction.

DIFFERENCES AT THE LEVEL OF INDIVIDUAL ATTRIBUTES

It might be thought that the areal differences first reported could be reduced further to demographic or socioeconomic attributes of individuals. This was not the case. For example, when the "income areas" discussed earlier were included in a multiple classification analysis along with respondent reports of their own family incomes, the areal measure was improved slightly as a predictor on four of the five questions, while the individual-level measure showed negligible relationships to the same four dissatisfaction questions. This was also true when respondents' education was included with either income areas or integration areas. These individual-level socioeconomic variables generally showed no consistent association with dissatisfaction over city services.

The one exception to the preceding summary is instructive, for it involves respondent education in relation to the schools' question. For both blacks and whites, though especially for the former, dissatisfaction with schools increases with *increasing* education of respondents. (This was not a result of area of residence, for the relationship increased for blacks and was maintained for whites when "integration area" was controlled.) It appears that those whose own education makes them place a high value on good schooling are the persons most apt to be critical of the current state of the schools in their neighborhood.

Furthermore, this relationship is stronger for blacks than for whites, and thus, the difference between black and white dissatisfaction levels increases sharply as one goes up the educational ladder. However, the overall effect of this increase tends to be canceled out because the two races are distributed differently over the educational levels. Black college graduates are particularly dissatisfied with schools, but they constitute a much smaller proportion (less than 5 percent) of the total black sample than do white college graduates (more than 12 percent) of the total white sample. We can expect black criticism of the quality of schools to increase in the coming years as black education itself increases.

IDEOLOGICAL FACTORS IN DISSATISFACTION

At the beginning of this chapter we raised the question of ideological versus objective factors in racial differences in dissatisfaction with city services. Most of our evidence thus far is consistent with the assumption that services actually are worse in certain areas and that this causes variations in dissatisfaction. We failed to demonstrate such a relationship directly, however, since strong associations did not emerge between objective indicators of services and subjective dissatisfactions. This leaves a more ideological explanation as an important possibility. Perhaps blacks (and especially blacks in segregated areas) are simply more negative about government in general, and this negativism is added to "normal" dissatisfaction to produce the racial differences recorded in Table 11.1.

The best measures available to us of ideological disenchantment with government for both blacks and whites were questions on the city mayor and the federal government:

How about the Mayor of [city name]? Do you think he is trying as hard as he can to solve the main problems of the city or is he not doing all he could to solve these problems? [If not doing all he could] Do you think he is trying fairly hard or not hard at all?

The question on the federal government was the same except that "federal government in Washington" was substituted for "mayor," and "they" for "he."

Both items are related moderately to the four dissatisfaction items (data not shown). If the causal direction is simply that poor city services lead to criticism of government heads, then the relation should be stronger for the mayor than for the federal government, since the mayor is the person most directly responsible for the quality of services. However, the relations are about equally strong for the mayor and the federal government. This leaves as the more likely possibility the existence of an ideological propensity to be critical of both the products and the leaders of government.

Does this ideological propensity contribute somehow to the *greater* dissatisfaction of blacks? Apparently not. When ideology is held constant (for example, when we look only at those who feel the mayor is not trying hard at all), the gap between black and white dissatisfaction scores is not reduced. "Ideology" seems to elevate *equally* both black and white dissatisfaction levels, but is not a source of the racial *difference* in such levels. Moreover, there is no evidence that ideology is involved in the relationship between dissatisfaction scores and the racial mix of the neighborhood: when either the mayor or federal government items are introduced as controls, the basic associations are unchanged; namely, satisfaction tends to increase with whiteness of neighborhood.

SOME CONCLUSIONS AND PRACTICAL IMPLICATIONS

Our analysis indicates that the primary source of racial difference in dissatisfaction with city services lies in variations by neighborhood within cities. These variations are essentially along a status dimension defined in our study by race and social class. It is not one's own race or class that is more relevant, however, but that of one's neighborhood. Persons living in largely black and lower-income areas are most dissatisfied with the services they receive regardless of their race or income; persons living in largely white and upper-income areas are most satisfied with their services, again regardless of their own race or income.

We cannot determine whether these neighborhood differences are due primarily to discriminatory treatment by city administrations or primarily to racial composition in a more direct sense. Both may well be involved. On the one hand, for example, an increase in lower-class blacks in an area is associated with a rise in certain types of crime; at the same time, police patrols may become less visible and concerned in such a neighborhood, at least from the standpoint of the average citizen. *Both* changes would lead to dissatisfaction with the "quality of police protection in this neighborhood."

Other variables were also identified as sources of dissatisfaction with city services. In particular, cities themselves differ in levels of dissatisfaction—enough so that despite the general trend of racial difference, whites in some cities are more dissatisfied than are blacks in other cities. Thus while city variation does not account at all for racial *differences,* it is an important factor in producing variation in satisfaction for *both* races. We suspect that these city differences in subjective evaluations are due to objective differences in the delivery of municipal services, but we were only slightly successful in documenting this crucial point. Future research on attitudes in this area needs also to identify and measure more clearly the objective characteristics of neighborhoods and of cities that are presumed to underlie reported dissatisfactions.

The main competing explanation of dissatisfactions with services assumes that they are simply facets of a broader alienation from government. Our study provides some evidence that general ideology is involved in dissatisfaction, but not that it is an important factor in racial differences. Whites show much the same relationship between general ideology and specific dissatisfactions as do blacks. Alienation, therefore, acts largely as a constant factor raising dissatisfaction for both races, but not greatly affecting the gap between them.

Beyond our interest in raising civic satisfaction, the measures we have focused on may have a larger importance. After the 1967 urban riots, a search went on to identify the type of city or of area within city in which riots were more likely to occur. The search was generally unsuccessful, and it was soon recognized that almost any large city could have a riot. Somewhat more success was obtained by separating out the parts of cities in which riots occurred, but even here the economic differences appeared much less sharp than had been expected. Indeed, other than having a disproportionately large black population, it is not clear that so-called disorder areas differed socioeconomically from the rest of the city once race was held constant. But such areas did differ in level of dissatisfaction with city services. Blacks in riot tracts were noticeably more dissatisfied than blacks in the same cities living outside such tracts. The relationships are reduced when integration areas and income areas are controlled, as might be expected, but this does not change the descriptive fact that black citizens living in riot areas experienced greater dissatisfaction with city services than blacks living elsewhere in the same cities. Assuming that these dissatisfaction levels are not simply a result of the riots, but preceded them, we may have here one factor providing legitimacy for the kind of behavior and ideology that characterized the riots. In particular, the belief that the city administration discriminates against one's neighborhood in the provision of basic services could be used to justify actions ordinarily viewed as criminal. We shall not pursue the finding further in this paper, but it points up some possible implications of citizen dissatisfaction with municipal services.

12

Joe T. Darden

ENVIRONMENTAL PERCEPTION BY GHETTO YOUTHS IN PITTSBURGH

The summer of 1967 brought racial disorder to nearly 150 American cities. In April of 1968 the city of Pittsburgh, Pennsylvania, joined the ranks. Why did it happen? What can be done to prevent it from happening again?

To answer these questions at that time, the President of the United States, Lyndon B. Johnson, appointed a special commission to investigate the "quality of the environment" in which the disorders occurred. The commission became formerly known as the National Advisory Commission on Civil Disorders. The investigators spent many days and nights in the field, analyzing the attitudes and behavior of the people in the "disturbed areas."

Their study, however, was made after the "fact." Had studies been made in the past of the perception of ghetto residents toward the quality of their environment, such behavior as did occur possibly could have been predicted and thus with a change in the quality of the environment even prevented. Therefore, the significance of studies of this nature cannot be overemphasized.

This particular study, however, is in no way comprehensive, but merely aims to serve as a pilot for further research in the future. It is hoped that this article will stimulate more social scientists to explore perceptual problems in greater depth, particularly those relevant to a better under-

Reprinted from *Pennsylvania Geographer*, Vol. 8 (1) (April 1970), pp. 19–22, by permission of the publisher.

standing of social issues. The problem of this study concerns itself with determination of the attitude of high school seniors residing in a ghetto of Pittsburgh toward the quality of their environment.

DEFINITION OF CONCEPTS

For the purpose of this study, the term *attitude* is considered synonymous with "belief" or "opinion." It describes a preference held by a person with respect to an object, an area, or a concept. It does not in itself constitute a value. It is the result of a valuation process of some kind. Insofar as it applies to an environment, it requires perception of that environment. By *perception* is meant the complex process by which people select, organize, and interpret sensory stimulation into a meaningful and coherent picture of the world.

The definition of *ghetto* is the one used by the National Advisory Commission on Civil Disorders. As defined by the commission, a ghetto is an area within a city characterized by poverty and acute social disorganization, and inhabited by members of a racial or ethnic group under conditions of involuntary segregation.

The term *environment* is considered one that is wholly private to the perceiver and part of his/her phenomenology. *Phenomenology* means how the environment appears to the individual; in other words, how he/she sees or apprehends it, without check or control by any criteria of denotation or objectivity.

OBJECTIVE AND METHODOLOGY

The objective is to determine whether ghetto high school seniors believe their environment is of good quality or bad quality. The hypothesis is that Pittsburgh's ghetto high school seniors believe their environment is of bad quality. This study is based on primary data gathered in the field. The technique used to gather the data was the interview, which consisted of the following seven statements: (1) I will definitely not remain in this area (environment) in the future; (2) I have thought about leaving the area (environment); (3) This area (environment) is not worth living in, but I have *not* thought about leaving it; (4) I am uncertain about my position in this area (environment); (5) This area (environment) is worth living in but causes lots of trouble; (6) The pleasure of living in this area (environment) far outweighs the pain; (7) My satisfaction with this area (environment) could not be any greater. Each student was asked to check only *one* of the statements—the one that most closely applied to him. After checking the statement, the student was asked to state briefly the reason or reasons for his choice.

THE SAMPLE POPULATION AND THE STUDY AREA

The sample for this study was drawn from Fifth Avenue High School which is located in the Middle Hill District of Pittsburgh. In 1965, this school was 92.9 percent black. The total population of the Middle Hill in 1969 was 27,076 with a total number of housing units 8,525. Only 1,395 people owned their homes which carried an average value of $8,446. There were 1,400 houses listed as deteriorating and 539 dilapidated.

The Middle Hill, like other ghettos across the country, occupies the bottom level of a really stratified society. The following statistics are given as evidence of this fact. The median education of Middle Hill residents was 9.7 grade, compared to 10.0 grade for the city of Pittsburgh. The same unequal situation applied to other aspects of social life. The median income of the Middle Hill was $3,252 compared to $5,605 for Pittsburgh. Employment was 79.6 percent for the Hill and 91.0 for Pittsburgh. In the area of housing, the Hill had 65.9 percent that was *none* defective, compared to 77.0 for Pittsburgh. These statistics reveal the real situation or condition in the Middle Hill, which as we will see later correlates very well with the perception held by those who lived there.

It is customary, however, when one leaves his environment and observes it from outside that his once mere perception becomes a known reality. This is best manifest by the case of a sixteen-year-old boy who left Fifth Avenue High School to attend Yale University for a summer. Upon his return to his community (the Hill District), he revealed his experience in a speech delivered before the Urban Youth Action Committee. He said:

"I left Yale with new ideas and a different outlook on life. Coming back to my community, I realized what my community is lacking and how our people are being 'short changed.' I feel we are missing the benefits of an integrated society. From my experience, I learned that men of different races can live together in peace. Because we are missing this, the average Negro in the Hill District does not feel that racial barriers can be broken down. . . .

We, the people of this community are cheated and deprived in many ways and we should do something—we must do something— to eliminate these disadvantages, to make our society a better place to live in."

PRESENTATION OF FINDINGS

The researcher's survey of the attitude of high school seniors residing in the ghetto toward the quality of their environment revealed the following result: That ghetto high school seniors believe their environment is of bad quality. This fact validates the basic hypothesis.

A total of 100 seniors were interviewed from a class of 154. Only 95 interviews were acceptable. Five were discarded due to error caused by a failure of the students to follow instructions. Their responses resulted in the following tabulation:

Table 12.1: Responses of Ghetto Seniors

Question	Number	Percent
1	43	45.3
2	22	23.2
3	8	8.4
4	9	9.5
5	3	3.1
6	2	2.1
7	8	8.4
TOTAL	95	100.0

As the table indicates, 43 students or 43.3 percent said they definitely will not remain in the Hill District in the future. Twenty-two students or 23.2 percent said they have thought about leaving the area. Eight students or 8.4 percent said the area is not worth living in, but they have *not* thought about leaving it. Nine students or 9.5 percent said they were uncertain about their status in the area. Three students or 3.1 percent said the area is worth living in but causes lots of trouble. Two students or 2.1 percent said the pleasure of living in the area far outweighs the pain, and eight students or 8. 4 percent said their satisfaction with the area could not be any greater.

What is the significance of these responses? The significance is that the majority of the students are expressing a *negative attitude toward the quality of their environment*. In other words 76.9 percent are dissatisfied with the area in which they live. Only 13.6 percent expressed a positive attitude toward the quality of their environment or satisfaction with their area. The remaining 9.5 percent preferred to remain neutral.

Why are they dissatisfied? An answer to this question proved to be more difficult to ascertain. Forty-five or 47.4 percent gave no reason for their dissatisfaction. The reasons given by the remaining fifty students or 52.6 percent are ranked in the following order of frequency:

A. At least three students listed the following reasons:
1. Inadequate housing
2. Just tired of living in the same area
3. Lack of job opportunities or opportunities for success
4. Leaving for college
5. Poor streets

B. At least two students listed the following reasons:
1. Desire to go to another country (the countries listed were Mexico or the continent of Africa)
2. Poor living conditions
3. Too many thieves in the area
4. Too many addicts in the area
5. Desire to explore other areas
6. The area needs improvement

C. At least one student listed the following reasons:
1. Violence in the area
2. Too many other people coming in causing trouble
3. Lack of recreational facilities
4. Not enough things here
5. Bad area, lack of places to go
6. Lack of protection
7. Run-down neighborhood
8. Too many Uncle Toms, welfare recipients, and filthy killers
9. Troublesome area
10. Area unfit to raise my future family
11. Prefer a better area
12. Because it is a ghetto and I hate it

The above list suggests a negative attitude toward the quality of the environment. The following list indicates the opposite.

At least one student listed the following reasons for his satisfaction with his environment:
1. People nice and area nice.
2. The working opportunities are here.
3. I have lived here so long, I enjoy it.
4. The Hill is just the way I like it, just the way it has been, and just the way it will always be.

The majority of the high school seniors residing in the ghetto (Hill District) believe their environment is of bad quality. The reasons for their belief vary. They can best be characterized a mild, not hostile, not anti-establishment, and not antiwhite. Instead their ultimate action appears to be focused on an elevation of themselves as individuals without condemnation or contempt for others. They felt that self-improvement can best be obtained by leaving their present environment. In other words, *"spatial mobility"* is the key to their future success in environmental adjustment. The minority who wish to remain are either indifferent, satisfied with the present conditions, or hope to improve the local environment—none wish to destory it. Their future hope lies in the lowering of the racial barriers which presently exist.

PART SEVEN

THE POLITICAL SYSTEM
AND GHETTO RESIDENTS

INTRODUCTION

Poor ghetto residents are the most powerless of urban dwellers. The reasons for such absence of political power are revealed in the article that follows by Clinton Jones. Jones uses an applied approach at the national or macro level to demonstrate how blacks in cities throughout the United States are disenfranchised in the form of at-large election systems. He devised a black representation ratio based on data derived from The Municipal Yearbook, The National Roster of Black Elected Officials, *and the United States Census Reports to conclude that at-large systems of elections reduce black political representation on city councils. The black representation ratios reflect empirically the serious underrepresentation of black Americans on city councils regardless of election system. The election system does influence black representation, however. According to Jones, at-large election systems, particularly in the South, are a form of institutional racism severely limiting the electoral chances of black residents.*

13

Clinton Jones

THE IMPACT OF LOCAL ELECTION SYSTEMS ON BLACK POLITICAL REPRESENTATION

Black American efforts to enter the American political system, free of racial restrictions, may be described as a cyclical process that involves the persistent search for an effective strategy; the resulting failure of that strategy; and the renewed strategy search, characterized by both random and planned testing of the American political system, in hopes of somewhere striking a responsive cord.

For example, even though the civil rights movement of the 1960s succeeded in removing overt, legal restrictions from black political participation, it failed to bring about black political representation commensurate with the size of the black population. Subsequent analyses of reasons for the continued political underrepresentation of blacks have led to the identification of other, more subtle restraints on black political participation, often referred to as "institutional racism." Institutional racism has been defined as:

Racism attributable to the fundamental operating rules of an institution, and which on the basis of race preempts blacks from effective access to the decision-making process.

At-large systems of electing persons to city councils, along with other institutional features of "reform" government, are often posited as examples of institutional racism.

Reprinted from *Urban Affairs Quarterly*, Vol. 11 (March 1976), pp. 345–356, by permission of the publisher and author.

Whether at-large elections serve to minimize black political representation is a debatable proposition that may be tested empirically. It is clear, however, that at-large systems were not adopted with the specific intent of weakening black political influence. The at-large method of electing city council members was popularly proposed by middle- and upper-class Americans during the late nineteenth and early twentieth centuries as a device to destroy one of the institutional bases for urban political-machine domination by eliminating the feudalistic ties of the predominately white urban masses to the urban political machine. Proponents of at-large systems hoped to establish apolitical, efficient, and businesslike city governments that would respond to overall community needs and not to the particularistic needs and interests of the various ethnic and economic communities.

There are, at the same time, documented instances where cities have changed to at-large systems as tactics to dilute black political influence although from 1962 to 1972 only a few cities in this sample with rapidly growing black populations changed from district to at-large systems. The more common election-system controversies do not involve cities with rapidly growing black populations seeking to establish at-large systems to dilute black political influence, but rather the efforts of blacks to replace existing at-large systems with district systems. The concern of this paper is not, however, whether at-large systems were consciously adopted to discriminate against blacks, but whether they are in fact barriers to black political representation in urban communities.

In addition to determining the validity of assertions that at-large systems discriminate against black Americans, this test of the relationship between election systems and black political representation will contribute to two categories of urban and political research. First, there is a body of research that analyzes black participation in the American electoral process. These studies discuss black voter behavior, explain the methodological weaknesses of employing a voter-behavior framework to describe black political behavior, review the political "payoffs" blacks may derive from voting, and the political effectiveness of "bloc" voting.

The second category of research consists of studies that treat governmental structures as independent variables and seek to identify the impact of governmental structures on public policy content. This is not, of course, so grand an effort as to measure "black political power." Black absence or presence on city councils may or may not be an accurate reflection of black political influence. Black presence on a city's council does, however, indicate black political accomplishment in the area of placing a black in public office, and may indicate, as well, a degree of institutional responsiveness to minority interests in that particular city. While the sample is limited to blacks, the findings should be suggestive for other racial-ethnic minorities who seek to capture elective office as representatives of racial-ethnic interests.

STUDY DESIGN

The data for this study was drawn from four sources: (1) *The Municipal Yearbook* (1972); (2) questionnaire; (3) *The National Roster of Black Elected Officials* (1972); and (4) United States Census Reports. Data from these sources are comparable because they were compiled during a similar time period.

The initial sample was to consist of all American cities with 50,000 or more residents and a black population of at least 5 percent. The 5 percent black population minimum, while essentially intuitive, was established to include only those cities in which blacks were a large enough percentage of a city's population to realistically expect to win an electoral victory as representatives of black interests. *The Municipal Yearbook* was employed as the primary source to identify each city's election system. Thirty-two cities which met the inclusion criteria were not listed in *The Municipal Yearbook*, and they were sent questionnaires to obtain the needed information. Seventeen of the thirty-two questionnaires were returned; cities that failed to return the mailed questionnnaires were omitted from the study. *The National Roster of Black Elected Officials* provided the names of blacks serving on each city's council. The final sample size is 171. The sample includes (1) 106 cities with at-large systems; (2) 30 cities with district (ward) systems; and (3) 35 cities with systems that combined at-large and district systems.

The independent variables are (1) at-large systems; (2) district systems; (3) number of seats in at-large systems; and (4) percentage of population in each district unit. The two variables—i.e., number of seats in at-large systems and percentage of population in each district—is an attempt to determine the effect of variation within at-large and district systems on black political representation.

The dependent variable is a measure of black representation on city councils labeled "black representation ratios." Black representation ratios were derived by dividing the black percentage of a city's population into the black percentage of that city's council seats. The black representation ratio is intended to illustrate the degree to which black membership on a city's council equals the black percentage of that city's population. If the black percentage of council seats is equal to the black percentage of a city's population, the black representation ratio will equal 1.00 The black representation ratio will be more or less than 1.00

depending on whether the black percentage of council seats is more or less than the black percentage of the city's population.

Geographical region is controlled to test each relationship. Region is controlled in this study because of assumptions that region is an abstraction that contains certain historical and demographical factors that affect political behavior, and especially because of the South's political history, which involves a systematic denial of the ballot and other forms of political participation to its black citizens. It is plausible that the South's political history has generated processes that continue, even after the 1965 Voting Rights Act, to hamper black political representation to an extent peculiar to the South.

The following set of working hypotheses concerning the relationship between local election systems and black representation were established: (1) the district system of electing city councils favors black membership on city councils; (2) the greater the number of seats in at-large systems, the greater black representation; and (3) the larger the percentage of a city's population contained in each district unit, the greater black underrepresentation.

To test the relative impact of at-large and district systems on black representation on city councils, the mean black representation ratios within at-large and district systems are compared. Simple correlation techniques (Pearson's) are employed to test the strength of the relationship between the number of seats in at-large systems and black representation on city councils, and the relationship between percentage of population in each district unit with black representation on city councils.

The above hypotheses rest on two assumptions: (1) that most American cities with sizable black populations are residentially segregated into black and white neighborhoods, and (2) that racial consciousness among black Americans is of such an intensity that if given the opportunity, blacks will choose members of their own race to represent them on city councils.

AT-LARGE AND DISTRICT SYSTEMS: A Comparison

One hundred thirty-six cities in this study elected their city councils by at-large and district methods; 106 at-large and 30 by district. The data support the hypothesis that at-large systems restrict black membership on city councils. The mean representation ratio for at-large cities is .43, compared to .61 for district cities, a difference of .18.

The negative consequences of at-large systems for black Americans become even more signficant when one realizes that more blacks, in this sample, live in at-large cities (i.e., 22 percent of population) than in district cities (i.e., 17 percent of population), but hold a lower percentage of council seats in at-large cities (i.e., 9 percent) than in district cities (i.e., 14 percent). Thus, if election systems are irrelevant to black representation, blacks should hold a higher percentage of council seats in at-large systems simply because blacks are a greater percentage of the population in those cities.

The black representation ratios indicate, as well, the serious under-representation of black Americans on city councils regardless of election system. The representation ratios point out that at-large systems work in conjunction with and supplement other factors that serve to restrict black membership on city councils.

When region is controlled, black representation on district city councils remains larger than in at-large cities in each region. As Table 13.1

Table 13.1: Black Representation Ratios within At-Large and District Systems Means and Standard Deviations

	North-Central N = 35	North-east N = 21	South N = 57	West N = 23
At-large N = 106	.44(.66) N = 20	.40 (.54) N = 16	.41 (.72) N = 53	.54 (.73) N = 17
District N = 30	.49 (.55) N = 15	.70 (.68) N = 5	.74 (.61) N = 4	.75 (.58) N = 6

indicates, at-large restrictions on black representation are more severe in Southern cities than in cities in other regions. To compound problems for Southern black representation, the South, more than any other region, favors the at-large system. Fifty-three Southern cities have at-large systems and only four have district systems. As an indication of the relative advantage of district systems to Southern black representation, the black representation ratio for Southern cities with district system (.74) is the second highest among the regions and only slightly less than the highest in the West (.75).

THE RELATIONSHIP BETWEEN NUMBER OF SEATS IN AT-LARGE
SYSTEMS AND BLACK MEMBERSHIP ON COUNCILS

The second hypothesis posited a relationship between number of seats within at-large systems and black representation. While election system has been shown to influence black representation, it must also be recognized that the number of seats available within an at-large system can affect representation prospects. If only a small number of seats are available, at-large systems may be even more disadvantageous to a minority's electoral chances. Table 13.2 outlines the correlations between number of council seats and black representation ratios.

Without controlling for region, the correlation score is extremely high (.93). When region is controlled, the predominating influence of the South on the strength of the relationship is revealed. The South represents one-half of the at-large cities in this study and shows such a strong relationship between number of council seats and black political represen-

Table 13.2: Correlation Coefficients between Number of Seats and Black Political Representation

	All Regions N = 105	North-Central N = 20	North-east N = 16	South N = 53	West N = 17
Correlation Coefficients	.93	.69	-.08	.96	.30

tation that it distorts the strength of the relationship when region is not controlled. In a number of other regions the relationship becomes weak when the effects of regional variations are controlled.

The relationship between number of seats and black membership on city councils in the North-Central region, however, remains high (.69). The relationships in the Northeast and West are much more ambiguous. In the Northeast the relationship proved negative, and in the West the relationship is relatively weak.

The data supporting hypothesis two in the South suggest that the size of city councils in at-large systems is an important form of institutional racism simply by severely limiting the electoral chances of a minority.

The same observation holds, though to a lesser extent, in the North-Central region of the United States.

Several specific examples of black underrepresentation in the South may help to explain the unusually high coefficient of correlation score resulting from relating number of council seats to black representation on city councils. Table 13.3 depicts cities with large black populations that have few council seats with no blacks on their city councils.

Table 13.3: Correlation Coefficients between Percent of Black Population in Districts and Black Representation Ratios

	All Regions N = 65	North-Central N = 25	North-east N = 15	South N = 17	West N = 8
Correlation coefficients	-.27	-.19	-.37	-.17	-.01

DISTRICT SIZE AND BLACK REPRESENTATION

To test the relationship between district size and black representation, the mean percent population per district was calculated and correlated with the black representation ratios. The sample size is 65, including

Table 13.4: Southern At-Large Cities with Few Council Seats No Black Members

	Black Percent of Population	Black Seats	Total Seats
Chattanooga, Tennessee	35	0	4
Columbia, South Carolina	39	0	4
Jackson, Mississippi	39	0	3
Mobile, Alabama	35	0	2
Montgomery, Alabama	33	0	3
Tuscaloosa, Alabama	26	0	3

all cities with either district systems or combination systems that include some districts.

The hypothesis that district size is inversely related to black representation on city councils is confirmed. However, as Table 13.4 indicates, the correlation coefficients are consistently low. Why district size is not as strongly related to black political representation as number of seats in at-large systems is not clear. The two independent variables—i.e., district size and number of seats in at-large systems—test the same type of relationship; that is, they both test the relationship between the number of council seats and black political representation. One possible explanation is that the representation of distinct community (district) interest, an inherent feature of district systems, eliminates the most discriminatory features of election systems, and that where district systems are in operation, variations in district size have some, but limited, effect on black political representation.

Regional controls reveal little variance from national findings. Contrary to the findings in the earlier test of the relationship between number of seats in at-large systems and black political representation, a weak relationship was found to exist between district size and black representation in the South.

The findings of this study support assertions that black Americans are underrepresented on city councils and that at-large systems are institutional barriers to black political representation. Variations within at-large and district systems were also found to affect black representation on city councils. The relationship between number of seats and black political representation approached an almost perfect relationship for Southern cities. While district size was shown to affect black representation, the coefficients of correlation were not as high as those portraying the strength of relationship between number of seats in at-large systems and black political representation.

This study provides evidence that supports the adoption of the following election-system reforms if black representation on city councils is to be increased: (1) replacement of at-large systems with district systems, especially in the South and Northeast; (2) increasing the number of council seats, if elimination of at-large systems is not politically feasible; and (3) decreasing the district size in cities utilizing the district system.

However, disaggregation of the data revealed several deviations from the aggregate findings that suggest that election systems should not be emphasized as panaceas for black underrepresentation on city councils. Clearly there are factors at work, in addition to election systems, that affect black representation. For example, there is an at-large city within each region in which blacks, based on black representation ratios, are overrepresented on its city council (to wit, Berkeley, California; Indianapolis, Indiana; San Antonio, Texas; and New Rochelle, New York). A series of case studies of at-large cities with black overrepresentation would yield valuable information about black political representation.

Notwithstanding the exceptions to the general findings, the evidence supports the proposition that the method of electing city councils, especially the number of council seats in at-large systems, affects black political representation.

PART EIGHT

ALTERNATIVE SOLUTIONS TO GHETTO PROBLEMS
Economic Development or Spatial Redistribution

INTRODUCTION

The preceding chapters have focused primarily on ghetto problems; the succeeding chapters focus on solutions. The search for solutions to the problems of American ghettos has involved at least two strategies. One strategy, advocated in the first article by Peter Labrie, recommends that the ghettos be economically developed despite the limited resources available. Such development is to occur through the encouragement of ghetto residents' initiatives toward community control. Specifically, it involves the development of ghetto-controlled municipal corporations to eliminate the poverty and to restructure the economic base of the ghetto, i.e., increase the ghetto's capital and employment base. It also involves the development of ghetto economic and higher educational institutions. Labrie's strategy is based on the premise that the economic poverty and consequent social problems of the ghetto are a function of profound imbalances in the national urban economy and of monopolistic interests accumulated by the white community. Thus, relieving the problems of the ghetto must involve eliminating the monopolistic control that nonghetto residents hold over the ghetto structure and mobilizing unprecedented resource subsidies at national and local levels for resolving imbalances affecting the ghetto. Labrie's solution is consistent with those who view the ghetto as an internal colony, a colonial appendage of the dominant white metropolitan community that drains the ghetto of its ability to develop its own capital and resource base.

In the second article, John Kain and Joseph Perksy disagree with the economic-development strategy. They argue that those who advocate

191

programs for improving the ghetto through economic development, renewal, and reconstruction make a false *analogy when they depict the ghetto as an underdeveloped country in need of economic development. This view, according to the authors, is an oversimplified and misleading one which ignores the strong linkages that tie the ghetto to the metropolitan area and the nation. The purpose of their paper is to describe these linkages. Kain and Persky view the ghetto's existence as the source of the problem and hold that the problems of high unemployment, poor education, etc., will continue as long as the ghetto exists. According to Kain and Persky, the problem can be handled in the short run by various schemes of redistributing governmental revenues; a preferable long-run solution would involve a complete change in the structure of the metropolitan area involving a major dispersal of low-income populations and, in particular, the black population. Tools must be provided to enable individuals to break out of the present ghetto structure.*

Kain and Persky provide a step-by-step program for doing so. It involves improvements in the employment situation through improved information systems and improved transit access between central-city ghettos and outlying employment areas; expanding the supply of low-income housing outside of the ghetto; the suburbanization of the black population; and compensatory education and school desegregation.

Finally the authors argue that the benefits to both the ghetto and the metropolitan area by dispersal of the ghetto population cannot be realized and may even be hindered by programs (such as those described by Labrie) which are aimed at economically developing the ghetto.

The reader should decide which strategy—economic development or spatial redistribution—is the most practical, feasible, and sound for solving the problems of the ghetto. For additional references on this issue, consult the Bibliography at the end of this volume.

14

Peter Labrie

BLACK CENTRAL CITIES
Dispersal or Rebuilding (Part II)

It is a widespread practice to hold the ghetto responsible for much of the burgeoning financial burden which metropolitan areas are currently experiencing. The increasing fiscal and administrative pressures placed upon central city governments to enable them to provide adequate municipal facilities and services for their large black and lower income resident population, and the demand for more expensive transportation systems to handle the expanding traffic flows between the central city and the fringe, are examples of these burdens. Indeed, John F. Kain states that the ghetto has "produced" these imbalances [see Chapter 15]. But this is not historically accurate. Imbalances among population, housing, and employment growth have always been a part of American urban development. Housing production has always lagged behind population growth, both nationally and locally. The physical and social manifestations of housing shortages predominate, of course, in the overcrowded and deteriorated residential areas of the central cities. The point is that the black population has been a prime recipient of imbalances inherent in American urban growth. Problems resulting from these imbalances have been compounded by the black population's greater degree of poverty inherited from slavery and the plantation system of the South and the huge volumes and rapid rates of their urban migrations. These complications have undoubtedly accelerated the white suburban flow,

Reprinted from *The Review of Black Political Economy*, Vol. 1, No. 3 (Winter–Spring 1971), pp. 78–99, by permission of the publisher.

aggravated metropolitan transportation problems, and increased the fiscal and administrative burdens of central-city governments. However, it will help to take a closer look at the underlying ramifications of some of these problems.

It has been pointed out, for example, that the increase of blue-collar jobs in the suburbs and of white-collar jobs in the central cities is ironically creating numerous travel difficulties for both lower-income central-city residents traveling to work in the suburbs and upper-income suburban residents traveling to work in central cities. It would, of course, be more efficient to have the population living near its place of employment. But to what extent have urban areas ever developed efficiently? Don't urban residents continually absorb public inefficiencies to realize private choices? They have continually shown this by their widespread preference for the automobile over public transportation, which produces increased congestion and numerous other traffic problems. After all, as is so often stated, transportation is a function of land use. Transportation problems are a function of a host of land-use choices made by urban residents, private enterprises, and public agencies. In the case of the metropolitan racial situation, the trend toward predominantly white upper-income suburbs and predominantly black lower-income central cities evidently means that residents are willing to absorb the transportation costs and difficulties in order to maintain their respective residential environments. Planners may entertain the possibilities of rearranging residential land uses to meet this particular transportation problem, but it would mean putting the cart before the horse. It would be absurd to hold that land uses can or should be considerably rearranged to satisfy transportation efficiencies, even if these efficiencies could be adequately defined.

THE GHETTO AND THE DECLINE OF THE CENTRAL CITY

Another point needs to be considered in regard to claims that the huge influx of black and other lower-income groups to the central city coupled with the exodus of the upper-income white groups to the suburbs has led to the decline and decay of the central city. Many analysts go so far as to state that the spread of metropolitan economic growth outward to the suburbs means that the central cities have no more potential for further growth. For example, some authors have written that "the decentralizing forces of American economic life are not reversible. The absence of vacant land within central cities, coupled with the existence of an enormous supply of vacant land on the urban periphery, will not permit a major expansion of the employment capacity of central cities. Public programs that seek only to rebuild the central-city housing stock and to encourage industry to locate within central cities and within ghettos run counter to the movement of the private economy."

Yet more intensive analyses of metropolitan economic decentralization have revealed that there is potential for growth in the central cities but that meaningful policies for realizing this potential are lacking. To be sure, the land situation in the central cities is tight and the suburbs offer more room for development. The economic function of the central city is declining both relatively and absolutely in relation to the suburbs, but this does not mean it is on the verge of collapse. For example, re-distribution of more central business-district businesses to the suburbs does not mean that the central business district will not retain a central economic focal point in metropolitan structure. Undoubtedly many businesses will remain and continue to expand in the urban core. The central cities may not capture quite as high a proportion of such (office) activity as they have in the past, but there is not much doubt that absolute increases in such employment will occur. Nor is there much doubt that, to the extent that they occur, they will offer a continued stimulus to some central business districts.

The problem areas in the central city are those older residential com-munities and business districts surrounding the central business district. It is here where blight and decay are setting in and where most black ghettos are located. As the structures in these areas become so old and dilapidated that they are no longer useful, a potential for reuse appears. But so far very few local governments have developed meaningful renewal policies for developing this reuse potential. It is widely acknowledged by housing experts and specialists that thus far the federal renewal program has been manipulated in such a manner as to hamper, if not set back, the redevelopment of declining central-city areas. The many destructive consequences of the program in reducing the amount of housing accessible to minority and lower-income groups—thereby increasing the amount of overcrowding and blight—have been widely publicized.

But it should be remembered that what is lacking is not the need for central-city renewal itself, but the adoption of realistic and effective policies for achieving renewal. Indeed, the need for realizing the potential of central-city renewal is especially pressing. Without positive action the urban center may wither and the metropolis may become a vast, amorphous, headless amoeba. A strong center is needed socially, economically, and psychologically, for it is here that urban life is lived in full, and virtually all activities in the metropolitan area focus toward it. In the next section of this paper it is proposed that ghetto rebuilding become a major component of a general metropolitan effort to build a strong urban center.

THE POSITION OF THE GHETTO IN METROPOLITAN STRUCTURE
Monopolistic Control

In order to get at the more vital linkages between the ghetto and metropolitan structure, it is necessary to move away from the views, fostered by the case for ghetto dispersal, concerning metropolitan imbalances "produced" by the ghetto. Instead we must delve more closely into the economic imbalances which surround the emergence of the ghetto. We know that a vast majority of the black population entered the cities at the bottom of the economic structure and has remained there throughout its urban history. Also, it is widely acknowledged that whites who parted from the areas occupied by black migrants nonetheless retained control over the areas' business and real estate. This can be readily seen in many examples: slum landlords who capitalize on the general metropolitan housing shortage to squeeze excess rent from black tenants for substandard dwellings; marginal central-city businesses which rely upon the "cheap" labor supply in the ghetto for employment; the mortgage-lending policies of FHA which enabled millions of white families to move from the central cities and maintain segregated suburban communities. In effect, the severe competitive disadvantage of the black community in the political economy of the cities has provided a base for the acquisition of varied economic and political interests by the white community. Over the years the accumulation of these interests becomes institutional and structural; the interests become monopolistic.

Quantitative evidence on monopolistic advantages achieved by the white community is supported by the investigations of Lester Thurow reported in his recent book, *Poverty and Discrimination*. Using econometric techniques to investigate the relationship between poverty and discrimination in the United States, he shows that black poverty is considerably more extensive and enduring than white poverty and, more importantly, that various economic gains acquired by the white community result in economic losses for the black community. In light of such facts it is misleading to view economic discrimination through the lens of formal bourgeois economic theory which traditionally conceived of economic discrimination in terms of physical distance, in terms of the white population's willingness to pay for not associating with blacks. As Thurow and others have pointed out, it is more realistic to view it in terms of social distance, in terms of whites defining black people's points of entry into the marketplace in order to reap substantial economic advantages. For example, employment discrimination consists not only in white employers' refusal to hire blacks but also in their relegation of blacks to inferior occupational and income positions, such as domestic servants, chauffeurs, messengers, file clerks, etc. The power to carry out such relegations is a function of the monopolistic institutional advantages acquired by whites relative to blacks.

Thurow's conclusions reveal: "Quantitatively the monopoly powers of the white community vis-à-vis the black community are a major force leading to lower Negro incomes and higher individual white incomes. Negro losses and white gains amount to approximately $15 billion per year." In discussing the policy implications of this conclusion, he makes the significant point that the "policy instruments must be color conscious. The package of programs that will cure white poverty will not cure Negro poverty. Something extra is needed."

Although he does not fully articulate it, the theoretical thrust of Thurow's findings points toward what many black community groups have been maintaining for several years; namely, that the ghetto functions as a colonial appendage of the dominant white metropolitan community, which drains the ghetto of its ability to develop its own capital and resource base. This view carries much more theoretical and empirical weight than the references to ghetto-produced imbalances made in the case for ghetto dispersal. American metropolitan growth has never been balanced in either the economical sense of an efficient utilization of resources or the normative sense of an equitable distribution of resources. The locus of metropolitan imbalances associated with the ghetto structure can usually be traced to the monopolistic control over the ghetto structure by the white community.

THE GHETTO AND SOCIAL PATHOLOGIES

In examining the pathologies of the ghetto, it is necessary first to distinguish between the ghetto and pathologies. After all, a ghetto is not synonymous with the pathologies of social and economic deprivation, as John Kain and others seem to imply. A ghetto is only a residential area inhabited by a common ethnic group. Economic poverty, for instance, is not a necessary characteristic of ghettos. Many Jewish ghettos in Europe have maintained a higher standard of living than most of the surrounding European population.

Moreover, while black ghettos in America manifest many social pathologies, these represent only one aspect of black urban life and do not characterize all of their residential areas within the central cities. Kain, instead of referring to the works of Kenneth Clark and Claude Brown to characterize the ghetto as "institutionalized pathology," would have done better to refer to the works of E. Franklin Frazier who has done more comprehensive and thorough studies of black urban communities over a longer period of time than either Clark or Brown. His studies on the ecological settlement of the black population in Harlem and Chicago have revealed that neighborhood differentiation by family organization and socioeconomic status tends to follow in broad outline the same general pattern within black residential areas as it does within white residential areas. The ghetto slum areas which Clark and Brown refer to would constitute only one type of black residential neighborhood. Moreover, the increased suburbanization of the white population since 1950 has opened up more and better residential areas within the central cities for black families and households. Thus, one finds greater neighborhood differentiation among the black central-city population today than existed at the time Frazier conducted his studies. The hard-core slum ghetto is no more characteristic of black urban communities than skid row is of the white central-city communities.

In looking at the pathologies associated with the polarization of the races, it is important to recognize the difference between polarization in terms of racial attitudes and the actual forces of ecological segregation between blacks and whites. Polarization of the races did not occur with the black concentration in the central cities and the white flight to the suburbs. The races have always been polarized in a moral and social sense that has little to do with spatial segregation. In fact, blacks were probably most integrated in a spatial sense during the slavery and early postslavery periods when their servant dwellings were freely intermixed with the mansions of their white masters and employers. The current crisis of racial polarization simply reflects the extent to which the white population has recently become aware of the plight of the black community. In regard to the ghetto, it is crucially important to recognize that it represents a form of moral and social isolation more than a physical or spatial isolation. Moreover, rather than producing this social isolation, the ghetto structure is an important shield from its damaging effects. Consider very carefully the words of Frazier in referring to the plight of the Negro middle class:

> The middle class owes its growth and form of existence to the fact that the Negro has been isolated mentally, socially, and morally in American society. Therefore, in some respects, the Negro community may be regarded as a pathological phenomenon. It is not surprising, then, that

the Negro middle class shows the mark of oppression . . . in its mental and psychic make-up. The middle-class Negro shows the mark of oppression more than the lower-class Negro who finds a shelter from the contempt of the white world in his traditional religion, in his songs, and in his freedom from a gnawing desire to be recognized and accepted. Although the middle-class Negro has tried to reject his traditional background and racial identification, he cannot escape from it. Therefore, many middle-class Negroes have developed self-hatred.

The ghetto, of course, is the primary locational base for the "shelter" institutions of the black lower class referred to by Frazier. These institutions are vital to the social sustenance of a vast majority of the black population. In light of the profound historical roots of the American racial problem, it is doubtful that the ghetto will lose its "shelter" function in the foreseeable future.

To recognize positive functions of the ghetto is not to deny its many problems. The point is that the problems should be put in their proper perspective. Thus, such problems as those of the central-city ghetto schools cannot be seen simply as a product of the expanding boundaries of segregation. It is not the expansion itself which leads to high dropout rates, insufficient college preparation, poor classroom environments, etc. Solutions to such problems are too complex to be found in policy structures of school integration. Indeed, in the South and various parts of the North and West, white politicians and educators have used the federal guidelines on school desegregation to make integration a one-way street, in which black students, teachers, and principals are transferred to white schools and the black school system is eliminated, bringing about loss of occupational mobility for black teachers and educators. And in large black ghettos, such as those in Washington, Los Angeles, and Chicago, it is doubtful that school integration is attainable in the near future. Thus it is not surprising that, in the past couple of years, interest of many black community groups in the school issue has shifted from integration to community control. As manifested in the widely publicized Ocean Hill–Brownsville school crisis in Brooklyn in 1968, ghetto parents are increasingly recognizing that many of the formal educational problems of their children are closely related to the lack of control which they can exert on the school board and other local institutions that determine the development of public-school facilities and educational programs.

THE FALSE SEARCH FOR MARKET BALANCE

In sum, the case for ghetto dispersal rests upon a false search for metropolitan market balance. The studies tend to connect the growth of metropolitan structure to the movement of the market mechanism. They view the private economy of the metropolis as shifting toward the suburbs and postulate, therefore, that ghetto inhabitants should also shift in order to have access to growing metropolitan resources. Not only do such analyses reflect an incomplete and inaccurate assessment of the metropolitan economy and the problem of accessibility to its resources, they also underrate the scale and nature of the ghetto's economic and employment situation and completely ignore its vital geosocial functions. More importantly, by continually drawing simplistic and naive connections between economic needs and resources, they are deterred from the most fruitful course to their ultimate objective of recommending policies for change. As Gunnar Myrdal has stated, in *The Political Element in the Development of Economic Theory,* "In most questions of economic policy there are conflicts of interests. This in fact cannot be concealed by obscure talk of *a priori* principles. In those cases neither an economist nor anybody else can offer a 'socially' or 'economically correct' solution. . . . It should be one of the main tasks of applied economics to examine and to unravel the complex interplay of interests, as they sometimes, converge, sometimes conflict."

The object of this critique has been to indicate that the relationship of the ghetto to metropolitan structure can only be understood in all of its dimensions: economical, political, social, and cultural. The problems inherent in ghetto-metropolitan linkages involve institutional and interest conflicts that permeate all these dimensions. The black ghetto is a pathological community because the political, economical, and social deprivations experienced by its inhabitants are a function of monopolistic interests built upon its structure by various groups of the white metropolitan community. Such a relationship has severely dissipated and constricted the ghetto's political and economic institutions.

To remove these constrictions does not imply a large-scale displacement and removal of ghetto blacks to the suburbs. The high rates of natural increase among the central-city black population will undoubtedly lead to increase in the rate of black suburbanization. But this does not mean that the central-city ghetto will suddenly wither away. Quite to the contrary, the ghetto is seen as a highly durable community which will be around for some time to come. The problem then is one of creating conditions which remove the political and economic constrictions on existing ghettos and encourage their inhabitants to assert themselves in the control and management of their community environment. Such control and management are at the very heart of the black struggle to achieve a wholesome and decent community life.

POLICY CASE FOR GHETTO REBUILDING

Our program proposals for reconstituting the black central-city communities do not in any sense reflect a belief that their successful implementation would secure full collective freedom for black people. It is our firm conviction that the substantial majority of black people cannot gain relief from their oppression, from their material and spiritual degradations and frustrations, until they completely sever their subjection to the tentacles of the dominant white society. To us, this necessarily means the achievement of black nationhood, the formation of a black nation-state with its own land base. To deny the possibility of this achievement is to deny history. Yet at the same time one must also recognize certain minimal preconditions to the formation of black nationhood: the existence of a mass consensus for black nationhood with strong unified leadership to implement it; sophisticated black political and economic institutions that command respect and exert influence among other nations of the world; and favorable domestic and international circumstances which make it opportune for blacks to acquire a land base. To us, all the evidence suggests that the maturation of these preconditions is at least another generation away; hence our current energies are directed to their fulfillment. It is in this light that our ghetto-rebuilding programs are proposed. They represent interim "middle range" objectives which black people can strive toward until they are able to bend national and international circumstances to the interest and fulfillment of black nationhood.

Also, although our proposed programs deal primarily with urban areas, this does not mean we view the cities as the most suitable environments even for black interim objectives. Nor does it mean that we deny the need for a substantial black rural-development program. But the central cities are where most black people now reside. Furthermore, their large-scale urban concentrations are the product of tremendous migrations which began during World War I and gave no indication of leveling off until the past decade. The rates and volumes of these migrations are the most rapid and largest in modern world history and have caused considerable disruption and uprooting of black social and cultural ties. Thus in many regions, particularly in the relatively new black communities of the West, many blacks are still involved in the process of establishing themselves in the cities. To advocate programs involving further substantial migrations within the confines of white America would appear to be out of touch with the tempo and process of black community settlement unless the programs can guarantee definite improvements in black living situations.

In assessing the economic resources available for black development, one should not get hung up on "facts" and "figures" used to show the paucity of resources available to black people in the central city. It is true that they are meager. According to most established economic indices and criteria, central cities are relatively insignificant units in the total economic system and offer no genuine access to the chains of command in white America's dominant institutions. But these facts have nothing to say about the potential of black central-city development. The "hard" facts of economics should not make one lose sight of the more basic fact that economic activities, like all other societal activities, are no more than a function of human behavior, a product of the human will. People do not simply live according to general economic stages and systems. People possess economies. The flexibility of people in providing for their material welfare can never be absolutely circumscribed. The ability of black people to provide for themselves in the central city will ultimately depend on the caliber of their own community organization and leadership. This necessarily means that the black leadership must demonstrate considerable shrewdness and tenacity in extracting resource subsidies from white public and private institutions to help support direly needed community-development projects, such as housing renewal and construction, day-care centers, community colleges, and business and commercial endeavors. The central city is no more undesirable for meeting these challenges than any other locational base within the confines of white America. The white suburban residents and businesses who have left the central city in an impoverished state may neglect it, but they cannot write it off. The central city is still an indispensable unit in the overall distribution of metropolitan activities. Important financial and commercial offices, strategic government and military functions, public-utility and -transportation facilities, and many other integral metropolitan facilities and services are concentrated in central cities and offer potential leverage to their black inhabitants in extracting overdue economic support from the white metropolitan community. Moreover, whether blacks ultimately remain in the United States or separate to another land, they can never escape the delicate and difficult problems of contending amid moral forces to provide for and protect their material and social interests. The central cities are just as good a place as any to realize the far-reaching implications of a statement made by Frederick Douglass over a century ago: "Society is a hard-hearted affair. With it the helpless may expect no higher dignity than that of the paupers. The individual may lay society under obligation to him or society will honor him only as a stranger and sojourner."

POLICY FRAMEWORK FOR GHETTO REBUILDING

The policy proposals that follow consist of four program elements considered to be essential to any national effort to bring about effective renewal of ghetto communities. They apply primarily to those major central cities and smaller towns and villages in various parts of the country which contain a significant proportion of black people and whose communities are marked by a predominance of low incomes, substandard housing, low indigenous capital base, and deteriorated physical environments.

The proposals do not go into specific program designs in terms of indicating detailed fiscal and organizational alternatives for implementation. This would be a considerable task that goes far beyond the scope of this paper. Within each proposal element, much applied research and planning needs to be done. The proposals themselves simply represent the general ends and organizational forms toward which many existing black community-development efforts can be directed. Due to the tremendous, deeply rooted problems within the ghetto and the powerful, complex political and economic forces impinging upon its structure, ghetto rebuilding must necessarily be conceived of as a fairly long-run process consisting of a host of sustained organizational efforts and involving major political struggles and conflicts within the metropolitan and national structures.

A primary feature of the proposals is their reliance upon existing and incipient ideas and organizational resources within the black community. The programs are conceived of as being built from the bottom up rather than from the top down. Hopefully this approach would avoid many of the "community participation" difficulties that permeate existing efforts, such as the Model Cities program, which attempts to solicit community support for a program conceived in Washington and offers no real promise of physical and social improvement. Only one of the proposals is original to the writer. The others reflect a synthesis of various ideas and organizational thrusts that have emerged from the black community over the past decade. In effect, ghetto rebuilding is simply an encouragement of black initiatives toward community control.

Develop Black Municipal Corporations. This means the creation of a protomunicipal structure within specified ghetto boundaries of each urban area. It would involve the development of a black municipal authority elected by and responsible to ghetto inhabitants. This black municipal authority would be the primary body responsible for the general physical, social, and economic reconstruction of the ghetto. Its board of councilmen, and perhaps its mayor, would be responsible for the provision of all basic community services, from housing and urban renewal to public education to law enforcement.

In large urban areas, such as Detroit and Chicago, the corporation could exist along with regular city government, but it would assume responsibility for most of the services usually provided by that government. Also, it would be the primary body representing the black community in any discussions and negotiations between city hall and the ghetto. Of course, in small, unincorporated, all-black towns of the rural South it would simply be a matter of acquiring legal corporation and setting up the administrative machinery for municipal government, a trend which has already begun in Mississippi, Alabama, and other Southern states.

The black municipal structure would also serve as the prime recipient of funds from the Departments of Housing and Urban Development and of Health, Education and Welfare, and from other federal agencies, to provide basic community improvements in the ghetto. This arrangement would eliminate many of the conflicts that now occur between the black community and city hall when funds "disappear" as they filter indirectly to the community through city hall. In a sense, the black municipal corporation might sponsor the same broad set of community services that the Model Cities program is trying to provide. Only its organizational structure would maintain closer links to the residents and a more reliable system for the accounting and provision of community services.

Movements in this direction are evident in many places. Most notable are the achievements of the Nation of Islam, which has an internal system of black self-development. Relying primarily upon the self-sacrifice and devotion of its members, it is building through a central organizational mechanism a number of schools, farms, businesses, and educational and health centers in various parts of the country. As an actual model of black community development, it is similar in broad outline to the development approaches taken by certain developing countries. China and Tanzania, for example, stress reliance upon the indigenous resources of their predominantly rural populations to embark on the arduous road to industrialization and modernization. One can also see the trend toward black municipal organization in the black neighborhood organizations that have been developed in Oakland, Brooklyn, Harlem, Chicago, and other urban areas. One can further see it in the Afro-American police societies organized across the Northeast and Midwest, one of their main objectives being to work for the patrol of black communities by black policemen. The black municipal authority then would strengthen and legitimize these incipient black efforts in law enforcement, public education, and the whole range of community services. It would support, coordinate, and channel the increasing indigenous efforts toward community control into the tremendous task of rebuilding the social and physical fabric of the ghetto.

Build Black Economic Development Institutions. One of the primary challenges and responsibilities facing the black municipal corporations would be to eliminate the poverty and restructure the economic base of the ghetto; that is, to increase the ghetto's capital and employment base, diversify and enlarge the productive capacity of its businesses, and provide for black control and determination over the ghetto economy. This responsibility could be met by the establishment of community-based development corporations operating under carefully prepared and organized economic programs to increase the standard of living among ghetto inhabitants. Two of the most widely discussed proposals for bringing about such innovations are the CORE Community Self-Determination Bill, sponsored before the 1968 session of Congress, and the Ghediplan, devised by black economist Dunbar S. McLaurin. These proposals call for the creation of an elaborate system of community corporations, banks, and other entrepreneurial mechanisms to establish a capital base in the ghetto and carry out far-reaching programs of black economic development. While they differ in many respects and would have to be modified to fit the particular local conditions and circumstances of a given black community, they do offer a fertile basis for examining ways in which black groups can use their organizational and political strength to help achieve ghetto economic control and growth.

For example, one of the main features of the Ghediplan is the design of a framework by which ghetto development corporations can productively utilize fiscal and economic resources from government, business, and labor institutions to acquire the necessary capacity and experience for large-scale productive activity. It rests not so much upon direct grants from the government as on creative utilization of existing governmental fiscal resources to provide "guaranteed" markets and financing for ghetto businesses and industries. A significant proportion of the city, state, or national government's purchase contracts, for instance, would be allotted to ghetto corporations to provide their businesses with a built-in market for the sale of their products and services. Such an act by the government, it is felt, would probably include similar acts from large private businesses and labor unions. Likewise, "guaranteed financing" could be provided by governmental bodies using their security bonds and other deposits to encourage banks and financial institutions to furnish the necessary credit and loan capital for ghetto-development business ventures. The commitment of these marketing and financial resources from the government and other dominant institutions would provide some of the vital economic ingredients required by the black business and industries at their early stage of growth.

Well-organized black municipal corporations and political organizations would be in a strategic position to help extract and mobilize the types of fiscal and economic supports mentioned in the Ghediplan. In cases where such organizations achieve control over the management and operation of various city services, they could act as primary agents in providing the "guaranteed" markets and financing to the development corporations. In addition, black organizational pressure, in the form of economic boycotts, strikes, and other confrontation tactics might be used against large white businesses and labor unions to garner their support. Black community organizations could also be instrumental in bringing pressure to bear on elected political officials of predominantly black constituencies to endorse and help mobilize resources for their economic-development programs. Too often these elected officials use the fragmented organizational state of their constituencies and the prestige and power of their positions to set themselves above the people, advocating all sorts of ill-conceived and worthless programs for "curing" poverty. Unified black community groups with well-defined economic programs and strong political organization would narrowly limit the range of irresponsible actions and maneuvers their politicians are accustomed to performing.

Regardless of the various tactics used from locality to locality, the ultimate objective is one of establishing a black institutional and organizational base for carrying out thorough and diversified economic development of the ghetto. Moreover, it is important that black municipal and political organizations play a strategic role in this process, stimulating and catalyzing it by using political leverage to extract support from the dominant white institutions and acting in a regulatory capacity over the development corporations so as to ensure their commitment and responsibility to the economic improvement of ghetto inhabitants.

Combine Ghetto Rebuilding with Central-City Renewal. This program could serve as one of the primary development activities of the black municipal and private corporate structures. It would involve the black municipal and development corporations acting as primary partners in a general metropolitan effort to revitalize declining areas of the central city, particularly the central business district, with the black corporations assuming complete responsibility for the physical, economic, and social renewal of specified portions of the district.

It was mentioned earlier that, in most metropolitan areas with large black populations, various commercial and industrial areas within the central city are declining both economically and physically, marked by empty office space and marginal businesses with high turnover rates, as a result of the business exodus to the suburbs. Since the expansion of commercial and financial offices remaining in the urban core will occupy a relatively small amount of space, a potential demand is developing, but so far there has been little actual demand for reuse. The need for land-development outlets by black municipal and development corporations could readily fill much of this demand. Access to these declining areas would provide much-needed space for their residential renewal and business-development activities. In residential renewal it would enable the construction of significant numbers of new dwellings to house both new black family formations and those households displaced by clearance of the worst ghetto areas. Also it would furnish space for the community-development corporations to launch major industrial and commercial enterprises. By establishing these business enterprises within or near the central business district, the corporations would be in a strategic location to capture significant proportions of the metropolitan economic market, for despite its decline the central business district still attracts for a variety of reasons a major part of the metropolitan population.

In addition to these economic benefits there would be important social and cultural benefits. It is widely recognized by urban analysts that the urban core must renew its role as a political, economic, and cultural center if the metropolis is to be prevented from becoming "headless" and monotonous, a city without diversity and excitement. Also, it is apparent that one must begin to think in terms of new images regarding the city center. A center within a decentralized metropolitan structure will necessarily have to be different from one in a centralized structure. A new city center cannot restrict itself to large-scale commercial development but must cater to a wider variety of smaller attractions. The center might increasingly provide a variety of cultural, recreational, and tourist retail enterprises. While these enterprises would be small relative to the huge corporations of the white community, they would be of an attractive size for the developing black corporations. What better way to revitalize the city center than by providing for the development of black cultural centers, theaters, restaurants, Afro-Asian import and export exchanges, and various other enterprises? It is widely recognized that the black population, the largest and except for the Indian the oldest nonwhite ethnic group in the country, has made unique and permanent social and cultural contributions to the development of the society. What better way to acknowledge these contributions than by the development of major black political, cultural, and commercial establishments at the heart of the metropolitan area? Too often when people think of interracial communication, they think in small group terms, in terms of black and white residents living together in interracial housing projects or students going to integrated schools. But perhaps more important is the communication one receives through public images, the urban sights one sees while walking along city streets, attending musical and theatrical performances, and eating at restaurants. City centers with black people managing and operating their own establishments would stand in sharp contrast to those of today with black people serving primarily as waiters, cooks, and stock and file clerks for predominantly white establishments.

Develop Black Institutions of Higher Education. A crucially important need generated by the above programs would be increased demands for black skills in all phases of urban and rural development; engineers, accountants, community planners, statisticians, public and business administrators, agricultural economists, research analysts, etc. While increased black access to the educational resources of predominantly white colleges would be needed to meet some of these demands, it would also be essential that predominantly black colleges and universities be overhauled and developed to meet the skill demands and needs for ghetto rebuilding. All-black college development programs would of course have to be coordinated by a national group of black educators and administrators who have an experienced and sincere interest in the higher education of the black population.

The first focus of any general black college development program should be the existing predominantly black colleges and universities in the Southern and border states. It is acknowledged by black and white educators that these colleges have been beset by a host of major problems in the postwar period due primarily to large migrations of blacks from the South to the North and West and to the rapid pace of social and technological changes in the society. Handicapped by low budgetary funds, increased educational costs, and excessive control by paternalistic white boards of trustees and state officials, many have become increasingly unable to make necessary improvements in their facilities and instructional programs. As a result, they have been severely hampered in preparing students for worthwhile tasks in the modern world. Despite this decline, most of the colleges will survive, one way or another, because of the sheer growth pressures of the rapidly increasing black student population. Yet there is no reason why they should not be upgraded to meet the modern skill demands and requirements of the black population. Many have unique and valuable assets to rebuild upon. Tuskegee has important schools in agriculture and veterinary science built upon the scientific accomplishments of the late George Washington Carver. Atlanta University, Fisk, and many others have valuable library and research materials on the black community. With the abundant resources in this country there is no reason why these colleges should be allowed to decline. What more reliable avenue for the flow of public and private subsidies than to institutions whose administrative machinery is already intact? Programs and struggles to break the tight control over these colleges by paternalistic whites and increase the flow of funds for overhauling their administrative and educational structures would have the impact of greatly accelerating the number of black college students with the necessary skills and motivation to accomplish the task of rebuilding their communities.

A second focus should be on the creation of black community colleges in every urban area with a large black population. In the North and West some have already started, such as Malcolm X University in Chicago and Nairobi College in East Palo Alto, California. Colleges such as these could supply training in a range of essential practical skills that are not provided by prestigious white universities. It is no secret that college-educated blacks have been traditionally shunted into nonpractical subjects, such as sociology, political science, and English literature, most of which reflect white ethnocentric intellectual biases and are not relevant to black world views and skill needs. What would be needed in abundance are more useful skills, such as how to manage and operate a business cooperative, building-construction contracting and management, bookkeeping, etc. The training in many such skills could be provided within a year or two and would be highly relevant opportunities for many black youths seeking a "second chance" in life. Black community colleges situated in the ghetto would be in a strategic position to provide such opportunities.

Owing to the discordance and unevenness that emerge in critical discussions such as this paper, we will now attempt to tie together the main points in capsule form. In general the case for ghetto rebuilding rests upon a different conception of the relationship between the ghetto and metropolitan decentralization than does the case for ghetto dispersal.

The case for ghetto dispersal holds that the dominant movements of the white population and economic resources to the suburban fringe have isolated the black ghettos in the central city and limited their residents' geographic accessibility to direly needed social economic resources. The isolation is seen as accentuating the economic poverty and social pathologies of the ghetto in addition to creating imbalances in metropolitan growth. If these problems are to be resolved, then it is considered imperative that barriers which limit the ghetto residents' access to the suburbs be eliminated so that they can move to the dominant resources on the fringe. Therefore the focus is on the creation of conditions which make for the dispersion of the black population from the central-city ghettos to the suburbs.

The case for ghetto rebuilding does not see the social and economic deprivations of the ghetto as a product of its geographic isolation from the suburbs, but as a product of much more complex forces at work within the metropolis and the nation as a whole. First as a different set of historical experiences resulting from conditions of slavery and servitude in the rural South, the black population has never been fully assimilated into the cultural fabric of the country. This cultural difference has been reinforced by the social economic position which blacks inherited when they moved in large number to the cities. Their general economic position has always been at the bottom of the urban structure, which means that they have continually suffered from housing and employment shortages and imbalances that have continually existed in the national urban economy and that the structure of their ghetto community has provided a basis upon which white community groups have built monopolistic economic and political interests. Thus, the economic poverty and consequent social pathologies of the ghetto are a function of profound imbalances in the national urban economy and of monopolistic interests accumulated by the white community.

Relieving the problems of the ghetto is not so much a question of eliminating barriers to black movement to the suburbs as it is that of eliminating the monopolistic control which white groups hold over the ghetto structure and mobilizing unprecedented resource subsidies at national and local levels for resolving the economic imbalances affecting the depressed situation of the black community. While these problems are not spatially determined, they do tend to have a fixed spatial character. The national economic imbalances find their primary locational bases in the declining commercial, industrial, and residential areas of the city center, in which most urban blacks reside. Thus problems of improving the ghetto are closely related to those of revitalizing the city center. To try to resolve these problems by returning white middle-

and upper-income families to the city center and dispersing black families to the suburbs not only runs counter to historical forces of ecological segregation in American cities but in all probability would neither relieve the social and economic deprivations of the black population nor renew the city center. Hence the problems have to be faced where they are. Such a situation naturally points to ghetto rebuilding as the more effective and desirable alternative.

Ghetto rebuilding is seen as a process already at work in existing efforts by black community groups to attain control over various governmental, business, and educational activities within ghetto areas. The proposals for ghetto rebuilding consist simply of recommending the long-run organizational forms toward which these efforts should be directed if blacks are to attain firm control over their community environment and effectively utilize resource subsidies for its physical and social reconstruction. The proposals recommend the development of black municipal and business corporate structures as the primary instruments for carrying out the ghetto-reconstruction process. To enhance the social and economic viability of this process, it is recommended that ghetto rebuilding be part of a general metropolitan effort to revitalize the city center. The final proposal recommends the overhauling of existing predominantly black colleges and universities and the creation of new community colleges in black urban areas to help supply the skills required by the ghetto-rebuilding effort.

15

John F. Kain and Joseph J. Persky

ALTERNATIVES TO THE
GILDED GHETTO

We are faced today with a spate of proposals and programs for improving the ghetto through economic development, renewal, and reconstruction [see Chapter 14]. The intellectual basis of many of these proposals stems from a false analogy of the ghetto to an underdeveloped country in need of economic development. This oversimplified and misleading view ignores the strong linkages that tie the ghetto to the remainder of the metropolis and to the nation. When the nature of these linkages and the complex relationship between the ghetto and metropolitan development is understood, the potential destructiveness of these proposals becomes apparent. In this article we attempt to describe these interrelationships and the ghetto's consequent culpability for an expanded list of urban problems.

THE GHETTO AND THE METROPOLIS

If we begin with the usual list of "ghetto problems"—unemployment, low income, poor schools, and poor housing—it is easy to see the appeal of proposals aimed at making the ghetto livable. Moreover, casual observation of the slow pace of school desegregation, residential integration, and fair-employment practices would indicate that the promise of

---

Reprinted from *Public Interest*, Vol. 14 (Winter 1969), pp. 74–87, by permission of the publisher and authors.

integration and the gains achievable from the process are to be made only at an obscure point in the future. Thus, in the short run, the argument for ghetto improvement would have us view the ghetto as something of a community unto itself, a community that could substantially benefit from economic development and especially heavy investments of physical capital.

The weakness of this argument, however, is attested to by a growing body of evidence that indicates that (1) the above list of ghetto problems is much too short, because it ignores the serious implications of the growing ghetto for the metropolis as a whole and that (2) the ghetto itself is responsible for, or seriously aggravates, many of the most visible problems of urban Negroes.

The central Negro ghetto has produced a significant distortion of metropolitan development, which has added substantially to problems in central-city finance, metropolitan transportation, housing, and urban renewal. The decline of central cities has been hastened by a conviction in the white community, both individual and corporate, that the ghetto would continue its rapid expansion, carrying along its associated problems of concentrated poverty and social disorganization.

Although historically lower-income groups have tended to live in central cities, this residential pattern was the result of a highly centralized employment structure. Low-income households, constrained by limited housing and transportation budgets, clustered tightly around the work places in the densest accommodations available. High-income households, by contrast, with more disposable income and preferences for less-congested living conditions, found it expedient to commute to suburban areas where land costs were lower. These lower housing costs in suburban locations more than compensated them for the time, inconvenience, and out-of-pocket costs of commuting. Today, it still remains true that low-income households cluster more closely around their work places than do high-income households. However, with the accelerating pace of suburbanization of industry and jobs—itself no doubt due partly to the ghetto's expansion—these jobs are found less frequently in cities. Thus the poor are found less frequently in the central city; it is mainly the Negro poor who are found there. The inference is inescapable; *central cities are poor largely because they are black, and not the converse.*

The residential locations of whites in similar income groups support this contention. For example, 45 percent of Detroit's poor white families live in suburbs, but only 11 percent of its poor Negro families do so. These figures belie the argument that Negroes are concentrated in central cities because they are poor. This finding is consistent with the work of numerous researchers who have concluded that little of the existing pattern of Negro residential segregation can be explained by income or other socioeconomic characteristics. One of the authors of this article has elsewhere estimated that, on the basis of Negro employment locations and of low-income white residential choice patterns, as many as 40,000 Detroit Negro workers and 112,000 Chicago Negro workers would move out of central ghettos in the absence of racial segregation.

This residential pattern imposed on the Negro has led to an unduly large proportion of poverty-linked services being demanded of central cities. At the same time, the expansion of the ghetto has encouraged the exodus of middle-income whites. The result has been rapid increases in local government expenditures and a severe constraint on the ability of central cities to raise revenues. Hence, the current crisis in city finances. Although the problem can be handled in the short run by various schemes of redistributing governmental revenues, a preferable long-run solution would involve a major dispersal of the low-income population, in particular the Negro. Central cities will continue to have a high proportion of the poor as long as they contain a large proportion of metropolitan jobs. However, there is no rationale for exaggerating this tendency with artificial restraints.

HOUSING, TRANSPORTATION, SCHOOLS

Housing segregation has also frustrated efforts to renew the city. At first sight the logic of renewal is strong. By offering federal subsidies to higher-income whites locating within their boundaries, central cities have hoped to improve their tax base. The same logic underlies community efforts to woo industry. However, to the extent that these groups consider the city an inferior location, because of the existence of the ghetto, such subsidies will continue to fail. As long as the ghetto exists, most of white America will write off the central city. Spot renewal, even on the scale envisioned in the Model Cities program, cannot alter this basic fact.

In this context, even the small victories of central cities are often of a pyrrhic nature. So long as the central business district (CBD) manages to remain a major employment location, the city is faced with serious transportation problems, problems that would be substantially reduced if more of the centrally employed whites were willing to reside in the city. To a great extent, the CBD stakes its existence on an ability to transport people rapidly over long distances. Pressures for more expressways and high-speed rail transit are understandable—and yet both encourage the migration to the suburbs. The city must lose either way, so long as the ghetto is a growing mass that dominates the environment of its core and the development of its metropolitan area.

From the above argument, it is clear that the impact of the ghetto on the processes of metropolitan development has created or aggravated many of our most critical urban problems. These costs are borne by Negroes and whites alike. However, the same interaction between the ghetto and the metropolis has produced other important distortions whose costs fall almost exclusively on the Negro community. The ghetto has isolated the Negro economically as well as socially. In the first place, the Negro has inadequate access to the job market. For him, informal methods of job search, common to low-skilled employment, are largely limited to the ghetto. Jobs may be plentiful outside of the ghetto, yet he will know little or nothing of these opportunities. Moreover, the time and cost necessary to reach many suburban jobs, frequently compounded by the radial character of public transit services, often will discourage Negroes from taking or even seeking such jobs. Granted that the ghetto generates a limited number of service jobs, this effect is more than offset by the discriminatory practices of nonghetto employers. Research on the distribution of Negro employment in Northern metropolitan areas indicates the importance of these factors, by demonstrating that the proportion of Negroes in an area's work force is dependent on that area's distance from the ghetto and the racial composition of the surrounding residential neighborhoods. These distributional characteristics also affect the level of Negro employment. Estimates indicate that as many as 24,000 jobs in Chicago and 9,000 in Detroit may be lost to the Negro community because of housing segregation. These figures are based on 1956 and 1952 data and may well underestimate the current situation. The continuing trend of job decentralization also may have aggravated the situation.

De facto school segregation is another widely recognized limitation of Negro opportunities resulting from housing market segregation. A large body of evidence indicates that students in ghetto schools receive an education much inferior to that offered elsewhere. Low levels of student achievement are the result of a complex of factors including poorly trained, overworked, and undermotivated teachers, low levels of per student expenditures, inadequate capital plants, and the generally low level of students' motivation and aspiration. This last factor is, of course, related to the ghetto's poverty and social disorganization.

The continued rapid growth of central-city ghettos has seriously expanded the realm of *de facto* segregation and limited the range of possible corrective actions. For example, in 1952, 57 percent of Cleveland's Negro students went to schools with more than 90 percent Negro enrollment. In 1962, 82 percent went to such schools. By 1965, Chicago,

Detroit, and Philadelphia all had more than 70 percent of their Negro students in these completely segregated schools.

In addition to sharply curtailing Negro economic and educational opportunity, the ghetto is an important disorganizing force. It represents the power of the outside community and the frustration of the Negro. The sources of nourishment for many of the psychological and sociological problems too common to Negro Americans can be found here. Drug addiction, violent crime, and family disorganization all gain a high degree of acceptance, creating a set of norms that often brings the individual into conflict with the larger society. Kenneth Clark puts the case well: "The dark ghetto is institutionalized pathology; it is chronic, self-perpetuating pathology . . ." Although this pathology is difficult to quantify, it may well be the ghetto's most serious consequence.

In reviewing our expanded list of problems, it may seem that we have made the ghetto too much the villain. Physical segregation may have only been the not-so-subtle way to avoid discriminatory practices that might otherwise be rampant. Many ghetto problems might still exist in some other guise. Nevertheless, the problems as structured *now* must continue as long as the metropolis harbors this "peculiar institution."

Nothing less than a complete change in the structure of the metropolis will solve the problem of the ghetto. It is therefore ironic that current programs which ostensibly are concerned with the welfare of urban Negroes are willing to accept, and are even based on, the permanence of central ghettos. Thus, under every heading of social welfare legislation—education, income transfer, employment, and housing—we find programs that can only serve to strengthen the ghetto and the serious problems that it generates. In particular, these programs concentrate on beautifying the fundamentally ugly structure of the current metropolis and not on providing individuals with the tools necessary to break out of that structure. The shame of the situation is that viable alternatives *do* exist.

Thus, in approaching the problems of Negro employment, first steps could be an improved information system at the disposal of Negro job seekers, strong training programs linked to job placement in industry, and improved transit access between central ghettos and outlying employment areas. Besides the direct effects of such programs on unemployment and incomes, they have the added advantage of encouraging the dispersion of the ghetto and not its further concentration. For example, Negroes employed in suburban areas distant from the ghetto have strong incentives to reduce the time and cost of commuting by seeking out residences near their work places. Frequent, informal contact with white coworkers will both increase their information about housing in predominantly white residential areas and help to break down the mutual distrust that is usually associated with the process of integration.

Prospects of housing desegregation would be much enhanced by major changes in urban renewal and housing programs. Current schemes accept and reinforce some of the worst aspects of the housing market. Thus, even the best urban renewal projects involve the government in drastically reducing the supply (and thereby increasing the cost) of low-income housing—all this at great expense to the taxpayer. At best there is an implicit acceptance of the alleged desire of the poor to remain in central-city slums. At worst, current programs could be viewed as a concerted effort to maintain the ghetto. The same observation can be made about public-housing programs. The Commission on Civil Rights in its report on school segregation concluded that government policies for low-cost housing were "further reinforcing the trend toward racial and economic separation in metropolitan areas."

An alternative approach would aim at drastically expanding the supply of low-income housing *outside* the ghetto. Given the high costs of re-claiming land in central areas, subsidies equivalent to existing urban-renewal expenditures for use anywhere in the metropolitan area would lead to the construction of many more units. The new mix by type and location would be likely to favor small, single-family homes and garden apartments on the urban periphery. Some overbuilding would be desirable, the object being the creation of a glut in the low-income suburban-housing market. It is hard to imagine a situation that would make developers and renters less sensitive to skin color.

These measures would be greatly reinforced by programs that increase the effective demand of Negroes for housing. Rent subsidies to individuals are highly desirable, because they represent the transfer of purchasing power that can be used anywhere in the metropolitan area. Other income-transfer programs not specifically tied to housing would have similar advantages in improving the prospects of ghetto dispersal. Vigorous enforcement of open-housing statutes would aid the performance of the "impersonal" market, perhaps most importantly by providing developers, lenders, and realtors with an excuse to act in their own self-interest.

SUBURBANIZATION OF THE NEGRO

Even in the face of continuing practices of residential segregation, the suburbanization of the Negro can still continue apace. It is important to realize that the presence of Negroes in the suburbs does not necessarily imply Negro integration into white residential neighborhoods.

Suburbanization of the Negro and housing integration are not synonymous. Many of the disadvantages of massive, central ghettos would be overcome if they were replaced or even augmented by smaller, dispersed Negro *communities*. Such a pattern would remove the limitations on Negro employment opportunities attributable to the geography of the ghetto. Similarly, the reduced pressure on central-city housing markets would improve the prospects for the renewal of middle-income neighborhoods through the operations of the private market. Once the peripheral growth of central-city ghettos is checked, the demands for costly investment in specialized, long-distance transport facilities serving central employment areas would be reduced. In addition programs designed to reduce *de facto* school segregation by means of redistributing, busing, and similar measures would be much more feasible.

Although such a segregated pattern does not represent the authors' idea of a more open society, it could still prove a valuable first step toward that goal. Most groups attempting to integrate suburban neighborhoods have placed great stress on achieving and maintaining some preconceived interracial balance. Because integration is the goal, they feel the need to proceed slowly and make elaborate precautions to avoid "tipping" the neighborhood. The result has been a small, black trickle into all-white suburbs. But if the immediate goal is seen as destroying the ghetto, different strategies should be employed. "Tipping," rather than something to be carefully avoided, might be viewed as a tactic for opening large amounts of suburban housing. If enough suburban neighborhoods are "tipped," the danger of any one of them becoming a massive ghetto would be small.

Education is still another tool that can be used to weaken the ties of the ghetto. Formal schooling plays a particularly important role in preparing individuals to participate in the complex urban society of today. It greatly enhances their ability to compete in the job market with the promise of higher incomes. As a result, large-scale programs of compensatory education can make important contributions to a strategy of weakening and eventually abolishing the Negro ghetto. Nevertheless, the important gains of such compensatory programs must be continually weighed against the more general advantages of school desegregation. Where real alternatives exist in the short run, programs consistent with this latter objective should always be chosen. It is important to note that truly effective programs of compensatory education are likely to be extremely expensive and that strategies involving significant amounts of desegregation may achieve the same educational objectives at much lower costs.

Busing of Negro students may be such a program. Like better access to suburban employment for ghetto job seekers, busing would weaken the geographic dominance of the ghetto. Just as the informal experience of integration on the job is an important element in changing racial attitudes, integration in the classroom is a powerful learning experience. Insofar as the resistance of suburban communities to accepting low-income residents and students is the result of a narrow cost-minimization calculus that attempts to avoid providing public services and in particular education, substantial state and federal subsidies for the education of low-income students can prove an effective carrot. Title I programs of the Elementary and Secondary Education Act of 1965 and grants to areas containing large federal installations are precedents. Subsidies should be large enough to cover more than the marginal cost of educating students from low-income families, and should make it *profitable* for communities and school districts to accept such students. The experience of the METCO program in Boston strongly suggests that suburban communities can be induced to accept ghetto schoolchildren if external sources of financing are available.

Because the above proposals would still leave unanswered some immediate needs of ghetto residents, a strong argument can be made for direct income transfers. Although certain constraints on the use of funds, for example, rent supplements, might be maintained, the emphasis should be on providing resources to individuals and not on freezing them into geographic areas. The extent to which welfare schemes are currently tied to particular neighborhoods or communities should be determined, and these programs should be altered so as to remove such limitations on mobility. Keeping in mind the crucial links between the ghetto and the rural South, it is essential that the Southern Negro share in these income transfers.

THE GHETTO AND THE NATION

Although there are major benefits to be gained by both the Negro community and the metropolis at large through a dispersal of the central ghetto, these benefits cannot be realized and are likely to be hindered by programs aimed at making the ghetto a more livable place. In addition to the important objections discussed so far, there is the very real possibility that such programs will run afoul of major migration links with the Negro population of the South. A striking example of this problem can be seen in the issue of ghetto job creation, one of the most popular proposals to improve the ghetto.

Although ghetto job creation, like other "gilding" programs, might initially reduce Negro unemployment, it must eventually affect the system that binds the Northern ghetto to the rural and urban areas of the South. This system will react to any sudden changes in employment and income opportunities in Northern ghettos. If there are no offsetting improvements in the South, the result will be increased rates of migration into still-restricted ghetto areas. While we need to know much more than we now do about the elasticity of migration to various economic improvements, the direction of the effect is clear. Indeed it is possible that more than one migrant would appear in the ghetto for every job created. Even at lower levels of sensitivity, a strong wave of in-migration could prove extremely harmful to many other programs. The South in 1960 still accounted for about 60 percent of the country's Negro population, more than half of which lived in nonmetropolitan areas. In particular, the number of *potential* migrants from the rural South has not declined greatly in recent years. The effect of guaranteed incomes or jobs available in the metropolitan ghetto can be inferred from an analysis of the patterns of migration from the South.

Historically, the underdeveloped nature of the Southern region has proven a spur to the migration of *both* whites and Negroes. What recent progress has been achieved is overwhelmingly "whites only." The 1950s were the first decade in this century in which there was net white in-migration of the Southern region as a whole. This change is very likely the result of the expansion of industrial activity throughout the South and particularly its border areas. White male agricultural employment losses of about 1 million were more than offset by strong gains in manufacturing, wholesale and retail trade, and professional and related services. By way of contrast, Negroes concentrated in the slowest-growing and most discriminatory states in the Deep South showed no major gains to offset the almost 400,000 jobs lost in agriculture. Thus, despite rapid contraction of the agricultural sector, 1960 still found 21 percent of all Southern Negro males employed in agriculture as compared to 11 percent of Southern whites. It is not surprising, in terms of this background, that nearly 1.5 million Negroes (net) left the South in the 1950s.

The major result of the massive migrations of the 1940s and 1950s was to make the metropolitan areas of the North and West great centers of Negro population. In 1940 these areas accounted for only 20 percent of all Negroes in the country, whereas in 1960 37 percent of all Negroes lived in these same areas. Moreover, statistics on the migration of Negroes born in Southern states indicate a definite preference for the largest metropolitan areas of the country over small cities.

DEVELOPING THE SOUTH

Some appreciation for migration's contribution to the growth of Northern ghettos is provided by a comparison of the components of Negro population increase. Fifty-four percent of the 2.7 million increase in Northern Negro populations from 1950 to 1960 was accounted for by net in-migration of Southern Negroes. Although the data on more recent population changes are scanty, the best estimates suggest that Negro net migration from the South averaged about 100,000 per year for the period 1960 to 1966. It therefore appears that the contribution of Southern migration to the growth of Northern ghettos, even though it may now be on the decline, remains substantial.

The pattern of Negro migration is in sharp contrast with the pattern of white out-migration from the same areas of the South. Thus, there are about 2.5 million Southern-born whites and 2.5 million Southern-born Negroes in non-Southern metropolitan areas greater than 1 million, but 1.42 million whites and 4.2 million Negroes in non-Southern cities of 250,000 to 1 million. Cities greater than 250,000 account for 89 percent of Negroes who have left the South, but only 60 percent of whites. The framework of opportunities presented to the individual Negro migrant is such as to increase the desirability of a move out of the South and to stress the comparative desirability of large cities as against rural areas and medium-sized cities.

Although the differential in white and Negro migration is clearly related to differential economic opportunity, the overall level of Southern out-migration must be ascribed to the underdeveloped nature of the region. A more rapid pace of Southern economic development could change these historic patterns of Negro migration. Tentative research findings indicate that both manufacturing growth and urbanization in the South reduce Negro out-migration. Although the holding effect of these changes is not so strong for Negroes as for whites, the difference between the two responses can be substantially narrowed. If development took place at a higher rate, the job market would tighten and thus encourage Negroes to stay. Moreover, the *quid pro quo* for large-scale subsidies for Southern development might be strong commitments to hire Negro applicants. A serious program of Southern development is worthwhile in its own right as a cure to a century of imbalance in the distribution of economic activity in the nation. From the narrow viewpoint of the North, however, the economic development of the South can play a crucial role in providing leverage in the handling of metropolitan problems.

Belated recognition of the problems created for Northern metropolitan areas by these large-scale streams of rural migration have led in recent months to a large number of proposals to encourage development in rural areas. Not surprisingly, the Department of Agriculture has been quick to seize the opportunities provided. A "rural renaissance" has been its response. Full-page advertisements headed, "To save our cities, We must have rural-urban balance," have appeared in a large number of magazines under the aegis of the National Rural Electric Cooperative Association. These proposals invariably fail to recognize that Negro migration from the rural South differs in important respects from rural-urban migration and has different consequences. Failing as they do to distinguish between beneficial and potentially disruptive migration, these proposals for large-scale programs to keep people on the farms, everywhere, are likely to lead to great waste and inefficiency, while failing to come to grips with the problem that motivated the original concern.

IMPROVING SKILLS

A second important approach to easing the pressure on the ghetto is to improve the educational and skill level of incoming migrants. An investment in the underutilized human resource represented by the Southern white and Negro will pay off in either an expanded Southern economy or a Northern metropolitan job market. Indeed, it is just this flexibility that makes programs oriented to individuals so attractive in comparison to programs oriented to geography. To the extent that a potential migrant can gain skills in demand, his integration into the metropolis, North or South, is that much eased. In light of these benefits, progress in Southern schools has been pitifully slow. Southern Negro achievement levels are the lowest for any group in the country. Southern states with small tax bases and high fertility rates have found it expedient in the past to spend as little as possible on Negro education. Much of the rationalization of this policy is based on the fact that a large proportion of Southern Negroes will migrate and thus deprive the area of whatever educational investment is made in them. This fact undoubtedly had led to some underinvestment in the education of Southern whites as well, but the brunt has been borne by the Negro community.

Clearly it is to the advantage of those areas that are likely to receive these migrants to guarantee their ability to cope with an urban environment. This would be in sharp contrast to migrants who move to the ghetto dependent on the social services of the community and unable to venture into the larger world of the metropolis. Nor are the impacts of inadequate

Southern education limited to the first generation of Negro migrants. Parents ill-equipped to adjust to complex urban patterns are unlikely to provide the support necessary for preparing children to cope with a hostile environment. The pattern can be clearly seen in the second generation's reaction to life in the ghetto. It is the children of migrants and not the migrants themselves who seem most prone to riot in the city.

Thus, education of potential migrants is of great importance to both the North and South. The value of the investment is compounded by the extent to which the overall level of Negro opportunity is expanded. In the North, this is dependent on a weakening of the constricting ties of the ghetto. In the South it depends on economic development per se.

This article has considered alternative strategies for the urban ghetto in light of the strong economic and social link of that community to the metropolis in which it is embedded and to the nation as a whole. In particular, the analysis has centered on the likely repercussions of "gilding programs."

Included prominently among these programs are a variety of proposals designed to attract industry to metropolitan ghettos. There have also been numerous proposals for massive expenditures on compensatory education, housing, welfare, and the like. Model-cities programs must be included under this rubric. All such proposals aim at raising the employment, incomes, and well-being of ghetto residents *within* the existing framework of racial discrimination.

Much of the political appeal of these programs lies in their ability to attract support from a wide spectrum ranging from white separatists to liberals to advocates of Black Power. However, there is an overriding objection to this approach. "Gilding" programs must accept as given a continued growth of Negro ghettos, ghettos which are directly or indirectly responsible for the failure of urban renewal, the crisis in central-city finance, urban transportation problems, Negro unemployment, and the inadequacy of metropolitan school systems. Ghetto gilding programs, apart from being objectionable on moral grounds, accept a very large cost in terms of economic inefficiency, while making the solution of many social problems inordinately difficult.

A final objection is that such programs may not work at all, if pursued in isolation. The ultimate result of efforts to increase Negro incomes or reduce Negro unemployment in central-city ghettos may be simply to induce a much higher rate of migration of Negroes from Southern rural areas. This will accelerate the already rapid growth of black ghettos, complicating the already impressive list of urban problems.

Recognition of the migration link between Northern ghettos and

Southern rural areas has led in recent months to proposals to subsidize economic development, educational opportunities, and living standards in rural areas. It is important to clarify the valuable, but limited, contributions well-designed programs of this kind can make to the problems of the metropolitan ghetto. Antimigration and migrant improvement programs cannot in themselves improve conditions in Northern ghettos. They cannot overcome the prejudice, discrimination, low incomes, and lack of education that are the underlying "causes" of ghetto unrest. At best they are complementary to programs intended to deal directly with ghetto problems. Their greatest value would be in permitting an aggressive assault on the problems of the ghetto—their role is that of a counterweight which permits meaningful and large-scale programs within *metropolitan* areas.

What form should this larger effort take? It would seem that ghetto dispersal is the only strategy that promises a long-run solution. In support of this contention we have identified three important arguments:

1. None of the other programs will reduce the distortions of metropolitan growth and loss of efficiency that result from the continued rapid expansion of "massive" Negro ghettos in metropolitan areas.

2. Ghetto dispersal programs would generally lower the costs of achieving many objectives that are posited by ghetto improvement or gilding schemes.

3. As between ghetto gilding and ghetto dispersal strategies, only the latter is consistent with stated goals of American society.

The conclusion is straightforward. Where alternatives exist, and it has been a major effort of this article to show they do exist, considerable weight must be placed on their differential impact on the ghetto. Programs that tend to strengthen this segregated pattern should generally be rejected in favor of programs that achieve the same objectives while weakening the ghetto. Such a strategy is not only consistent with the nation's long-run goals, but will often be substantially cheaper in the short run.

PART NINE

SUGGESTED REFERENCES
FOR FURTHER STUDY OF THE GHETTO

INTRODUCTION

Although the ghetto is a very old phenomenon, few studies of it existed prior to 1966. The years 1966 to 1970 were the peak period for research on the ghetto. In fact, 44.2 percent of the 312 studies in this Bibliographic Guide that follows were published during that time. Furthermore, 80 percent of these works were published from 1966 to 1975. Publications on the ghetto then dropped from 138 during 1966 to 1970 to 112 in 1971 to 1975 and to only 35 in 1976 to 1980.

It seems evident from this record that research on the ghetto is strongly influenced by societal events. During the period from 1966 to 1970 which was one of maximum protest and violence in the ghetto a considerable number of researchers were engaged in attempting to understand the causes of this disquiet and unrest. The period from 1971 to 1975, which was one of continued slight political gains for ghetto residents and of a decline in social assistance programs saw a slackening in this effort. By 1976, when the socioeconomic status quo prevalent before the riots once again prevailed, fear of renewed ghetto protest and violence had diminished and so did interest and concern about conditions in the ghetto.

Although not annotated, the works in the Bibliographic Guide, which follows, have been very carefully selected. Albeit an attempt was made to be comprehensive, almost all subsidiary items were intentionally excluded. Thus each entry listed is focused at least 99 percent on the ghetto.

In order to assist the reader in further study and research on various aspects of the ghetto, the Bibliographic Guide has been organized around several themes, many of which are the same as those outlined in the preceding sections of this volume. The major themes are the Concept and Origin of the Ghetto, the Changing Population of the Ghetto: Ethnic Ghetto versus Racial Ghetto, the Spatial Diffusion of the Ghetto, the Economy of the Ghetto, the Political System of the Ghetto, Health, Education, and Transportation in the Ghetto, the Quality of Life in the Ghetto, and Civil Disorders in the Ghetto. The final section is labeled simply "Other Categories."

Although studies on the ghetto have declined since 1970 due in part to a lack of protest and violence, the problems of the ghetto have worsened. As long as such problems as differential high unemployment rates, poor education, health care, transportation, unequal justice and powerlessness remain, future racial conflict would seem inevitable. Any ghetto may explode at any time under such circumstances. The violence during the summer of 1980 in the ghettos of Miami, Orlando, and Chattanogga is evidence of that fact. It is hoped that this Bibliographic Guide will stimulate and facilitate further research and understanding of the problems of the ghetto and thereby aid in their long overdue solution.

16

Joe T. Darden

A BIBLIOGRAPHIC GUIDE
FOR THE STUDY OF THE GHETTO

1: THE CONCEPT AND ORIGIN OF THE GHETTO

Bracey, John H.; Maier, August; and Rudwick, Elliott, eds. *The Rise of the Ghetto.* Belmont, Cal.: Wadsworth Publishing Co., 1971.

Carr, Homer B. "Before the Ghetto: A Study of Detroit Negroes in the 1890's." M.A. Thesis, Wayne State University, 1968.

Ford, Larry, and Griffin, Ernst. "The Ghettoization of Paradise." *The Geographical Review* 69 (April 1979), pp. 140–158.

Foster, Madison. "Black Organizing: The Need for a Conceptual Model of the Ghetto." *Catalyst: A Socialist Journal of the Social Services* 1 (1978), pp. 76–90.

Greer, Scott A. *Neighborhood and Ghetto: The Local Area in Large-Scale Society.* New York: Basic Books, 1974.

Hammerz, Ulf. *Southside, An Inquiry into Ghetto Culture,* pp. 13–21. New York: Columbia University Press, 1969.

Hicks, Charles, et al. "Black Ghettos and Uncertain Futures." *Faculty Research Journal* [of St. Augustine College] (January 1971), pp. 18–25.

Humphrey, Norman D. "Black Ghetto in Detroit." *Christian Century* (January 15, 1947), pp. 78–79.

Ipcar, Charles. "The Ghetto: A Critique of Conceptual Approaches." Department of Geography, Michigan State University, 1971 (mimeographed).

Katzman, David M. *Before the Ghetto: Black Detroit in the Nineteenth Century.* Urbana: University of Illinois Press, 1973.

Kusmer, Kenneth L. *A Ghetto Takes Shape: Black Cleveland, 1870–1930.* Urbana: University of Illinois Press, 1976.

Lammermeier, Paul J. "Cincinnati's Black Community: The Origins of a Ghetto, 1870–1880." In *The Rise of the Ghetto,* pp. 24–28. Edited by John Bracey, August Meier, and Elliot Rudwick. Belmont: Wadsworth Publishing Co., 1971.

Lofland, J. "The Youth Ghetto." *Journal of Higher Education* 39 (1968), pp. 131–143.

Lubetkin, Zwiak. "The Last Days of the Warsaw Ghetto." *Commentary* 3 (1947), pp. 401–411.

Mason, P. F. "Some Characteristics of a Youth Ghetto in Boulder, Colorado." *Journal of Geography* (December 1972), pp. 526–533.

Sachar, A. L. *A History of the Jews,* pp. 251–255. New York: Alfred A. Knopf, 1966.

Seig, Louis. "Concepts of Ghetto: A Geography of Minority Groups." *Professional Geographer* 23 (January 1971), pp. 1–4.
Spear, Allan. "The Institutional Ghetto." In *The Rise of the Ghetto,* pp. 170–174. Edited by John Bracey, August Meier, and Elliott Rudwick. Belmont: Wadsworth Publishing Co., 1971.
———. "The Origins of the Urban Ghetto, 1870–1915." In *Key Issues in the Afro-American Experience,* pp. 153–166. Edited by Nathan Huggins, Martin Rilson, and Daniel Fox. New York: Harcourt Brace Jovanovich, 1971.
Weaver, Robert. *The Negro Ghetto.* New York: Harcourt, Brace and Co., 1948.
Wheeler, James O., and Brunn, Stanley D. "An Agricultural Ghetto: Negroes in Cass County, Michigan, 1845–1968." *Geographical Review* 59 (July 1969), pp. 317–329.
Wirth, Louis. *The Ghetto.* Chicago: University of Chicago Press, 1928.
———. "The Ghetto." *American Journal of Sociology* 33 (July 1927), pp. 57–71.

2: THE CHANGING POPULATION OF THE GHETTO
Ethnic Ghetto versus Racial Ghetto

Blassingame, John W. "Before the Ghetto: The Making of the Black Community in Savannah, Georgia, 1865–1880." *Journal of Social History* 6 (1973), pp. 469–481.
Blumburg, Leonard, and Lalli, Michael. "Little Ghettos: A Study of Negroes in the Suburbs." *Phylon* 27 (1966), pp. 117–131.
Clark, Dennis. *The Ghetto Game: Racial Conflicts in the City.* New York: Sheed and Ward, 1962.
Connally, Harold X. *A Ghetto Grows in Brooklyn.* New York: New York University Press, 1977.
Different Strokes: Pathways to Maturity in the Boston Ghetto: A Report to the Ford Foundation. Boulder: Westview Press, 1976.
Elgie, Robert. "Rural Immigration, Urban Ghettoization and Their Consequences." *Antipode* 2 (December 1970), pp. 35–54.
Feagin, Joe R. *Ghetto Social Structure: A Study of Black Bostonians.* San Francisco: R. and E. Associates, 1975.
Forman, Robert. *Black Ghettos, White Ghettos and Slums.* New York: Prentice-Hall, 1972.
Goldfield, David R. "The Black Ghetto: A Tragic Sameness." *Journal of Urban History* 3 (May 1977), pp. 361–371.
Gordon, Gregory, and Swanson, Albert. *Chicago: Evolution of a Ghetto.* Chicago: Home Investments Fund, 1976.
Gregorovius, Ferdinand A. *The Ghetto and the Jews of Rome.* New York: Schocken Books, 1948.
Hapgood, Hutchines. *The Spirit of the Ghetto: Studies of the Jewish Quarter in New York.* New York: Funk and Wagnalls Co., rev. ed., 1909.
Hesse-Biber, Sharlene. "The Ethnic Ghetto as Private Welfare: A Case of Southern Italian Immigration to the United States, 1880–1914." *Urban & Social Change Review* 12 (Summer 1979), pp. 9–15.
Hill, Herbert. "Demographic Change and Racial Ghettos: The Crisis of American Cities." *Journal of Urban Law* 44 (Winter 1966), pp. 231–285.
Hirsch, Arnold. "Making the Second Ghetto: Race and Housing in Chicago, 1940–1960." Ph.D. dissertation, University of Illinois, Chicago Circle, 1978.
Katz, Jacob. *Out of the Ghetto: Social Background of Jewish Emancipation, 1770–1870.* Cambridge: Harvard University Press, 1973.
Kelly, Gregory P. "The Westside: The Making of a Ghetto." *The Lansing Star* (August 30, 1978), p. 4.

Krout, Maurice H. "A Community in Flux, The Chicago Ghetto Resurveyed." *Social Forces* 5 (1926), pp. 273–282.

McColl, Robert W. "Vietnam, Cuba and the Ghetto." In *Invitation to Geography*, pp. 112–117. Edited by David A. Lanegian and Risa Palm. New York: McGraw-Hill, 1973.

Meier, August, and Rudwick, Elliott. *From Plantation to Ghetto.* New York: Hill and Wang, rev. ed., 1970.

Osofsky, Gilbert. *Harlem: The Making of a Ghetto.* New York: Harper and Row, 1966.

Partridge, William. *The Hippie Ghetto: The Natural History of a Subculture.* New York: Holt, Rinehart and Winston, 1973.

Philpott, Thomas L. *The Slum and the Ghetto: Neighborhood Deterioration and Middle-Class Reform, Chicago, 1880–1930.* New York: Oxford University Press, 1978.

Radzialowski, Thaddeus. "The View from a Polish Ghetto: Some Observations on the First One Hundred Years in Detroit." *Ethnicity* 1 (July 1974), pp. 125–150.

Ramirez, Manuel. "Identity Crisis in the Barrios." In *Pain and Promise*, pp. 57–60. Edited by Edward Simer. New York: New American Library, 1972.

Reiss, L. S. "Five Ghettos of the Modern Exodus." *Survey* 51 (October 1923–March 1924), pp. 447–452.

Rose, Peter I. *The Ghetto and Beyond: Jewish Life in America.* New York: Random House, 1969.

Spear, Allan H. *Black Chicago: The Making of a Negro Ghetto, 1880–1920.* Chicago, University of Chicago Press, 1967.

Ward, David. "The Emergence of Central Immigrant Ghettoes in American Cities, 1840–1920." *Annals of the Association of American Geographers* 58 (1968), pp. 343–359.

Wye, Christopher G. "Midwest Ghetto: Patterns of Negro Life and Thought in Cleveland, Ohio, 1929–1945." Ph.D. dissertation, Kent State University, 1973.

Zeublin, Charles. "The Chicago Ghetto," in *Hull House Maps and Papers*, pp. 91–111. Chicago: Thomas Y. Crowell Co., 1895.

3: THE SPATIAL DIFFUSION OF THE GHETTO

Adams, John B., and Sanders, Robert. "Urban Residential Structure and the Location of Stress in Ghettos." *Earth and Mineral Sciences* 38 (January 1968), pp. 29–32.

Bailey, Robert M. "The Cutting Edge of the City's Expanding Ghetto." *Planning* (ASPO) 40 (1974), pp. 10–13.

Boyce, Ronald R. "Is There a Geographically Based Solution to the Problems of the Negro Ghetto." *Geographic* 2 Western Geographic Series. British Columbia, Canada: Department of Geography, University of Victoria, 1973.

Browne, Robert S. "Building Viable Ghettos," in *The Urban Scene in the Seventies*, pp. 229–237. Edited by James Blumstein and Eddie Martin. Nashville: Vanderbilt University Press, 1974.

Bryne, D. "Allocation, The Council Ghetto, and the Political Economy of Housing." *Antipode* 8 (March 1976), pp. 24–29.

Deskins, Donald R., Jr. "Interaction Patterns and the Spatial Form of the Ghetto." Special Publication No. 3. Evanston: Department of Geography, Northwestern University, 1969.

Edel, Matthew. "Development vs. Dispersal: Approaches to Ghetto Poverty." In *Readings in Urban Economics.* Edited by Matthew Edel and Jerome Rothenberg. New York: Macmillan, 1972.

Edwards, O. L. "Patterns of Residential Segregation Within a Metropolitan Ghetto." *Demography* 7 (May 1970), pp. 185–193.

230 / BIBLIOGRAPHIC GUIDE

Hansell, C. R., and Clark, W. A. V. "The Expansion of the Negro Ghetto in Milwaukee." *Tydschrift Voor Economishe in Sociale Geografie* 61 (1970), pp. 267-277.
Harrison, Bennett. "Suburbanization and Ghetto Dispersal: A Critique of Conventional Wisdom." In *Controversies of State and Local Government.* Edited by Mavis Mann Reeves and Parris Glendening. Boston: Allyn and Bacon, 1971.
Harvey, David. "Revolutionary and Counter Revolutionary Theory in Geography and the Problem of Ghetto Formation." *Antipode* 4 (July 1972), pp. 1-13.
Hodgart, Robert L. "The Process of Expansion of the Negro Ghetto in Cities of the Northern United States: A Study of Cleveland, Ohio." M. A. thesis, Pennsylvania State University, 1969.
Ingram, Gregory. "An Analysis of Ghetto Housing Prices Over Time." In *Residential Location and Urban Housing Markets,* chapter 4. Studies in Income and Wealth 43. Cambridge: Ballinger Publishing Co., 1979.
Kern, Clifford R. *Racial Discrimination and the Price of Ghetto Housing in City and Suburb: Some Recent Evidence.* Cambridge: Dept. of City and Regional Planning, Harvard University Discussion Paper No. D 77-2 (March 1977).
Labrie, Peter. "Black Central Cities: Dispersal or Rebuilding." Part II, *Review of Black Political Economy* 1 (Winter-Spring 1971), pp. 78-99.
Laguerre, Michel. "Internal Dependency: The Structural Position of the Black Ghetto in American Society." *Journal of Ethnic Studies* 6 (Winter 1979), pp. 29-44.
Loury, Glenn C. "The Minimum Border Length Hypothesis Does Not Explain the Shape of Black Ghettos." *Journal of Urban Economics* 5 (April 1978), pp. 147-153.
McColl, Robert W. "Creating Ghettos: Manipulating Social Space in the Real World and the Classroom." *Journal of Geography* 71 (November 1972), pp. 496-502.
Meyer, David R. *Spatial Variation of Black Urban Households.* Chicago: University of Chicago Press, Department of Geography Research Paper No. 129, 1970.
Morrill, Richard L. "The Negro Ghetto: Problems and Alternatives." *Geographical Review* 55 (1965), pp. 339-361.
———. "The Persistence of the Black Ghetto as Spatial Separation." *Southeastern Geographer* 11 (November 1971), pp. 149-156.
———. "A Geographic Perspective of the Black Ghetto." In *Geography of the Ghetto,* pp. 28-58. Edited by Harold M. Rose. DeKalb: Northern Illinois University Press, 1972.
Rose, Harold M. "The Development of an Urban Subsystem: The Case of the Negro Ghetto." *Annals of the Association of American Geographers,* (March 1970), pp. 1-17.
———. "The Black Ghetto as a Territorial Entity." Special Publication No. 3, Department of Geography, Northwestern University, 1969.
Rothman, Jack. "The Ghetto Makers." In *Housing Urban America.* Edited by Jon Pynoos, Robert Schafer, and Chester Hartman. Chicago: Aldine Publishing Co., 1973.
Sanders, Ralph A., and Adams, John S. "Age Structure in Expanding Ghetto Space, Cleveland, Ohio, 1940-1965." *Southeastern Geographer* 11 (November 1971), pp. 121-132.
Sands, Gary. "Ghetto Development in Detroit." In *Metropolitan America: Geographic Perspectives and Teaching Strategies,* pp. 175-197. Edited by Robert D. Swartz et al. Oak Park: National Council for Geographic Education, 1972.
Schnare, Ann, and Struyk, Raymond J. "An Analysis of Ghetto Housing Prices Over Time." In *The Economics of Residential Location and Urban Housing Markets.* Edited by G. Ingram. New York: National Bureau of Economic Research Conference on Income and Wealth (May 1975).

Tata, Robert J.; Van Horn, Sharyn; and Lee, David. "Defensible Space in a Housing Project: A Case Study from a South Florida Ghetto." *Professional Geographer* 27 (August 1975), pp. 297–303.
Wassenich, Mark. *New Towns from the Point of View of the Ghetto Resident: Phase II.* Chapel Hill: University of North Carolina, Center for Urban and Regional Studies, 1970.
Weaver, Robert C. "Non-White Population Movements and Urban Ghettos." *Phylon* 20 (Autumn 1959), pp. 235–241.
Wieand, K. "Housing Price Determination in Urban Ghettos." *Urban Studies* 12 (1975), pp. 193–204.
Williams, Joyce. *Black Community Control: A Study of Transition in a Texas Ghetto.* New York: Praeger, 1973.

4: THE ECONOMY OF THE GHETTO

Adams, Arvil V., and Nestel, Gilbert. "Interregional Migration, Education and Poverty in the Urban Ghetto: Another Look at Black-White Earnings Differentials." *Review of Economics and Statistics* 58 (May 1976), pp. 156–166.
Adjei-Barwuah, Barfour. "Socio-Economic Regions in the Louisville Ghetto." Ph.D. dissertation, Department of Geography, Indiana University, 1972.
Aldrich, Howard E. "Employment Opportunities for Blacks in 'the Black Ghetto: The Role of White-Owned Businesses." *American Journal of Sociology* 78 (1973), pp. 1403–1425.
Allen, Louis L. "Making Capitalism Work in the Ghettos." *Harvard Business Review* (May–June 1969), pp. 83–92.
Barrera, Mario; Munoz, Charles; and Ornelas, Charles. "The Barrio as an Internal Colony." In *People and Politics in Urban Society*, pp. 465–498. Urban Affairs Annual Reviews 6. Beverly Hills: Sage Publications, 1972.
Bauman, John F. "Poverty in the Urban Ghetto." *Current History* (November 1970), pp. 283–289.
Bell, Carolyn S. *Economics of the Ghetto.* New York: Pegasus Publishing Co., 1970.
Berk, Richard A. "The Role of Ghetto Retail Merchants in Civil Disorders." Ph.D. dissertation, Johns Hopkins University, 1970.
Berndt, Harry E. *New Rules in the Ghetto: The Community Development Corporation and Urban Poverty.* Westport, Conn.: Greenwood Press, 1977.
Berry, Brian J. L. "Ghetto Expansion and Single Family Housing Prices, 1968–1972." *Journal of Urban Economics* 3 (October 1976), pp. 397–423.
Bloom, Gordon F. "Black Capitalism in Ghetto Supermarkets: Problems and Prospects." *Industrial Management Review* 2 (Spring 1970), pp. 37–48.
Brown, James K., and Lusterman, Seymour. *Business and the Development of Ghetto Enterprise.* New York: Conference Board, 1971.
Browne, Robert S. "Cash Flows in a Ghetto Community." *Review of Black Political Economy* 1 (Winter/Spring 1971), pp. 28–39.
"Chained to the Ghetto: Fair Housing Laws, United States." *Economist* 219 (April 9, 1966), pp. 137–138.
Cross, Theodore L. *Black Capitalism.* New York: Atheneum, 1969.
Davies, Shane, and Huff, David L. "Impact of Ghettoization on Black Employment." *Economic Geography* 48 (1972), pp. 421–427.
Doeringer, Peter B. "Ghetto Labor Markets: Problems and Programs," Program on Regional and Urban Economics, Discussion Paper No. 35, Harvard University, 1968.
–––. "Manpower Programs for Ghetto Labor Markets." In *Proceedings of the 21st Annual Winter Meeting, Industrial Relations Research Association*, pp. 257–267. Madison, Wis.: n.p., 1969.

Donaldson, Loraine, and Strangways, Raymond S. "Can Ghetto Groceries Price Competitively and Make a Profit?" *Journal of Business* 46 (January 1973), pp. 61-66.

Drake, St. Clair, and Cayton, H. R. *Black Metropolis,* pp. 174-213. New York: Harcourt Brace and Co., 1945.

Eiben, Crowell, Jr. "Insurers Invest in the Ghetto." *Civil Rights Digest,* 1 (Summer 1968), pp. 11-15.

Evans, Lelia, "Neo-Colonialism and Development of the Black Ghetto: Model Cities." *Black Lines: A Journal of Black Studies* 1 (1970), pp. 17-26.

Ferman, Louis. "The Irregular Economy: Informal Work Patterns in the Urban Ghetto." (mimeographed) n.d.

Fusfeld, Daniel R. "Transfer Payments and the Ghetto Economy." In *Transfers in an Urbanized Economy,* pp. 78-92. Edited by Kenneth Boulding, Martin Pfaff, and Anita Pfaff. Belmont: Wadsworth Publishing Co., 1973.

———. "The Economy of the Urban Ghetto." In *Financing the Metropolis,* pp. 369-399. Urban Affairs Annual Reviews, 4. Edited by John P. Crecine. Beverly Hills, Cal: Sage Publications, 1970.

Garrity, John T. "Red Ink for Ghetto Industries," *Harvard Business Review* (May-June 1968), pp. 158-161, 171.

Gordon, D. M. "Class, Productivity and the Ghetto." Ph.D. dissertation, Harvard University, 1971.

———. "A Graph Theoretic Approach to the Ghetto Marketplace." Paper presented at 41st Annual Meeting of the Operations Research Society of America, Atlantic City, N.J., November 1972.

Harris, Donald. "The Black Ghetto as Colony: A Theoretical Critique and Alternative Formulation." *Review of Black Political Economy* 2 (1972), pp. 3-33.

Harrison, Bennett. "Education and Underemployment in the Urban Ghetto." In *Problems in Political Economy,* pp. 181-190. Edited by D. M. Gordon. Lexington, Mass.: D. C. Heath and Co., 1971.

———. "Ghetto Economic Development: A Survey." *Journal of Economic Literature* (March 1974), pp. 1-36.

Harwood, Edwin. "Youth Unemployment: A Tale of Two Ghettos." *Public Interest* 17 (Fall 1969), pp. 78-87.

Hefner, James. "Ghetto Economic Development—Content and Character of the Literature." *Review of Black Political Economy* 1 (1971), pp. 43-71.

Heilburn, James, and Wellisz, Stanislaw. "An Economic Program for the Ghetto." *Proceedings of the Academy of Political Science* 29 (1968), pp. 72-85.

Heilburn, J., and Conant, R. R. "Profitability and Size of Firm as Evidence of Dualism in the Black Ghetto." *Urban Affairs Quarterly* 7 (March 1972), pp. 251-284.

Heins, Marjorie. *Strictly Ghetto Property.* Berkeley: Ramparts Press, 1972.

Henderson, William L., and Ledebur, L. C. "The Viable Alternative for Black Economic Development (Three Programs: Jobs and Training, Black Capitalism, Ghetto Eradication or Dispersal)," *Public Policy* 18 (Spring 1969), pp. 429-449.

Jones, Mary Gardner. "The Revolution of Rising Expectations: The Ghettos Challenge to American Business." Address before the 34th Annual Meeting of the National Association of Food Chains, November 16, 1967.

Kain, J. F. *Coping with Ghetto Unemployment.* Cambridge: Harvard University Press, 1968.

———. *The Effect of the Ghetto on the Distribution and Level of Non-White Employment in Urban Areas.* Santa Monica, Cal.: Rand Corporation Bulletin, 1965. Also in *Proceedings of the Social Statistics Section,* 1964, pp. 260-269.

———. "Coping with Ghetto Unemployment." *Journal of the American Institute of Planners* 35 (March 1969), pp. 80-89.

Karpel, Craig. "Ghetto Fraud on the Installment Plan." *New York* 2 (May 26, 1969), pp. 24-32, and 2 (June 2, 1969), pp. 41-44.

Levine, Charles. "Black Entrepreneurship in the Ghetto: A Recruitment Strategy." *Land Economics* 48 (August 1972), pp. 269–273.
Levitan, Sar A., and Taggart, Robert, III. "Developing Business in the Ghetto." *Conference Board Record* (July 1969), pp. 13–21.
Levitan, Sar A.; Manguin, Garth L.; and Taggart, Robert, III. *Economic Opportunity in the Ghetto: The Partnership of Government and Business.* Baltimore: Johns Hopkins University Press, 1970.
Llewellyn, J. B. "The Problem of Business Operations in the Ghetto." In *Minority Business Development.* Boston: Federal Research Bank of Boston, 1976.
McLaurin, Dunbar S. *Ghetto Economic Development and Industrialization Plan.* New York: Human Resources Administration, April 1968.
Marcus, Burton H. "Similarity of Ghetto and Non-Ghetto Food Costs." *Journal of Marketing Research* 6 (August 1969), pp. 365–368.
Mellor, Earl F. "A Case Study: Costs and Benefits of Public Goods and Expenditures for a Ghetto." In *Transfers in an Urbanized Economy,* pp. 38–57. Edited by Kenneth Boulding, Martin Pfaff, and Anita Pfaff. Belmont: Wadsworth Publishing Co., 1973.
Mercer, John. "Housing Quality and the Ghetto." In *Geography of the Ghetto,* pp. 144–167. Edited by Harold M. Rose. De Kalb: Northern Illinois University Press, 1972.
–––. "Monopoly Profits and Ghetto Food Merchants: An Empirical Test." Unpublished paper, Columbia University, 1973.
Myers, Samuel L. "The Economics of Crime in the Urban Ghetto." *The Review of Black Political Economy* 9 (Fall 1978), pp. 43–59.
National Committee Against Discrimination in Housing. "Black Unemployment in the Ghetto." In *Racial Discrimination in the United States,* pp. 152–158. Edited by Thomas Pettigrew, New York: Harper and Row, 1975.
Oakland, W. H.; Sparrow, F. T.; and Stettler, H. L. "Ghetto Multipliers: A Case Study of Hough." *Journal of Regional Science* 11 (1971), pp. 337–345.
Price, William A. "Economics of the Negro Ghetto." *National Guardian* (September 3, 1966), p. 4.
Raine, Walter J. "The Ghetto Merchant Survey." A report prepared for the Office of Economic Opportunity, Nathan E. Cohen, Coordinator. Los Angeles: University of California, Institute of Government and Public Affairs (June 1, 1967).
Reiss, Albert J., Jr., and Aldrich, Howard. "Absentee Ownership and Management in the Black Ghetto: Social and Economic Consequences." *Social Problems* 18 (Winter 1971), pp. 319–339.
Rosen, S. M. "Better Mousetraps: Reflections on Economic Development in the Ghetto." *Urban Review* 4 (May 1970), pp. 14–18.
Sengstock, Mary C. "The Corporation and the Ghetto: An Analysis of the Effects of Corporate Retail Grocery Sales on Ghetto Life." *Journal of Urban Law* 45 (1968), pp. 673–703.
Sexton, Donald E. *Groceries in the Ghetto.* Lexington, Mass.: D. C. Heath and Co., 1973.
Sowell, Thomas. "A Neo-Mercantilist Model for Maximizing Ghetto Income." *The Review of Black Political Economy* 1 (1971), pp. 22–27.
Sturdivant, Frederick D. "Better Deal for Ghetto Shoppers." *Harvard Business Review* 46 (March–April 1968), pp. 130–139.
Sturdivant, Frederick, ed. *The Ghetto Marketplace.* New York: Free Press, 1969.
Tabb, William K. "Black Power–Green Power: The Economics of the Ghetto." In *Explorations in Urban Land Economics,* pp. 56–80. Edited by John L. Sullivan. Hartford: University of Hartford, 1970.
–––. "A Cost-Benefit Analysis of Location Subsidies for Ghetto Neighborhoods." *Land Economics* 48 (1972), pp. 45–52.
–––. *The Political Economy of the Black Ghetto.* New York: W. W. Norton and Co., 1970.

Vietorisz and B. Harrison. "Ghetto Development, Community Corporations, and Public Policy." *Review of Black Political Economy* 2 (Fall 1971), pp. 28-43.
Wolfe, Joseph A. "Increasing Black Entrepreneurship in the Ghetto: An Exploratory Study of a Management Training Program for Harlem Blacks." Ph.D. dissertation, New York University Graduate School of Business Administration, 1971.
"Writing a Policy for the Ghetto." *Business Week* (September 9, 1967), p. 34.

5: THE POLITICAL SYSTEM OF THE GHETTO

Adrian, Charles R. "The States and the Ghettos." In *Politics and the Ghettos*, pp. 82-103. Edited by Roland Warren. New York: Atherton Press, 1969.
Binstock, Robert. "The Ghettos, the New Left and Some Dangerous Fallacies." In *Politics and the Ghettos*, pp. 191-196. Edited by Roland L. Warren. New York: Atherton Press, 1969.
Chisholm, Shirley. "Ghetto Power in Action: The Value of Positive Political Action." In *The Black Politician: His Struggle for Power*, pp. 40-42, 123-131, part 2. Edited by Marvyn Dymally, Scituate, Ma.: Duxbury Press, 1971.
Cloward, Richard A., and Elman, Richard M. "Advocacy in the Ghetto." *Transaction* (December 1966), pp. 27-35.
Cooper, John L. *The Police and the Ghetto*. Port Washington: Kennikat Press, 1979.
Dumpson, James R. "Fantasy and Reality in the Ghetto Problem." In *Politics and the Ghettos*, pp. 71-79. Edited by Roland L. Warren. New York: Atherton Press, 1969.
Feagin, Joe R., and Hahn, Harlan. *Ghetto Revolts: The Politics of Violence in American Cities*. New York: Macmillan Co., 1973.
Glickman, Elliott B., and Jones, Vera M. "Consumer Legislation and the Ghetto." *Journal of Urban Law* 45 (Spring and Summer 1969), pp. 705-712.
Grier, George C. "The Negro Ghettos and Federal Housing Policy." *Law and Contemporary Problems* 32 (Summer 1967), pp. 550-560.
Groves, W. E. "Police in the Ghetto." In *Perspectives on Urban Politics*, pp. 169-198. Edited by J. S. Goodman. Boston: Allyn and Bacon, 1970. Reprinted from *Supplemental Studies for the National Advisory Commission on Civil Disorders*, pp. 103-114. Washington, D.C.: U.S. Government Printing Office, 1968.
Hill, Richard J., and Larson, Calvin J. "Differential Ghetto Orgainization." *Phylon* (Fall 1971), pp. 302-311.
Jones, Delmos J. "Incipient Organizations and Organizational Failures in an Urban Ghetto." *Urban Anthropology* 1 (Spring 1972), pp. 51-67.
Kapsis, Robert. "Black Ghetto Diversity and Anomie: A Sociopolitical View." *American Journal of Sociology* 83 (March 1978), pp. 1132-1153.
Kilson, Martin. "Political Change in the Negro Ghetto, 1900-1940s." In *Key Issues in the Afro-American Experience*, pp. 167-192. Edited by Nathan I. Huggins, Kilson Martin, and Daniel Fox. New York, vol. 2, 1971.
Long, Norton E. "Politics and Ghetto Perceptuation." In *Politics and the Ghettos*, pp. 31-43. Edited by Roland L. Warren. New York: Atherton Press, 1969.
Lyons, S. R. "Political Socialization of Ghetto Children: Efficacy and Cynicism." *Journal of Politics* 32 (May 1970), pp. 288-304.
O'Loughlin, John. "Malapportionment and Gerrymandering in the Ghetto." In *Urban Policy Making and Metropolitan Dynamics*. Edited by John S. Adams. Cambridge: Ballinger Publishing Co., 1978.
Rein, Martin. "Social Stability and Black Ghettos." In *Politics and the Ghettos*, pp. 44-58. Edited by Roland L. Warren. New York: Atherton Press, 1969.
Rossi, Peter H., and Berk, Richard A. "Local Political Leadership and Popular Discontent in the Ghetto." *Annals of the American Academy of Political and Social Science* 391 (September 1970), pp. 111-127.

Rossi, Peter, et al. *The Roots of Urban Discontent. Public Policy, Municipal Institutions and the Ghetto.* New York: John Wiley and Sons, 1974.

Savich, Harold. "Powerlessness in an Urban Ghetto: The Case of Political Biases and Differential Access in New York City." *Polity* 5 (Fall 1972), pp. 19–56.

Schulman, Jay. "Ghetto-Area Residence, Political Alienation and Riot Orientation." In *Riots and Rebellion: Civil Violence in the Urban Community*, pp. 261–284. Edited by Louis H. Masetti and Don Bowen. Beverly Hills: Sage Publications, 1968.

Schulz, David A. *Coming Up Black: Patterns of Ghetto Socialization.* Englewood Cliffs, N.J.: Prentice-Hall, 1969.

–––. "Some Aspects of the Policeman's Role as it Impinges Upon Family Life in a Negro Ghetto." *Sociological Focus* 2 (Spring 1969), pp. 63–72.

Warren, Roland L., ed. *Politics and the Ghetto.* New York: Atherton Press, 1969.

Wood, Robert C. "The Ghettos and Metropolitan Politics." In *Politics and the Ghetto*, pp. 59–70. Edited by Roland L. Warren. New York: Atherton Press, 1969.

6: HEALTH, EDUCATION, AND TRANSPORTATION IN THE GHETTO

Bauman, Gerald, and Grimes, Ruth. *Psychiatric Rehabilitation in the Ghetto: An Educational Approach.* Lexington, Mass.: D. C. Heath and Co., 1974.

Bogue, D. J. "Family Planning in the Negro Ghettos of Chicago." *Milbank Memorial Fund Quarterly* 48 (April 1970), pp. 283–307.

Campbell, Robert. *The Chasm: The Life and Death of a Great Experiment in Ghetto Education.* Boston: Houghton Mifflin, 1974.

Davis, James W. "Decentralization, Citizen Participation and Ghetto Health." *American Behavioral Scientist* 15 (September–October 1971), pp. 94–107.

Elam, Lloyd C. "What Does the Ghetto Want from Medicine?" In *Medicine in the Ghetto.* Edited by John Norman. New York: Appleton-Century-Crofts, 1969.

Everett, John R. "The Decentralization Fiasco and Our Ghetto Schools." *Atlantic Monthly* 222 (December 1968), pp. 71–73.

Farrell, Gregory R. "Resources for Transforming the Ghetto." In *The Schoolhouse in the City*, pp. 86–96. Edited by Alvin Toffler. New York: Praeger, 1968.

Gardner, Burleigh B., et al. "The Effect of Busing Black Ghetto Children Into White Suburban Schools." (July 1970) (ERIC Ed. 048-389).

Harrison, Bennett. *Education, Training and the Urban Ghetto.* Baltimore: Johns Hopkins University Press, 1972.

Harrison, N. "Education and Earnings in the Urban Ghetto." *American Economist* (Spring 1970), pp. 12–22.

Johnson, E. T. "The Delivery of Health Care in the Ghetto." *Journal of National Medical Association* 61 (1969), pp. 263–270.

Kupchik, George J. "Environmental Health in the Ghetto." *American Journal of Public Health* 59 (February 1969), pp. 220–225.

Labov, William. "A Note on the Relation of Reading Failure to Peer Group Status in Urban Ghettos." *Florida Reporter* (Spring/Summer 1969), pp. 54–57, 167–168.

Levy, Gerald. *Ghetto School: Class Welfare in an Elementary School.* New York: Pegasus Publishing Co., 1970.

Luchterhand, E., and Weller, L. "Social Class and the Desegregation Movement: A Study of Parents' Decisions in a Negro Ghetto." *Social Problems* 13 (Summer 1965), pp. 83–88.

Mackler, Bernard. "Grouping in the Ghetto." *Education and Urban Society* 2 (1969), pp. 80–96.

———. "Up from Poverty: The Price of Making It in a Ghetto School." In *Opening Opportunities for Disadvantaged Learners*, pp. 109–127. Edited by Harry Passow. New York: Columbia Teachers College Press, 1972.

Milio, Nancy. "Project in a Negro Ghetto." *American Journal of Nursing* 67 (May 1967), pp. 1006–1010.

Morgan, Gordon Daniel. *The Ghetto College Student: A Descriptive Essay on College Youth from the Inner City.* Iowa City: American College Testing Program, 1970.

Norman, John C. *Medicine in the Ghetto.* New York: Appleton-Century-Crofts, 1969.

Rist, Ray C. "Student Social Class and Teacher Expectations: The Self-Fulfilling Prophecy in Ghetto Education." *Harvard Educational Review* (August 1970), pp. 411–451.

Ruyle, Eugene A. "Ghetto and Schools in Kyoto, Japan." *Integrated Education* 11 (July–October 1973), pp. 29–34.

Soloman, Daniel; Hirsch, Jay; Scheinfeld, Daniel; and Jackson, John. "Family Characteristics and Elementary School Achievement in an Urban Ghetto." *Journal of Consulting and Clinical Psychology* 39 (1972), pp. 462–466.

Strauss, A. "Medical Ghettos." *Transaction* (May 1967), pp. 7–16.

Wheeler, James O. "Transportation Problems in Negro Ghettos." *Sociology and Social Research* 53 (1969), pp. 171–179.

———. "Work Trip Length and the Ghetto." *Land Economics* 44 (1968), pp. 107–112.

7: THE QUALITY OF LIFE IN THE GHETTO

Bartles-Smith, Douglas. *Urban Ghetto.* Guildford: Lutterwork Press, 1976.

Barton, Allen H. "The Columbia Crisis: Campus, Vietnam, and the Ghetto." *Public Opinion Quarterly* 32 (Fall 1968), pp. 333–351.

Battle, Sol, ed. *Ghetto '68.* New York: New World Press, 1968.

Bergsman, Joel. "Alternatives to the Non-Gilded Ghetto: Notes on Different Goals and Strategies." *Public Policy* 19 (Spring 1971), pp. 309–321.

Berry, Brian J. L. "Monitoring Trends, Forecasting Change and Evaluating Goal Achievements: The Ghetto v. Desegregation Issue in Chicago as a Case Study." In *Regional Forecasting.* Edited by M. Chisholm, A. E. Frey, and P. Haggett. London: Buttersworth, 1971. Also published in *Urban Social Segregation*, pp. 196–221. Edited by Ceri Peach. London: Langman, 1975.

Bullington, Bruce. *Heroin Use in the Barrio.* Lexington, Mass.: D. C. Heath and Co., 1977.

Bullough, Bonnie. "Alienation in the Ghetto." *American Journal of Sociology* 72 (March 1967), pp. 469–479.

Caplan, Nathan. "The New Ghetto Man: A Review of Recent Empirical Studies." *Journal of Social Issues* (1970), pp. 59–73.

Carey, George W. "Density, Crowding, Stress and the Ghetto." *American Behavioral Scientist* 15 (1972), pp. 495–509.

Clark, Kenneth B. *Dark Ghetto.* New York: Harper and Row, 1965.

Clarke, M. M. *Black-White Ghettos: Quality of Life in the Atlantic Inner City.* Oak Ridge National Laboratory – HUD (December 25, 1971).

Darden, Joe T. "Environmental Perception by Ghetto Youth in Pittsburgh." *Pennsylvania Geographer* (April 1970), pp. 19–22.

———. "The Quality of Life in a Black Ghetto: A Geographic View." *Pennsylvania Geographer* 12 (November 1974), pp. 3–8.

Drotning, Phillip T., and South, Wesley W. *Up from the Ghetto.* New York: Cowles Book Co., 1970.

Farrell, Walter. "Intra-Urban Mobility and Environmental Perception in a Black Middle-Class Ghetto: A Case Study in Flint, Michigan." Ph.D. dissertation, Department of Geography, Michigan State University, 1974.

——— and Brunn, Stanley. "Intraurban Mobility and Neighborhood Perception in Flint's Black Middle-Class Ghetto." *East Lakes Geographer* 13 (June 1978), pp. 4–19.

Foley, Eugene. *The Achieving Ghetto.* National Press, 1968.

Funnge, C. *Deghettoization: Specifics for Planning and an Examination of Elements of Urban Opportunity in New York City.* Brooklyn: Idea Plan Associates, 1966.

Goldfield, David, et al. *The Enduring Ghetto.* Philadelphia: Lippincott, 1973.

Hannerz, Ulf. "Roots of Black Manhood: Sex, Socialization and Culture in the Ghettos of American Cities." *Transaction* (October 1969), pp. 12–22.

Hapgood, Hutchines. "The Picturesque Ghetto." *Century* 94 (July 1917) pp. 469–473.

Hardy, Richard T., and Cull, John G. *Climbing Ghetto Walls.* Springfield, Ill.: Charles C. Thomas, 1973.

Hinckley, Katherine. "The Bang and the Whimper: Model Cities and Ghetto Opinion." *Urban Affairs Quarterly* 13 (December 1977), pp. 131–150.

Hippler, Arthur. *Hunter's Point: A Black Ghetto.* New York: Basic Books, 1974.

Kain, John F., and Persky, Joseph. "Alternatives to the Gilded Ghetto." *Public Interest* 14 (Winter 1969), pp. 74–87.

Kegels, S. Stephan. "A Field Experimental Attempt to Change Beliefs and Behavior of Women in an Urban Ghetto." *Journal of Health and Social Behavior* 10 (June 1969), pp. 115–125.

Kochman, Thomas. "Rapping in the Ghetto." *Transaction* 6 (February 1969), pp. 26–35.

Koestler, Frances A. "Pruitt-Igoe: Survival in a Concrete Ghetto." *Social Work* 12 (October 1967), pp. 3–14.

Kramer, Judith, and Leventman, Seymour. *Children of the Gilded Ghetto.* New Haven: Yale University Press, 1961.

Kuhn, M. W., and Mason, P. E. "Isla Vista, a Ghetto Model." Paper presented at the Association of Pacific Coast Geographers, Victoria, British Columbia, 1971.

McCord, William, et al. *Life Styles in the Black Ghetto.* New York: W. W. Norton and Co., 1969.

Mayer, John E., and Rosenblatt, Aaron. "Encounters with Danger: Social Workers in the Ghetto." *Sociology of Work and Occupations* 2 and 3 (August 1975), pp. 227–246.

Miller, Thomas V. *Ghetto Fever.* Milwaukee: Bruce Publishing Co., 1968.

Meister, Richard. *The Black Ghetto: Promised Land or Colony.* Lexington, Mass.: D. C. Heath and Co., 1972.

Moore, W., Jr. *The Vertical Ghetto.* New York: Random House, 1969.

Nesbitt, George A. "Breakup the Black Ghetto." *Crisis* 56 (February 1969), pp. 48–50.

"Oakland Presents Its Case for Salvaging a Ghetto." *Architectural Forum* 126 (April 1967), pp. 42–45.

Osofsky, Gilbert. "The Enduring Ghetto." *Journal of American History* (September 1968), pp. 243–255.

Rainwater, Lee. *Behind Ghetto Walls.* Chicago: Adine Publishing Co., 1971.

Rodman, H. "Family and Social Pathology in the Ghetto." *Science* 161 (August 23, 1968), pp. 756–762.

Rose, Harold M. *The Black Ghetto: A Spatial Behavioral Perspective.* New York: McGraw-Hill Co., 1971.

Steiss, Alan W., et al. *Dynamic Change and the Urban Ghetto.* Lexington, Mass.: D. C. Heath and Co., 1975.

Tucker, Sterling, *Why the Ghetto Must Go.* New York: Public Affairs Committee, 1968.

U. S. Commission on Civil Rights. *A Time to Listen . . . A Time to Act . . . Voices from the Ghettos of the Nation's Cities.* A Report of the Commission. Washington, D.C.: U. S. Commission on Civil Rights, November 1967.

Warner, Sam Bass, Jr., and Burke, Colin B. "Cultural Change and the Ghetto." *Journal of Contemporary History* 4 (October 1969), pp. 173–188.

Warren, Donald I. *Social Structural Processes Related to the Ghetto.* NIMH Research Grants of the Center for Minority Group Mental Health Programs, R01 16403, June 30, 1971.

Wilson, William. "Race Relations Models and Explanations of Ghetto Behavior." In *Nation of Nations: The Ethnic Experience and the Racial Crisis,* pp. 259–275. Edited by Peter Rose. New York: Random House, 1972.

8: CIVIL DISORDERS IN THE GHETTO

Abudu, Margaret J. G. "Black Ghetto Violence as Communication: A Case Study of Non-Conventional Political Protest." Ph.D. dissertation, Indiana University, 1971.

–––, et al. "Black Ghetto Violence: A Case Study Inquiry of Four Los Angeles Riot Event Types." *Social Problems* 19 (Winter 1972), pp. 408–426.

Berk, Richard A. "The Role of Ghetto Retail Merchants in Civil Disorders." Ph.D. dissertation, Johns Hopkins University, 1970.

Berkowitz, William R. "Socioeconomic Indicator Changes in Ghetto Riot Tracts." *Urban Affairs Quarterly* 10 (September 1974), pp. 69–94.

Blauner, Robert. "Internal Colonialism and Ghetto Revolt." *Social Problems* 16 (Spring 1969), pp. 393–408.

Boesel, David. "An Analysis of the Ghetto Riots." In *Cities Under Seige: An Anatomy of the Ghetto Riots, 1964-1968,* pp. 324–342. Edited by David Boesel and Peter Rossi. New York: Basic Books, 1971.

–––. "The Liberal Society, Black Youths, and Ghetto Riots." *Psychiatry* (May 1970), pp. 265–281.

––– and Rossi, Peter, eds. *Cities Under Siege: An Anatomy of the Ghetto Riots.* New York: Basic Books, 1971.

Boskin, Joseph. "The Revolt of the Urban Ghettos." *Annals of the American Academy of Political and Social Science* 382 (March 1969), pp. 1–14.

–––. "Violence in the Ghettos: A Consensus of Attitudes." *New Mexico Quarterly* 37 (Winter 1968), pp. 317–334.

Canfield, Roger B. *Black Ghetto Riots and Campus Disorders.* San Francisco: R and E Research Associates, 1973.

Caplan, N. S., and Paige, J. M. "A Study of Ghetto Rioters." *Scientific American* 219 (1968), pp. 19–25.

Cervantes, Alfonso J. "To Prevent a Chain of Super Watts: Rioting in the Ghettos of Our Great Cities Threatens to Become Epidemic Unless Business Takes a Greater Initiative." *Harvard Business Review* 45 (September–October 1967), pp. 55–65.

Crawford, Thomas J. "Police Perception of Ghetto Hostility." In *Perception in Criminology,* chapter 16. Edited by Richard L. Hershel and Robert Silverman. New York: Columbia University Press, 1975.

Etzkowitz, H., and Schaflander, O. M. *Ghetto Crisis: Riots or Reconciliation.* Boston: Little, Brown and Co., 1969.

Feagin, Joe R. "Social Sources of Support for Violence and Non-violence in a Negro Ghetto." *Social Problems* 15 (Spring 1968), pp. 432–441.
———, and Sheatsley, Paul B. "Ghetto Resident Appraisals of a Riot." *Public Opinion Quarterly* 32 (Fall 1968), pp. 352–362.
Gans, Herbert. "The Ghetto Rebellions and Urban Class Conflict." In *Urban Riots: Violence and Social Change,* pp. 45–54. Edited by R. H. Connery. New York: Vantage Press, 1969.
Geschwender, James A. *Black Revolt: The Civil Rights Movement, Ghetto Uprisings and Separatism.* Englewood Cliffs: Prentice-Hall, 1971.
Goldberg, Louis. "Ghetto Riots and Others: The Faces of Civil Disorder in 1967." *Journal of Peace Research* 5 (1968), pp. 116–131.
Hahn, Harlan. "Black Separatists: Attitudes and Objectives in a Riot Torn Ghetto." *Journal of Black Studies* (September 1970), pp. 35–53.
———. "Ghetto Sentiments on Violence." *Science and Society* 33 (Spring 1969), pp. 197–208.
———. "Violence: The View from the Ghetto." *Mental Hygiene* 53 (October 1969), pp. 509–512.
Levy, Burton. "Cops in the Ghetto." In *Riots and Rebellion: Civil Violence in the Urban Community,* pp. 347–358. Edited by Louis Masotti and Don R. Bowen. Beverly Hills: Sage Publications, 1968.
Lightfoot, Claude M. *Ghetto Rebellion to Black Liberation.* New York: International Publishers, 1968.
Mark, Ber. *Uprising in the Warsaw Ghetto.* New York: Schocken Books, 1975.
Mason, Peter F. "Some Spacial and Locational Relationships Relevant to Youth Ghetto Disorder." *Proceedings of the Association of American Geographers* 5 (1973), pp. 165–169.
Panker, G. J. *Black Nationalism and Prospects for Violence in the Ghetto.* Santa Monica: Rand Corporation, June 1969.
Report of the National Advisory Commission on Civil Disorders. New York: Bantam Books, 1968.
Rossi, Peter, et al. "Between Black and White—The Faces of American Institutions and the Ghetto." In *Supplemental Studies for the National Advisory Commission on Civil Disorders,* July 1968.
Rossi, Peter H., ed. *Ghetto Revolts.* Chicago: Aldine Publishing Co., 1970.
Williams, Walter. "Cleveland's Crisis Ghetto." In *Ghetto Revolts,* pp. 13–31. Edited by Peter Rossi. Chicago: Aldine Publishing Co., 1970.

9: OTHER CATEGORIES

Anchor, Shirley. *Mexican Americans in a Dallas Barrio.* Tucson: University of Arizona Press, 1978.
Atkinson, Paul; Reid, Margaret; and Sheldrake, Peter. "Creating a Company of Unequals: Sources of Occupational Stratification in a Ghetto Community Mental Health Center." *Sociology of Work and Occupation* 4 (August 1977).
Blair, Thomas L. *Retreat to the Ghetto: The End of a Dream?* New York: Hill & Wang, 1977.
Bloom, Solomon. "Dictator of the Lodz Ghetto." *Commentary* 7 (January–June 1949), pp. 111–122.
Clark, Kenneth. *Youth in the Ghetto.* New York: Harlem Youth Opportunities Unlimited, 1964.
Dembo, Richard and Burgos, William. "A Framework for Developing Drug Abuse Prevention Strategies for Young People in Ghetto Areas." Paper presented at the

annual meeting of the American Educational Research Association, San Francisco, April 19-23, 1976.

Downs, Anthony. "Alternative Futures for the American Ghetto." *Daedalus* 97 (Fall 1968), pp. 1331-1378.

Eripps, Thomas R. "Movies in the Ghetto, B.P. (Before Poitier)." *Negro Digest* 18 (February 1969), pp. 21-32.

Ettore, E. M. "Women, Urban Social Movements and the Lesbian Ghetto." *International Journal of Urban and Regional Research* 2 (October 1978), pp. 499-520.

Frankel, Barbara. *Childbirth in the Ghetto: Folk Beliefs of Negro Women in a North Philadelphia Hospital Ward.* San Francisco: R and E Research Associates, 1977.

Goldfarb, Ronald. *Jails: The Ultimate Ghetto.* New York: Anchor Press, Doubleday, 1975.

Hapgood, H., Epstein, J., and Golden, H. *The Spirit of the Ghetto.* Funk and Wagnalls Co., 1965.

Leah, Daniel, Jr. "All-Colored—But Not Much Different: Films Made for Negro Ghetto Audiences, 1913-1928." *Phylon* 36 (September 1975), pp. 321-339.

Muller, Thomas J. *The Ghetto of Indifference.* Nashville: Abingdon Press, 1966.

Nelson, Richard R. *The Moon and the Ghetto.* New York: W. W. Norton and Co., 1977.

Rasmussen, Karl R. "The Multi-Ordered Urban Area: A Ghetto." *Phylon* (Fall 1968), pp. 282-290.

Salisbury, Howard G. "The State Within a State: Some Comparisons Between the Urban Ghetto and the Insurgent State." *Professional Geographer* 22 (April 1971), pp. 105-112.

Smith, Christopher J. "Being Mentally Ill in the Asylum of the Ghetto." *Antipode* 7 (September 1975), pp. 53-59.

Taber, Richard. "A Systems Approach to the Delivery of Mental Health Services in Black Ghettos." *American Journal of Orthopsychiatry* 40 (1970), pp. 702-709.

Wilson, Robert A. "Anomie in the Ghetto: A Study of Neighborhood Type, Race, and Anomie." *American Journal of Sociology* 77 (1971), pp. 66-68.

Wolpert, Elaine, and Wolpert, Julian. "From Asylum to Ghetto." *Antipode* 6 (1974), pp. 63-76.

Zangwill, Israel. *Children of the Ghetto: A Study of a Peculiar People.* New York, Grosset and Dunlap, 1895.

———. *Dreamers of the Ghetto.* New York and London: Harper and Bros., 1898.

———. *Ghetto Comedies.* New York: Maxmillan and Co., Vol. 172, 1907.

———. *Ghetto Tragedies.* London: McClure and Co., 1893.

INDEX

Accommodation, 15
Advertising newspapers, 79, 99, 100-107
Antagonism, 69
Anti-Semitism, 65
Assimilation, 120; cultural, 120;
  model, 109

Busing, 218

Caste theory, 112
Centralization, 34, 81
City, as a dynamic organism, 33; central
  business district, expansion of, 37,
  86, 204, 214; city structure, theory
  on, 33; differences, 163-165; growth
  of, 14; internal spatial structure, 34,
  35; landscape interpretation, 33;
  microcosm of the, 14, 20, 32; model
  of, 12
Colonialism, as a process, 111, 114,
  117, 119; as a social system, 111;
  black ghettos, status of, 116-117;
  classical, 111-114, 119; colonization,
  121; concept of, 113, 115; culture,
  119, 120
Community, 18-20, 30; closed, 20;
  egalitarian, 67; immigrant, 73; open,
  68; self-determined, 155
Concentric Zone Theory, 34
Conflicts, economic, 65; social, 61
Coordinates, assignment of, 40;
  coordinate systems, 41; conversion
  to point data, 41; quadrant data, 41;
  street numbering systems, 40

Cultural impact, 114

Deprivation, 7, 160, 168
Discrimination, in housing, 69
Disorder, social, 7

Ecological theory, 34; processes, 35, 36
Economy, 120, 131; in ghetto, 137-
  139; income sources, 131; irregular
  economy, 134, 135, 150; labor
  market, 137; locations of business,
  140; low wage industries in,
  132-133; segregated, 138-141;
  risks, 138; sizes of business, 140;
  welfare system, 135, 136
Emancipation, proclamation of, 22
Employment, marginal, 7
Enclave, immigrant, 59; educational
  attainment, 62, 63, 66; ethnic
  group, distribution of, 59; employment opportunities, 63, 64; foreign
  language communities, 63, 64;
  housing of, 64; immigration, causes
  of, 63; neighborhoods, Italians of,
  63; Poles, history of, 62; social
  distance scales, 62, 63; social
  organization of, 67; social status of,
  65, 66; socio-economic status of,
  62

Environment, attitude toward, 174-176;
  dissatisfaction of the, 163; perception by ghetto youth, 174, 177, 179;
  quality of, 174, 176; urban centrifugal
  and centripetal forces in, 33